Generation Zero

How Fiat Destroyed the Working Class and How Bitcoin Fixes It

Grant Amagi

Amagi Press

GENERATION ZERO

How Fiat Destroyed the Working Class and How Bitcoin Fixes It

by

Grant Amagi

Published by Amagi Press

This book is for informational and educational purposes only. It does not constitute financial, investment, legal, or tax advice. The author is not a licensed financial advisor, broker, or tax professional. Any decisions you make regarding your finances are your own responsibility. Consult a qualified professional before making investment decisions.

ISBN: 979-8-9958447-2-3 (hardcover)
ISBN: 979-8-9958447-0-9 (paperback)
ISBN: 979-8-9958447-1-6 (ebook)

Cover Design By Julia Kuris, Designerbility

Printed in the United States of America

First edition, 2026

Contents

Acknowledgments

This book is dedicated to my father and late mother, as well to the working men and women of his generation. Of course, no book can be accomplished alone. I am grateful for the love and support of my family and friends. Having the love and support of my wife and children was essential to completing this work. It's also my hope that the book's completion serves as inspiration for them to achieve their goals one day.

Finally, I'd like to extend my gratitude to the many thoughtful people who have shaped my thinking over the years, and opened my mind to different, and often painful, ideas. Two people, however, stand out as the most influential and life changing.

I met retired Marine Corps Master Sergeant Al Willey at a training school about 25 years ago. He challenged my thinking in such a profound way that I was never the same. He didn't lecture or belittle me. He simply asked how do I really know what I think I know. Up until that time, I had lived my life in a comfortable shell. I had been taught many things, memorized a lot of it, and was fairly certain I had the world figured out. Plot twist, I did not and I was humbled to find that out. Al helped me start a journey of independent learning and discovery. That journey led me to write this book.

I would like to personally thank Dr. Ron Paul, former Congressman of the United States. I had the pleasure of meeting Dr. Paul on a couple of occasions over the years and his kind, patient explanation of the nature of politics and economics always resonated with me. This book builds on much of his work and study, and extends it into a future with Bitcoin. I am honored to continue his work of education.

Introduction: The Man Who Did Everything Right

In April of 1971, a young Marine led a fire team through the Vietnamese jungle. He was twenty years old. A fire team is four men—the smallest infantry unit the Marine Corps fields, often used for patrol and short-distance reconnaissance. The point man led the way, hacking through brush with a machete while placing each foot with the kind of care that keeps you alive. A few steps behind him walked a junior rifleman, whose job was to pour fire into anything that moved the moment contact was made. Behind the rifleman walked our young leader, nearly a year into his deployment but already an old man in this group. He carried the radio, which marked him for every enemy sniper in the province. At the rear, the most junior member of the team walked Tail-End Charlie—the last man in line, watching behind them for what the jungle might send.

The thing about being a great point man is that it's an all-or-nothing job. You are great until the moment you miss. And then you're dead. On this day, on this step, their point man missed the sign of danger. He was excellent at his job. Lives depended on it, and he knew that. But one step was all it ever took in a war that killed over 58,000 Americans just like him. He died instantly. So did the young rifleman a few feet behind.

The fire team leader was hit badly, but still breathing. Tail-End Charlie escaped harm. Together, they held down the position, radioed for help, and waited to see if enemy combatants had heard the explosion. Many against two. Maybe many against one and a half. The fire team leader's right leg was shattered. He was just trying to survive.

They were not overrun. But our main character's leg would be amputated above the knee. He spent the next year in a VA hospital learning to walk on a prosthesis. The two

Marines who died that day had families waiting for them. They deserved to come home, and they didn't, and that is a debt that no government check or ceremony can repay.

• • •

Then life resumed—or as close to it as life gets after something like that. He went to college on the GI Bill. He married. He had kids. He bought a house in a modest neighborhood and drove a used car to work every morning. He earned promotions. He moved the family to a slightly better neighborhood. He watched his children grow up, leave home, start lives of their own. He downsized to a condo. He never asked for anything. Maybe just leave him a handicapped parking space so the walk isn't too far. That's not much to ask from a country he'd bled for.

He did everything right. Not in a loose, motivational-poster sense. In a literal, verifiable, line-item sense. He contributed to his 401(k) every paycheck for decades. He lived within his means. He paid his mortgage on time, every time. He didn't gamble. He didn't speculate. He didn't blow it on boats or bad investments. The only thing he splurged on was his children. He followed the plan—the exact plan that every financial advisor, every HR department, every magazine article, and every well-meaning relative told him was the path to a secure retirement.

And when he got there, he discovered he had far less than he'd been promised.

• • •

My father did well. He's not destitute. His work ethic, his creativity, and his refusal to quit carried him further than most. He made smart decisions with limited information and stretched every dollar with the kind of discipline that only people who've seen real hardship seem to possess. By any normal standard, he succeeded.

But that's the problem. It should not require extraordinary effort, extraordinary discipline, and extraordinary creativity just to end up okay. Before 1971, it didn't. A man with an ordinary job, ordinary savings habits, and ordinary intelligence could build a life, own a home, raise a family on one income, and retire with dignity. That wasn't exceptional. That was the default. My father beat the odds—but there shouldn't have been odds to beat. And if you weren't as disciplined as he was, as resourceful, as relentlessly hardworking? You're probably in much worse shape. Most people are.

For those younger than my father—his children, his grandchildren, the young families reading this book—it's worse. And it gets harder with every passing year. The same forces that quietly eroded his savings are accelerating. A home that cost two and a half years of income in 1971 now costs nearly five.[1] A single hospital visit can erase a year of savings. A college degree that once paid for itself now buries young people in debt before their careers begin. Each generation inherits the same rigged game, except the rig gets tighter.

For most of my life, I assumed this was just how it went. You work, you save, you hope for the best, and sometimes the math just doesn't add up. Bad luck. Bad timing. The cost of living went up. That's the explanation most people accept, because it's the only one they've ever been offered.

It is also a lie.

My father didn't fall short because he failed. He fell short because the money itself was quietly, systematically, and deliberately made worth less—year after year, week after week, day after day—while he held it. Every dollar he saved bought a little less than the dollar before it. Every raise he earned was partially consumed before it arrived. The retirement he'd been building for forty years was hollowed out from the inside, and nobody told him it was happening, because the people doing it had every incentive to make sure he never found out.

This is not a story about one man's bad luck. This is the story of a system—a monetary system—that was fundamentally broken in 1971, the same year a twenty-year-old Marine was learning to walk again in a VA hospital. While he was relearning how to stand, the men in Washington were cutting the last thread that connected American money to anything real. They didn't ask his permission. They didn't ask anyone's. They just did it. And from that moment forward, every working family in America—every man and woman who earned a paycheck and tried to save it—was entered into a game they didn't know they were playing, governed by rules they were never taught, and rigged in favor of people they'd never meet.

That hard-working family man is my father. And his story is the story of millions of American families—families who did everything right and still watched the ground shift beneath them. Families who blamed themselves when the math didn't work. Families who were told to work harder, save more, spend less, as if the problem were effort and not the money itself.

---

1. In 1971, median U.S. household income was $10,290 (U.S. Census Bureau, Current Population Reports, P-60 series) and the median home sales price was $25,500 (Federal Reserve Bank of St. Louis, Median Sales Price of Houses Sold, MSPUS series, Q4 1971), a ratio of 2.5. By Q4 2025, median household income was $83,730 (U.S. Census Bureau) and median home sales price was $405,300 (MSPUS series), a ratio of 4.84. See Sources and Data for complete references.

• • •

This book is about what happened to those families. It's about why a man who did everything right ended up with less than he earned, and why the same thing is happening—faster now—to his children and grandchildren. It's about a system that was built to look like prosperity while quietly transferring wealth from the people who work to the people who print.

But this is not a book about despair. If it were, I wouldn't have written it.

This is a book about a way out. A tool that didn't exist when my father started saving, but exists now. A form of money that no government can print, no central bank can debase, and no politician can promise away. It is the first invention in the history of money that puts the working class on equal footing with the people who've been rigging the game since 1971.

If you're a working American—if you punch a clock, raise kids, pay a mortgage, and lie awake sometimes wondering why it feels like you're running harder every year just to stay in place—this book was written for you. Not for Wall Street. Not for Silicon Valley. Not for the people who are already rich. For you.

The path was broken in 1971. A better way is here.

Let me show you.

Chapter One

Kiwi Fruit

In March of 2024, Congressman Brad Sherman of California sat across from Jerome Powell, the Chairman of the Federal Reserve, in the wood-paneled hearing room of the House Financial Services Committee. Sherman had a question. Not a complicated one. Not a gotcha about derivatives or interest rate swaps or any of the other things Congress pretends to understand. Just a simple question about the single most important number in American monetary policy.[1]

Why two percent?

Why does the Federal Reserve — the institution that controls the money supply of the most powerful economy on earth, the institution whose decisions determine what your mortgage costs, what your savings earn, whether your employer can afford to keep you — why does it target two percent inflation? Why not one? Why not three? Why not zero? What is the scientific, economic, or empirical basis for the number that drives every major financial decision in the Western world?

Powell's answer was revealing. Not because of what he said, but because of what he couldn't say. He acknowledged that the target originated in New Zealand. He called it "a pretty durable standard." He noted that other central banks had adopted it too.[2]

That was it. The Chairman of the Federal Reserve, the most powerful central banker on the planet, justified the cornerstone of his institution's policy by pointing out that everybody else does it. That's not an answer. That's an evasion.

1. House Financial Services Committee hearing, March 6, 2024. Video available via the Committee's official recordings.

2. Powell's exact phrasing during the March 6, 2024 exchange with Rep. Sherman.

Here's what Powell didn't say, because it would have been too embarrassing to say in a room full of cameras.

The two percent inflation target was invented in 1989 by a man named Don Brash. Before becoming the head of the Reserve Bank of New Zealand, Brash's previous job was running the New Zealand Kiwifruit Authority. That is not a joke. The man who invented the most important number in global monetary policy used to be in charge of kiwis. The fruit. Not the people.[3]

New Zealand in the late 1980s was a mess. But it's worth understanding *how* it became a mess, because the story is a miniature version of everything this book is about.

In 1965, New Zealand was the sixth wealthiest country on earth per capita. Small, agricultural, prosperous — they shipped butter, lamb, and wool to Britain and life was good. Then three things happened in quick succession. In 1973, Britain joined the European Economic Community, and New Zealand lost its primary export market overnight. That same year, the OPEC oil embargo sent energy prices through the roof, and New Zealand — heavily dependent on imported oil — watched its cost of living explode. The terms of trade collapsed. A country that had been rich was suddenly scrambling.[4]

What happened next should sound familiar to anyone who's watched a government respond to a crisis it helped create. Prime Minister Robert Muldoon reached for every lever the fiat system gave him. He froze wages and prices — for over two years, one of the longest such freezes in the developed world. He launched a program called "Think Big," borrowing massively to build synthetic fuel plants, steel mills, and chemical factories that were supposed to make New Zealand energy-independent. Public debt quintupled from $4.2 billion to $21.9 billion during his tenure. Marginal tax rates hit sixty-six cents on the dollar. The economy was regulated, controlled, and micromanaged into paralysis.[5]

It didn't work. Between 1971 and 1988, inflation fell below ten percent in only four out of seventeen years. It hit 18.4% in 1980. New Zealand dropped from sixth wealthiest per capita to nineteenth — and kept falling. Young people fled to Australia by the tens of thousands. By 1984, the country was on the edge of economic collapse, buried under

---

3. Brash served as Chairman of the New Zealand Kiwifruit Authority before his appointment to the Reserve Bank. See his official biography at the Reserve Bank of New Zealand.

4. OECD historical GDP per capita rankings. New Zealand's relative position declined steadily from the mid-1960s onward.

5. Debt figures from New Zealand Treasury historical fiscal data. Muldoon's wage and price freeze ran from June 1982 to February 1984. Marginal tax rates from New Zealand Inland Revenue historical records.

debt from projects that came online just as oil prices crashed, governed by a man whose own cabinet nearly deposed him and whose final term ended in a currency crisis.[6]

That was the disaster zone Don Brash walked into. The government passed a new law giving the central bank independence, and it fell to Brash to pick an inflation target. In a television interview, a reporter asked him what he was aiming for. Brash, by his own later admission, panicked. He blurted out a range of zero to one percent. It wasn't a number derived from research or modeling or any empirical evidence. "The figure," Brash later confessed, "was plucked out of the air."[7]

The target eventually settled at two percent — partly because it sounded more reasonable than zero, and partly because it gave policymakers room to maneuver. New Zealand's Finance Minister at the time, David Caygill, admitted years later that the inflation target "wasn't from our point of view the main point of the act." It was an afterthought. A footnote. A number pulled from thin air by a man who'd spent his career grading fruit.[8]

And notice the circularity. New Zealand's crisis was caused by fiat money — by a government that could borrow without limit, print without constraint, freeze prices by decree, and bury the country in debt financing projects that the private sector wouldn't touch because they didn't make economic sense. The crisis was what fiat *does* when the people holding the levers panic. And the solution — the 2% target that now governs the entire Western financial system — didn't address any of that. It just added a new number to the dashboard of the same broken machine.

But here's where it gets absurd. Other central banks saw New Zealand's inflation come down — which had far more to do with a global disinflationary cycle than anything Brash did — and decided to copy it. Canada adopted a two percent target. Then England. Then the European Central Bank. By the time the Federal Reserve officially adopted it in 2012 under Ben Bernanke, two percent had become monetary gospel. Not because anyone had proven it was right. But because everyone had agreed to pretend it was.[9]

---

6. Reserve Bank of New Zealand historical CPI series. The 1984 constitutional crisis arose when Muldoon initially refused to devalue the dollar as demanded by the incoming Labour government.

7. Don Brash, speech to the Reserve Bank of New Zealand, 2002. Brash has repeated this account in multiple interviews and public remarks.

8. David Caygill, retrospective interview on the Reserve Bank of New Zealand Act 1989.

9. Canada adopted its 2% target in 1991, the United Kingdom in 1992, the European Central Bank in 1998 ("below but close to 2%"), and the U.S. Federal Reserve in January 2012 under Chairman Ben Bernanke.

The Fed's own staff knows this. In 2021, an internal paper published by Federal Reserve economists examined the theoretical foundation for the idea that inflation expectations — the very mechanism that makes a target useful — actually drive real-world inflation. Their conclusion? The belief "rests on extremely shaky foundations," and clinging to it "could easily lead to serious policy errors."[10]

Read that again. The Federal Reserve's own researchers published a paper saying the intellectual basis for the thing their boss talks about every six weeks in front of Congress is, essentially, bullshit.

But the best part — the part that should make you laugh if it didn't make you want to throw something — is that they can't even do it. Over the last forty years, the Consumer Price Index — the government's own measure of inflation, calculated by the government's own statisticians, using the government's own methodology — has averaged 3.94% per year. Not two. Nearly four. Almost double the target. And that's using the numbers they publish themselves, which most people who buy groceries or pay rent suspect are generous.[11]

The most powerful financial institution in the world built its entire policy framework around a number it can't justify, borrowed from a country smaller than most American states, based on the on-air panic of a man who used to work in produce — and then couldn't even hit it. Not even close. Not even by their own math.

And yet. Jerome Powell sits in that chair, under those lights, in front of those cameras, and says "two percent" like it's a law of physics. He says it seven times in a five-minute opening statement. He says it with the confidence of a man who has either never read his own institution's research, or has read it and decided it doesn't matter.[12]

Two percent inflation means the money in your pocket loses half its value roughly every 35 years. Your parents' savings. Your retirement fund. The twenty dollars your

10. Jeremy B. Rudd, "Why Do We Think That Inflation Expectations Matter for Inflation? (And Should We?)," Finance and Economics Discussion Series, Federal Reserve Board of Governors, 2021.

11. Calculated from the Bureau of Labor Statistics Consumer Price Index for All Urban Consumers (CPI-U), FRED series CPIAUCSL, 1972–2025.

12. Author's count from Powell's opening statements at Federal Open Market Committee press conferences, archived on the Federal Reserve's website.

grandmother tucked into your birthday card. All of it, melting. Slowly enough that you don't notice. Fast enough that it matters.[13]

And the man in charge of that melting can't tell you why.

So how did we get here?

How did a number invented on live television by a fruit executive become the organizing principle of the global financial system? How did a handful of unelected officials — who can't even justify their own target — end up with more power over your daily life than your congressman, your governor, or your boss?

The answer isn't complicated, but it is long. And it starts a lot further back than you'd think. Not with central banks. Not with paper money. Not even with gold coins or silver bars. It starts with people. Regular people, doing what regular people have always done — trying to figure out how to cooperate without getting screwed.

Around the Fire

Go back far enough and there is no money at all. No banks. No government. No Federal Reserve. Just small bands of humans — thirty, forty, maybe a hundred and fifty at the most — figuring out how to survive together.

The popular imagination, shaped by too many movies and not enough anthropology, pictures these people as brutes. Savages grunting over scraps of meat. The phrase "cave man" is meant to evoke something primitive, something lesser — as if the absence of institutions meant the absence of intelligence.

It's the opposite. These were among the most successful societies in human history, measured by the only metric that actually matters: sustainability. Hunter-gatherer bands persisted for tens of thousands of years. The average modern nation-state has lasted a few centuries, if it's lucky. The Federal Reserve has been around for just over a century and has already destroyed ninety-seven percent of the dollar's purchasing power. Maybe we should be a little more humble about who the primitives are.[14]

In those early bands, leadership was earned. The best hunter led the hunt — not because he had a title, but because he was the best hunter. If he got old, or lazy, or stupid, someone else took his place. Authority was competence, and competence was constantly tested against reality. You couldn't print your way to status. You couldn't regulate your

13. The Rule of 72: divide 72 by the annual rate to approximate the halving time. At 2%, 72 ÷ 2 = 36 years. This shortcut works for any compound rate and will reappear throughout this book.

14. Bureau of Labor Statistics CPI data, FRED series CPIAUCSL. A dollar in 1913, when the Federal Reserve was established, is worth approximately three cents in 2025 purchasing power.

competition out of existence. You either delivered or you didn't, and the group adjusted accordingly.

This was not utopia. Life was hard, often short, and frequently violent. But the core operating system — voluntary cooperation among people who could leave if the deal went bad — was remarkably effective. People specialized. The best flint-knapper made tools. The best tracker led the hunt. The best gatherer knew which plants wouldn't kill you. They traded, not because some economist told them to, but because trading made everyone better off.

Economists have a name for this, though the people doing it didn't need one. They call it the *economic means* — the method of acquiring wealth through production and voluntary exchange. You make something, or you do something, and you trade it for what someone else made or did. Both sides benefit or the trade doesn't happen. It's the default human operating system, and it ran the world for a very long time.

There is another way to acquire wealth. You can take it. By force, by threat, by fraud, or by decree. The political scientist Franz Oppenheimer called this the [15] *political means* — and he argued, convincingly, that the history of the state is the history of the political means gradually overtaking the economic means. Every tax, every tariff, every act of money printing is a variation on the same theme: some people getting rich not by creating value, but by extracting it from people who do.

For most of human history, the political means barely existed. Not because people were more virtuous, but because there wasn't enough to steal. A band of hunter-gatherers doesn't accumulate surplus. There's no warehouse full of grain to raid, no treasury to plunder. If a bully tried to dominate the group, the group could simply leave. The exit option was always available, and that single fact — the ability to walk away — kept power in check more effectively than any constitution ever written.

Then came agriculture. And everything changed.

Surplus and the State

Sometime around 8,000 BCE, give or take a few millennia, humans figured out how to grow food on purpose. This was, by any measure, the most consequential technological breakthrough in history. It was also, from the perspective of individual freedom, a catastrophe.

15. Franz Oppenheimer, The State (1908), translated by John Gitterman. Oppenheimer's distinction between the "economic means" and the "political means" is foundational to this book's argument.

Agriculture created surplus. For the first time, a community could produce more food than it needed to survive. That surplus could be stored, traded, and accumulated. It was the beginning of wealth — and the beginning of wealth worth stealing.

The anthropological record is clear about what happened next. Hierarchy hardened. The chieftain became the king. The king needed soldiers to protect his territory and administrators to manage his grain stores. He needed a way to pay them both, which meant he needed taxes. The state was born — not as a natural extension of human cooperation, but as a protection racket that became possible only when there was something worth protecting. Or, depending on your perspective, something worth taking.

We don't have to speculate about what these early rulers were like. We have the record. The oldest surviving work of literature on earth — older than the Bible, older than Homer — is the Epic of Gilgamesh, written on clay tablets in ancient Sumer around 2100 BCE. Gilgamesh was king of Uruk, one of the first great cities, and the poem opens by telling you exactly what kind of leader surplus agriculture produced. He claimed every bride for himself on her wedding night. He beat anyone who challenged him into submission. His own people cried out to the gods for relief from the man who was supposed to protect them. This is the *first* ruler whose story survived long enough for us to read.[16] And the story is: he was a tyrant who took what he wanted because no one could stop him.

And it only got worse from there. The Assyrian kings didn't just commit atrocities — they *bragged* about them. In their own official inscriptions, carved into palace walls and stone monuments for all eternity, they cataloged their violence the way a CEO catalogs quarterly earnings. Ashurnasirpal II, who ruled the Neo-Assyrian Empire in the ninth century BCE, left detailed accounts of what he did to cities that resisted him. After crushing a rebellion at the city of Tela, he had the inscriptions record that he flayed the chiefs alive and draped their skins over a pillar at the city gate. Some captives he impaled on stakes. Others he burned alive. He had noses, ears, and fingers cut off the survivors. He put out their eyes. He made separate pillars of the living and the dead. This wasn't hidden. It wasn't classified. It was the *official press release* — the king's own résumé, chiseled into stone so no one would forget.[17]

---

16. The earliest Sumerian poems about Gilgamesh date to approximately 2100 BCE. The standard Babylonian version was compiled around 1200 BCE. Translation: Andrew George, The Epic of Gilgamesh (Penguin Classics, 1999).

17. Ashurnasirpal II reigned 883–859 BCE. His annals are translated in A. Kirk Grayson, Assyrian Rulers of the Early First Millennium BC, Royal Inscriptions of Mesopotamia series (University of Toronto Press, 1991).

These weren't anomalies. This was standard practice across centuries of Assyrian rule, each king trying to outdo the last in documented savagery. Sennacherib boasted of deporting 200,150 people from Judah and shutting King Hezekiah inside Jerusalem "like a caged bird." The historical record of early statehood doesn't read like a story of wise governance and public service. It reads like a horror novel written by the villain, who thought he was the hero.[18]

Four thousand years later, the tools have gotten more sophisticated. The modern state doesn't impale anyone on stakes outside the city gate. It doesn't need to. It has something far more elegant: a money printer. But the job description — extract wealth from the people who produce it, punish anyone who resists, and frame the whole operation as noble and necessary — hasn't changed much.

The critical shift was the loss of the exit option. A forager could walk away from bad leadership. A farmer couldn't. His wealth was in the ground — literally. Once territory filled up and survival depended on land you couldn't carry with you, the ability to leave evaporated. And without the ability to leave, the balance between the economic means and the political means tipped permanently.

This is the part of the story that most books skip, or tell as progress. "Civilization arose!" they say, as if moving from voluntary cooperation to coerced taxation was an upgrade. In some ways it was — agriculture enabled cities, writing, specialization on a massive scale. But it also enabled something that hadn't existed before: a permanent class of people who lived not by producing, but by controlling what others produced.

Sound familiar?

18. Sennacherib's Annals, preserved on the Taylor Prism (British Museum) and the Oriental Institute Prism. Translation in James B. Pritchard, ed., Ancient Near Eastern Texts Relating to the Old Testament (Princeton University Press, 1969).

Chapter Two

The Open Hand

The Emergence of Money

Here's a fact that would surprise most people: money was not invented by a government. No king woke up one morning and declared, "Let there be currency." Money emerged the same way language emerged — from the bottom up, through the voluntary actions of millions of people trying to solve a practical problem.

The problem was simple. Barter sucks.

If you're a farmer with extra grain and you need a new axe, you have to find someone who makes axes and wants grain. Right now. In the right quantity. That's called the "coincidence of wants," and it's as clumsy as it sounds. It's like trying to run an economy on Craigslist, except everyone's illiterate and there's no internet.

People solved this problem the same way they solve most problems — by trial and error over generations. They discovered that certain goods worked better than others as a medium of exchange. Not because anyone decreed it, but because some things just have the right properties. Cattle worked for a while. So did salt — the word "salary" comes from the Latin *salarium*, a salt allowance paid to Roman soldiers. Shells worked in some places. Beads in others.

But over time, across dozens of civilizations that never communicated with each other, the same answer kept emerging: metal. Specifically, precious metal. And most specifically, gold.

Gold won the monetary competition not because it's pretty — though it is — but because it has a set of properties that no other substance on earth matches simultaneously. It doesn't rust, rot, or decay. You can melt it down and divide it into any size you need. It's dense enough to be portable — a lot of value in a small space. It's scarce enough that you can't just go dig up more of it whenever you feel like it. And it's almost impossible to counterfeit, because its density and malleability are unique.

These aren't abstract qualities. They translate directly into what money needs to do for regular people. Durable means your savings don't spoil. Divisible means you can buy a loaf of bread or a house with the same money. Portable means you can take your wealth with you. Scarce means no one — not your neighbor, not your king, not your central bank — can create more of it out of thin air and dilute what you already have.

That last property is the one that matters most, and it's the one that separates real money from everything that came after.

An economist named Ludwig von Mises formalized this observation in a way worth pausing on, if only because it demolishes the most common excuse for government-controlled money. Critics have always argued that money's value is circular — people accept it because other people accept it, which means someone has to step in and declare: *this is money*. A king. A government. An authority.

Mises proved that's wrong. In 1912, he showed that you can trace the value of any money backward through time, day by day, until you reach the moment when the commodity wasn't money at all — when people valued gold just because it was useful. Pretty. Workable. Good for jewelry, for dentistry, for not corroding in the rain. People didn't accept gold as payment because a king said so. They accepted it because *yesterday* it had value, and yesterday's value was based on the day before that, and so on, all the way back to the first person who wanted gold because it was gold. No decree. No central authority. Just people, over centuries, converging on the same answer because reality kept rewarding it.

Economists call this the regression theorem, and we'll come back to it later in this book, because it turns out to have a lot to say about Bitcoin. For now, the point is simple: the best money humanity ever found wasn't designed. It was discovered. And the discovery didn't require a government. It required the opposite — the freedom to choose.[1]

What Honest Money Does

Under a gold standard — or any system where money is hard to produce — prices are honest signals. When bread costs a certain amount, that price reflects the actual supply of

1. The Theory of Money and Credit by Ludwig von Mises, first published in German as Theorie des Geldes und der Umlaufsmittel (Munich: Duncker & Humblot, 1912). The regression theorem appears in Part One, Chapter 4: "The Relation of the Monetary Theory to the General Theory of Value." English translation by H.E. Batson (London: Jonathan Cape, 1934). Available in full at mises.org.

bread relative to the actual supply of money. If a baker raises his price, it's because bread got scarcer or demand went up. The price tells you something true about the world.

More importantly, savings mean something. If you work for twenty years and set aside a portion of your earnings, that gold — or that paper backed by gold — holds its value. You can pass it to your children and it buys roughly the same amount of stuff it bought when you earned it. A father's labor can cross generations. A family can build wealth not by gambling or speculating or getting lucky, but by working hard and spending less than they earn.

This sounds like theory. It isn't. There was a time in American history when this was just how life worked, and the evidence for it is so clear that economists still argue about how to explain it away.

Between 1873 and 1897 — a period that included two severe depressions — the real wages of American non-agricultural workers rose thirty percent. Read that again. Through twenty-four years that included financial panics, bank failures, and mass unemployment, the average worker's purchasing power grew by nearly a third. Prices fell, but wages held, which meant the money in your pocket bought more stuff with each passing year. Economists call this "benign deflation," and it is the most hated concept in modern central banking, because it proves that the thing they've spent a century telling you is catastrophic — falling prices — is actually the natural reward for a productive society operating on honest money.

This is what the gold standard felt like for ordinary people. Not for bankers. Not for railroad tycoons. For the carpenter, the seamstress, the factory hand, the nurse. Your wages might not go up much in nominal terms, but they didn't have to, because the cost of everything around you was gently falling. Your savings didn't melt. They *grew* — not because you were earning interest at some bank, but because the money itself was getting more valuable as the economy produced more goods. A dollar saved in 1880 bought more in 1890 than it did the day you earned it. That is an astonishing fact, and it is the exact opposite of how money works today.

What did this mean in practice? It meant that people at the very bottom of American society — people with every conceivable disadvantage stacked against them — could build wealth through nothing more than work and thrift. Not speculation. Not leverage. Not connections. Just the radical act of saving money that held its value.

From Slave to Tycoon

Biddy Mason was born into slavery on a plantation in Hancock County, Georgia, in 1818. She never learned to read or write. She was sold between masters in Georgia, South Carolina, and Mississippi before ending up as the property of a Mormon convert named Robert Smith, who decided to join Brigham Young's migration west. In 1848, Biddy Mason — thirty years old, mother of three daughters — walked seventeen hundred miles from Mississippi to the Salt Lake Valley. Not rode. Walked. Behind a three-hundred-wagon caravan, herding cattle, setting up camp, cooking meals, and delivering babies along the trail. She did all of this while enslaved, while caring for her children, and while having no legal claim to her own body.

Smith eventually moved the household to San Bernardino, California — a free state, though he neglected to mention that fact to the people he kept as property. When Smith tried to relocate to Texas to re-enslave his workers, Biddy Mason's friends intervened. A Los Angeles judge heard her case. California law at the time didn't allow Black people to testify against white people in court, and Smith had bribed her lawyer not to show up. The judge spoke to Biddy privately, asked her what she wanted, and she said the word: freedom. On January 21, 1856, the court declared Biddy Mason and her thirteen family members free.

She was thirty-eight years old, illiterate, Black, female, and alone in a frontier town with three daughters and no money. By every modern metric of disadvantage, she should have been the most vulnerable person in America.

What she had was the ability to save in real money.

Mason found work as a nurse and midwife for a local doctor, earning about $2.50 a day. She was meticulous, skilled, and apparently tireless — she would eventually deliver hundreds of babies across the Los Angeles basin, treating patients of all races, carrying a large black medical bag everywhere she went. The bag also held her freedom papers.

She saved everything. Every day's wages went into the same pot, denominated in dollars backed by gold, dollars that didn't lose their value while she slept, dollars that bought the same amount of flour and lumber in 1866 that they'd bought in 1856. After ten years of saving — ten years of $2.50 days — she walked into a land office and bought two lots on Spring Street in the pueblo of Los Angeles for $250. She signed the deed with an X.

She told her daughters: never sell this land.

Then she kept saving. She kept buying property. She made shrewd investments in what was then a dusty frontier outpost. The city grew around her. Her land became prime urban real estate. By the time Biddy Mason died in 1891, she had accumulated a fortune of nearly $300,000 — the equivalent of roughly six to ten million dollars today. She was the wealthiest Black woman west of the Mississippi, and she still couldn't write her own name.

But here's the part that matters more than the fortune. Look at what she did with it. She founded the First African Methodist Episcopal Church of Los Angeles — the first Black church in the city — organizing services in her living room in 1872 until she could finance a permanent building. She opened a daycare for working parents. She established a school for Black children. She fed and sheltered the poor of all races. When a flood left families homeless, she opened an account at a local store and told them to send the bills to her. Lines of people — Black and white — formed daily outside her house on Spring Street, seeking food, medical care, money, or just a place to rest. She visited prisoners. She funded charities. Her grandson, Robert Curry Owens, became the wealthiest Black man in Los Angeles and a prominent civic leader.

An illiterate formerly enslaved woman, armed with nothing but a midwife's skill and money that held its value, built a fortune, raised a family, founded institutions that outlived her, and became the anchor of an entire community. In thirty-five years. Starting from zero. Starting from *below* zero.

"If you hold your hand closed, nothing good can come in," Biddy Mason told people. "The open hand is blessed, for it gives in abundance, even as it receives."[2]

Now here is the question that should keep you up at night.

Could Biddy Mason do what she did today?

A Black woman working a comparable job in modern Los Angeles — home health aide, nursing assistant, midwife — makes somewhere around fifteen dollars an hour. Sounds like more than $2.50 a day. It isn't. Not even close. Her rent in Los Angeles consumes forty to fifty percent of her income before she buys a single meal. The M2 money supply — the total amount of dollars in circulation — has been growing at over six percent a year for four decades, which means her savings lose roughly half their purchasing power every eleven years. If she manages to set aside anything at all, it sits in a bank account

2. Biddy Mason (1818–1891). Biographical details from the Los Angeles Almanac; PBS SoCal, "Biddy Mason and the Founding of Los Angeles"; and Encyclopedia.com. Mason earned $2.50 per day as a nurse and midwife for Dr. John Strother Griffin, saved $250 over approximately ten years, and on November 28, 1866 purchased two lots on Spring Street in Los Angeles. Her estate at death approached $300,000. The Biddy Mason Memorial Park in downtown Los Angeles occupies the site of her original homestead.

earning half a percent while inflation runs at four. She is moving backward while standing still.

And the property? Biddy Mason bought two lots for $250 — roughly a hundred days' wages. A comparable property in modern Los Angeles would cost millions. The median home in LA County costs over ten times the median household income. Biddy Mason's path — save your wages, buy property, build wealth — isn't just difficult today. It is mathematically impossible for someone in her position. Not because today's Biddy Mason is less capable or less disciplined. Because the money doesn't work anymore.

So what replaced the ability to save? The welfare state. Food stamps, Section 8 housing, Medicaid, SNAP, WIC, TANF — an alphabet soup of programs designed to keep people alive in a system that has made it impossible for them to build wealth. These programs are not evil, and the people who depend on them are not lazy. But they are a substitute — an inferior, dependency-creating substitute — for what sound money used to provide naturally. The ability to save *was* the social safety net. It always was. When the government destroyed the money, it destroyed the safety net, and then it built a bureaucratic replacement and called it compassion.

The cruelest irony is who gets hurt most. The people furthest from the money printers are the last to benefit from new money and the first to suffer from the rising prices it causes. In America, by almost every measurable standard, that means urban Black communities. The same communities where Biddy Mason built her fortune on $2.50 a day now have a median household net worth that, in some cities, rounds to zero. Not because something went wrong with the people. Because something went wrong with the money.

Biddy Mason didn't need a welfare check. She needed money that worked. She had it, and she built an empire. Today's Biddy Masons have been given a currency that melts in their hands and a government program to catch them when it does. That is not progress. The arsonist is selling fire insurance, and he is marketing it as generosity.

Or consider a different kind of story — not about survival, but about ambition.

In 1892, two brothers in Dayton, Ohio, opened a bicycle repair shop. Wilbur and Orville Wright were not wealthy. They had no college degrees — Wilbur had finished high school but never attended university; Orville had dropped out of high school to start a printing business. Their father was a bishop in a small evangelical church. They were, by any measure, working-class kids with mechanical aptitude and a lot of curiosity.

The bicycle business was booming in the 1890s — the invention of the "safety bicycle" had replaced the absurd penny-farthing, and suddenly everyone wanted one. The Wrights repaired them, then started manufacturing their own models — the Van Cleve, which sold for around $65, and the cheaper St. Clair at $42.50. They were good at it. The shop turned a modest but reliable profit.

And here's the thing that matters: those profits held their value. A dollar saved from selling a Van Cleve in 1894 bought the same amount of steel, fabric, and lumber in 1899. The Wrights didn't have to invest their savings in the stock market to stay ahead of inflation. They didn't need a financial advisor. They just needed a drawer or a bank account, and time. Over the course of a decade, they saved roughly $5,000 from the bicycle business. Not a fortune. A working-class nest egg, accumulated a few dollars at a time, from a small shop in Ohio.

That money funded the invention of the airplane.

Let that land for a moment. The Wright brothers used savings from a bicycle shop — accumulated in gold-backed dollars that didn't lose their value — to build a wind tunnel, test over two hundred wing designs, make multiple trips to Kitty Hawk, North Carolina, construct a series of increasingly sophisticated gliders, and finally, on December 17, 1903, achieve the first powered, controlled, sustained flight in human history. Total cost of the research program, including travel: under $1,000.

While they were doing this with their bicycle savings, the United States government was funding a man named Samuel Langley, Secretary of the Smithsonian Institution, to build a competing flying machine. Langley received $50,000 in War Department money — taxpayer funds, allocated through political connections. His "Great Aerodrome" was launched from a houseboat on the Potomac River on December 8, 1903 — nine days before the Wright Flyer's success at Kitty Hawk. It nose-dived immediately into the river. A second attempt also failed. Fifty thousand dollars of public money produced a very expensive piece of river debris.

Two bicycle mechanics with no degrees, saving in honest money, outperformed the United States government by a factor of fifty to one. The economic means — production, savings, voluntary exchange — beat the political means so badly it would be funny if it weren't so perfectly illustrative. The Wrights didn't need a grant. They didn't need a subsidy. They didn't need a government program. They needed money that held its value long enough for their savings to mean something.

This is what honest money does. It turns work into savings, savings into capital, and capital into possibility. It doesn't care if you're an illiterate formerly enslaved woman or a bicycle mechanic without a diploma. It doesn't care about your race, your pedigree, or your connections. It is the most egalitarian technology ever discovered, because it lets the economic means — competence, discipline, production — win.

This is the part that gets lost in every economics textbook, and it's the part that matters most for the people this book is written for. Under honest money, the working class can save. The playing field isn't perfectly level — it never has been and never will be — but the rules are the same for everyone. A king's gold coin and a peasant's gold coin buy the same amount of bread. No one gets a special rate. No one gets to create money that dilutes yours.

For roughly five thousand years — from the first stamped coins in Lydia around 600 BCE through the early twentieth century — variations of this system held. It wasn't perfect. Governments clipped coins, debased alloys, and ran every scam they could think of to stretch their money supply. But they were constrained. You can shave a little off a gold coin, but you can't print a gold coin. The physical reality of the metal imposed discipline that no law or institution could.

Then someone figured out a workaround.

Chapter Three

The Trench

The Long Con

The theft of honest money didn't happen all at once. It happened in stages, each one building on the last, each one a little more abstract, a little harder to see. If you mapped it out, it would look less like a revolution and more like a slow-motion heist — the kind where the victim doesn't realize he's been robbed until decades later, and by then the thieves are long gone.

Stage Zero: The Shave.

Before there were paper receipts or central banks or quantitative easing, there was a simpler version of the same crime. If you controlled the mint, you could shave the coins.

The trick was old before Rome was young. A ruler collects taxes in gold or silver coins. He melts them down, mixes in a cheaper metal — copper, usually — and re-stamps them at the same face value. Now he has more coins than he started with. The extra coins pay for wars, palaces, and bribes. The people holding the debased coins don't notice immediately, because the coins still *look* the same. They carry the same stamp, the same face, the same denomination. But there's less silver in each one, which means each one buys a little less. The ruler got richer. Everyone else got poorer. And because the theft was hidden inside the coin itself, most people never figured out who robbed them.

The Roman Empire ran this play for three hundred years, and it tracks almost perfectly with the empire's decline. When Augustus minted the silver denarius, it was nearly pure — around 95% silver. It was honest money, and it was the backbone of the most powerful economy the ancient world had ever seen. A soldier's daily wage was one denarius. A loaf of bread cost a predictable fraction of one. Prices were stable because the money was real.[1]

Then Nero got his hands on it. In 64 AD, facing the expenses of rebuilding Rome after the Great Fire and funding his own spectacular appetites — including the Domus Aurea, a golden palace so obscene that his successors tore most of it down — Nero reduced the denarius to about 80% of its former silver content. It doesn't sound like much. It was enough. He'd figured out that he could spend money he didn't have by making everyone else's money worth less. The public didn't riot because the coins still looked like coins. They just noticed, vaguely, that things seemed to cost more.[2]

Every emperor after Nero faced the same temptation, and almost all of them gave in. Trajan shaved a little more. Marcus Aurelius a little more after that. By the time Septimius Severus took power in 193 AD, the denarius was down to about 50% silver. His son Caracalla, in 215 AD, pulled off one of the great monetary scams of antiquity: he introduced a new coin called the antoninianus, declared it worth two denarii, and minted it with only about one and a half denarii of silver. Classic government math. Buy one, get one free — if you're the government.

By the Crisis of the Third Century — a fifty-year stretch of civil wars, plagues, and invasions — the Roman mint had given up pretending. Under the emperor Gallienus, around 260 AD, the denarius contained roughly 5% silver. It was a copper slug with a silver wash so thin it sometimes rubbed off before the coin left the mint. The most powerful currency in the ancient world had become a token. Soldiers refused it. Merchants hid their goods. Entire regions of the empire reverted to barter.[3]

And then came the part that should sound very familiar. Emperor Diocletian, who inherited this disaster in 284 AD, decided the problem wasn't the money. The problem was greed. In 301 AD, he issued the Edict on Maximum Prices — a comprehensive list

---

1. Numismatic analyses of Augustan-era denarii consistently show silver content between 95% and 98%. See Kevin Butcher and Matthew Ponting, The Metallurgy of Roman Silver Coinage (Cambridge University Press, 2014).

2. Butcher and Ponting (2014). Nero's debasement reduced the denarius from approximately 3.9 grams of silver to roughly 3.4 grams, a reduction of about 12–15% in silver content per coin, compounded by a reduction in coin weight.

3. The progression from 95% silver under Augustus to roughly 5% under Gallienus is one of the most thoroughly documented monetary collapses in history. For a comprehensive metallurgical analysis of the denarius across three centuries of debasement, see Butcher and Ponting (2014) and Roger S. Bagnall, Currency and Inflation in Fourth Century Egypt (Scholars Press, 1985).

of price ceilings on over 1,400 goods and services, from barley to boots to the wages of a veterinarian bleeding a horse. The penalty for charging more than the maximum was death. The penalty for [4] *paying* more than the maximum was also death. The penalty for refusing to sell your goods at the listed price — you guessed it — death.

It failed immediately. Merchants pulled their goods off the market rather than sell at a loss. Black markets exploded. Goods that had been merely expensive became impossible to find. The price of gold in debased denarii rose 250% *after* the edict. By the end of Diocletian's reign in 305, the law was a dead letter. You cannot fix broken money with a death threat.[5]

A thousand years later, a French bishop named Nicole Oresme sat down and wrote the autopsy. His treatise *De Moneta* — "On Money," written around 1360 — is one of the most remarkable documents in economic history, and almost nobody has read it. Oresme argued, in terms that would get him called a Bitcoin maximalist if he were alive today, that money belongs to the [6] *community*, not to the prince. When the prince debases the coinage, he is stealing. Not metaphorically. Literally. He is taking the silver out of your pocket and putting it in his.

"I am of the opinion," Oresme wrote, "that the main and final cause why the prince pretends to the power of altering the coinage is the profit or gain which he can get from it." And if the prince can do it once, Oresme warned, he'll do it again, and again, "until he is at length able to draw to himself almost all the money or riches of his subjects and reduce them to slavery. And this would be tyrannical, indeed true and absolute tyranny."[7]

That was 1360. The man was describing quantitative easing six hundred and fifty years before it had a name.

---

4. Edictum de Pretiis Rerum Venalium (Edict on Maximum Prices), promulgated by Diocletian in 301 AD. The edict's preamble blamed rising prices on the "avarice" of merchants and speculators. The full text, including the veterinary fee schedule, survives in fragmentary inscriptions across the eastern Roman Empire. See Tenney Frank, ed., An Economic Survey of Ancient Rome, vol. 5 (Johns Hopkins Press, 1940).

5. Lactantius, De Mortibus Persecutorum ("On the Deaths of the Persecutors"), written c. 313 AD, provides a contemporary account of the edict's catastrophic failure, including the disappearance of goods from markets and the flourishing of black markets.

6. Nicole Oresme, De Moneta (c. 1360). The standard English translation is by Charles Johnson: The De Moneta of Nicholas Oresme and English Mint Documents (Thomas Nelson and Sons, 1956). Oresme was Bishop of Lisieux and one of the most original thinkers of the medieval period.

7. Oresme, De Moneta, Johnson translation. The passages quoted here are from chapters 15 and 17, where Oresme builds his case that debasement is a form of taxation without consent and therefore tyranny by definition.

Oresme meant it as a warning. Fiat money made it a blueprint. The system we live under today — where a central bank can create unlimited currency with a keystroke, no silver required, no coins to shave, no physical constraint of any kind — is the machinery that makes Oresme's nightmare not just possible but *inevitable*. The prince no longer needs to melt down your coins. He just prints new ones.

Oresme went further. He ranked debasement as *worse than usury* — worse than loan sharking — because at least a loan shark requires your consent. The prince debases the coin without asking. You wake up poorer, and no one told you. In Oresme's framework, every king who shaved his coins was not a wise steward managing the economy. He was a thief who happened to wear a crown.

The physical constraints of metal made this kind of theft difficult to scale. You can debase a coin, but you can't debase it past zero. You can shave it, but people eventually notice — the coins get lighter, the prices get higher, and if you push it too far, the whole system collapses, as Rome discovered. The metal imposed a floor. The cheating had limits.

What the modern era figured out was how to remove those limits entirely. And it started, as most great frauds do, with something that sounded perfectly reasonable.

Stage One: The Receipt.

Gold is heavy. If you're a merchant in Renaissance Italy or seventeenth-century London, carrying gold around is inconvenient and dangerous. So you deposit it with a goldsmith — an early version of a bank — and he gives you a paper receipt. That receipt says: "The bearer of this note is entitled to X ounces of gold, held in storage." You can trade the receipt instead of the gold. It's lighter, it's easier, and you can always go get your gold back.

This is fine. The paper isn't money. It's a claim on money. As long as the gold is sitting in the vault, the system works exactly the way it should.

Stage Two: The Lie.

The goldsmith notices something. Most people never come back for their gold. They just trade the receipts. So the goldsmith has an idea: what if he writes *more* receipts than he has gold? He could lend out these extra receipts and charge interest on them. As long as everyone doesn't show up at once demanding their gold, no one will ever know.

This is fractional reserve banking, and it is — stripped of its textbook respectability — fraud. The goldsmith is lending money that doesn't exist. He's creating purchasing power out of nothing and charging people for the privilege of borrowing it. If you or I did this, we'd go to prison. When a bank does it, we call it the financial system.

The risk, of course, is a bank run. If depositors lose confidence and everyone demands their gold at once, the goldsmith is exposed. He doesn't have it. This happened regularly for centuries, and every time it did, the response was the same: instead of outlawing the practice, governments formalized it. They passed laws making fractional reserve lending legal, and they created institutions to backstop the banks when the inevitable happened.

Stage Three: The Central Bank.

There is a scene in Stanley Kubrick's *Paths of Glory* — a film that should be required viewing and isn't — where French soldiers are ordered to charge a German position called the Ant Hill. Everyone knows the attack is suicidal. The general who orders it knows it too. He wants a promotion, and he needs the assault on his record, and the men are — in the arithmetic of the war — expendable. Kirk Douglas, playing Colonel Dax, leads his men over the top anyway, because refusing an order means execution. The soldiers climb out of the trenches and are cut to pieces by machine gun fire within minutes. The attack fails. The general, humiliated, orders three random soldiers court-martialed and shot for "cowardice" to cover his own incompetence.

The film is set in 1916. It was made in 1957. It is, frame for frame, one of the most devastating things ever put on screen, and it raises a question that almost no one in the audience thinks to ask: who paid for all of this? Not the human cost — Kubrick handles that. But the money. The bullets, the artillery shells, the trenches, the gas, the rations, the uniforms, the ships, the trains, the bureaucracy of industrialized death that kept the Western Front grinding for four years and consumed sixteen million lives. Where did the money come from?

The answer to that question begins in 1694, on Threadneedle Street in London.

A central bank is, at its core, a lender of last resort — an institution that can create money to bail out banks that have lent more than they have. The Bank of England, founded in 1694, was the first modern example, and its origin story tells you everything you need to know about why central banks exist.

King William III was fighting an expensive war against France. England had just suffered a humiliating naval defeat at the Battle of Beachy Head, and the country needed to rebuild its fleet. The problem was that William was broke. He went to the goldsmiths — the private bankers of the era — and they all said no. The Crown's credit was ruined.

Charles II had already burned them, borrowing lavishly and then simply refusing to pay it back because, well, he was the king.[8]

So William struck a deal with a Scottish merchant named William Paterson and a group of wealthy investors. They would lend the Crown £1.2 million — roughly £200 million in today's money — and in exchange, they would receive a royal charter creating a new institution: the Governor and Company of the Bank of England. The investors got 8% interest on their loan, and more importantly, the Bank got the right to issue banknotes. A circular distributed to attract subscribers said the quiet part out loud: the Bank would have "benefit of interest on all moneys which it, the Bank, creates out of nothing."[9]

The money was raised in just eleven days. The Bank opened for business on August 1, 1694. King William and Queen Mary themselves invested the maximum permitted amount.[10]

Read that structure carefully, because it's the same deal that exists today, just scaled up. The government gets to spend money it doesn't have. The bankers get to create money and charge interest on it. And the public — the people who actually work for a living — get to pay for all of it through taxes and the slow erosion of their savings.

The arrangement worked spectacularly — for the government and the bankers. England went from a second-rate European power to the dominant global empire in barely a century. And the key wasn't superior culture or some inherent genius of the English people. It was that England could finance wars that its rivals couldn't. While other nations were limited to whatever gold they had in their treasuries, England could borrow against the future labor of its citizens and use the Bank to conjure the money into existence. By 1815, England's national debt had ballooned from £1.2 million to £885 million — almost

---

8. The Battle of Beachy Head (July 10, 1690) was a decisive French naval victory in the Nine Years' War. The English and Dutch fleet lost twelve ships, leaving the English Channel temporarily under French control and creating the urgent need for naval financing that led directly to the Bank of England's founding.

9. The Bank of England was incorporated by royal charter on July 27, 1694. The £1.2 million was raised from 1,268 subscribers. See John Clapham, The Bank of England: A History (Cambridge University Press, 1944), vol. 1.

10. The phrase appears in a promotional circular distributed to potential subscribers to the Bank of England in 1694. Its exact provenance has been debated by historians, but the substance of the claim — that the Bank would profit from issuing notes beyond its reserves — is not disputed. See Clapham (1944).

entirely from compounding war debts. The lenders reaped enormous profits, and the indebtedness gave them extraordinary political leverage. War was now a business model.[11]

The rest of Europe noticed. Central banks spread across the continent like a contagion. France, Prussia, Austria, Russia — by the late nineteenth century, every major European power had one. And every single one of them existed for the same fundamental reason the Bank of England did: to give the government access to money it hadn't earned, to finance ambitions it couldn't afford, and to push the costs onto the public through a mechanism so complex that most people would never understand they were being robbed.

This brings us back to the Ant Hill.

In the summer of 1914, Archduke Franz Ferdinand was assassinated in Sarajevo, and within weeks, Europe tumbled into war. What everyone expected would be a short, decisive conflict — the British press called it "the August bank holiday war" — became instead the most catastrophic bloodbath in human history up to that point. Sixteen million people died. Four empires collapsed. An entire generation of European men was fed into the grinding machinery of trench warfare, poison gas, and machine guns.[12]

The question no one in the history books bothers to ask is: *how was this paid for?*

Under a genuine gold standard, World War I could not have lasted more than a few months. When a government's war chest runs dry, the war ends. That was how wars had always worked. Kings fought until they ran out of gold, and then they negotiated. The financial constraint acted as a natural limit on the duration and scale of human violence. You can only kill as many people as you can afford to kill.

But in August 1914, every major belligerent did the same thing almost simultaneously: they suspended gold convertibility. Britain, France, Germany, Austria-Hungary, Russia — all of them quietly closed the gold window so they could print money to finance the war. Citizens who showed up at banks wanting to convert their paper into gold were turned away. The tether was cut, and governments discovered they could finance the war not from their own treasuries, but from the wealth of their entire populations — extracted invisibly through inflation.

---

11. UK national debt figures from the Bank of England's historical database and B.R. Mitchell, British Historical Statistics (Cambridge University Press, 1988). The debt grew primarily through financing the Seven Years' War, the American Revolution, the French Revolutionary Wars, and the Napoleonic Wars.

12. Standard WWI casualty estimates range from 15 to 22 million total deaths (military and civilian). The four empires that collapsed were the Russian, Ottoman, Austro-Hungarian, and German. See John Keegan, The First World War (Alfred A. Knopf, 1999).

The story of how this happened in Britain is particularly illuminating, and the economist Saifedean Ammous tells it brilliantly in *The Fiat Standard*[13] . When the Bank of England first issued war bonds to fund the fighting, the sale was a disaster. Less than a third of the bonds were subscribed. The British public, it turned out, was not terribly enthusiastic about financing a war with their savings. So the Bank of England did what central banks do: it cheated. It secretly granted funds to its own chief cashier and his deputy to purchase the bonds under their own names, making it look like the issue was fully subscribed. The *Financial Times*, in what would become a century-long tradition of serving as the establishment's stenographer, dutifully published an article proclaiming the bond sale was oversubscribed. John Maynard Keynes, then working at the Treasury, sent a secret memo to the Bank praising what he called their "masterly manipulation." The [14] *Financial Times* would only issue a correction 103 years later, in 2017, when the scheme was finally uncovered in the Bank's own archives.[15]

Ammous calls this the "fiat white paper" — the moment the modern monetary system was truly born. Not in a legislative chamber. Not through democratic process. But through a fraud, committed by a central bank, covered up by a newspaper, and praised by the most celebrated economist of the twentieth century. Saifedean describes the Bank of England's instructions to its branches as something like: from now on, do not make payment in gold. Take payment in gold. Encourage your customers to turn in their gold and give them paper instead.

That is how central banks fund wars. Not through honest taxation, which would require the public to consent to the cost. Not through voluntary bond purchases, which would require the public to actually want the war badly enough to pay for it. But through monetary manipulation — creating money from nothing, diluting the savings of every citizen in the country, and hoping no one notices until the shooting stops.

---

13. Saifedean Ammous, The Fiat Standard: The Debt Slavery Alternative to Human Civilization (The Saif House, 2021). The account of the Bank of England's wartime bond fraud is in Chapter 3.

14. The Financial Times published its correction in 2017 after researchers discovered the deception in the Bank of England's internal records. The original 1914 article had falsely reported that the war bond issue was oversubscribed by public demand.

15. Keynes's memo is preserved in the Bank of England archives and was brought to wider attention by Ammous (2021). At the time, Keynes was a young Treasury official; he would go on to become the most influential economist of the twentieth century, a career built in no small part on his comfort with exactly this kind of monetary management.

Germany went even further. The Reichsbank created "loan banks" — essentially a shadow central banking system — that could issue their own paper notes with no reserve requirements at all. Germany's money supply grew by 440% during the war. Prices were kept artificially stable through rationing and price controls — Diocletian's trick again — but the inflation was merely hidden, not prevented. It would explode catastrophically after the war, famously reducing the mark to wallpaper.[16]

And here is the point that matters for this book: fiat money didn't just *finance* the war. It *transformed the nature of war itself.*

The Prussian military theorist Carl von Clausewitz had written in his masterwork *Vom Kriege — On War*, published in 1832 — that war was "a continuation of politics by other means." He discussed the concept of "absolute war," a theoretical extreme in which all of a nation's resources are mobilized for total destruction of the enemy. But Clausewitz treated this as an abstraction, a logical extreme that real wars would never quite reach, because real wars are constrained by politics, by friction, and — though he didn't frame it this way — by money.[17]

It took the twentieth century to prove him wrong. German General Erich Ludendorff, who had directed Germany's war effort through the brutal final years of World War I, published *Der totale Krieg — The Total War*[18] — in 1935. Where Clausewitz saw absolute war as an unreachable theoretical limit, Ludendorff saw it as a *goal*. He argued that the distinction between soldiers and civilians was obsolete. In total war, the entire nation is mobilized: its economy, its industry, its people, its morale. Every citizen is a combatant. Every factory is a target. War is no longer limited to the battlefield. The war *is* the nation.

This idea — that war should consume everything — is only possible if you have already disconnected money from reality. You cannot fight a total war on a gold standard, because

16. Gerald D. Feldman, The Great Disorder: Politics, Economics, and Society in the German Inflation, 1914–1924 (Oxford University Press, 1993). The wartime inflation was suppressed by price controls and rationing; the hyperinflation of 1921–1923 was the delayed consequence.

17. Carl von Clausewitz, Vom Kriege (On War), published posthumously in 1832. The standard English translation is by Michael Howard and Peter Paret (Princeton University Press, 1976). The famous formulation is from Book 1, Chapter 1.

18. Erich Ludendorff, Der totale Krieg (1935). Ludendorff inverted Clausewitz's framework, arguing that politics should serve war rather than the reverse — a vision that required the total mobilization of national resources, which in turn required fiat money.

gold imposes a hard limit on how much destruction you can finance. You fight until the gold runs out, and then you stop. But when money can be created from nothing, there is no natural stopping point. War ends only when the wealth of all citizens has been evaporated through currency destruction. As Ammous puts it: under a gold standard, governments fought until they ran out of money. Under a fiat standard, governments fight until their citizens' money runs out of value.

Ron Paul, perhaps the only member of Congress in the last century who understood any of this, put it simply: "It is no coincidence that the century of total war coincided with the century of central banking."[19]

Sixteen million dead in World War I. Sixty million more in World War II. Tens of millions more in Korea, Vietnam, Iraq, Afghanistan, and every other conflict that followed. Not one of these wars could have been sustained without the ability to print money. Not one of them would have lasted as long as it did if governments had been forced to finance them honestly — through direct taxation that the public could see, vote on, and refuse.[20]

Think about those soldiers in *Paths of Glory*. They were ordered to charge into machine gun fire for a general's vanity. When they failed, they were shot by their own side. And the entire apparatus that made it possible — the trenches, the shells, the bureaucracy, the years of grinding attrition — was financed by silently stealing from the savings of the very families those soldiers left behind.

Central banking didn't just change how governments manage money. It changed how governments wage war. And it is worth keeping this in mind, because when we get to Bitcoin, we'll come back to this point. A form of money that cannot be printed is also a form of money that cannot finance endless war. The implications of that are staggering, and they are almost never discussed.

But we're getting ahead of ourselves. The central banking model had crossed the Atlantic.

---

19. Ron Paul has used this formulation in multiple speeches and writings. See Ron Paul, End the Fed (Grand Central Publishing, 2009).

20. WWII casualty estimates range from 50 to 80 million total deaths, including the Holocaust and civilian casualties from bombing, famine, and disease. The figure of 60 million is a commonly cited midpoint. See Antony Beevor, The Second World War (Little, Brown, 2012).

Chapter Four

Slow Poison

Stage Four: The Federal Reserve.

America resisted central banking longer than most. Andrew Jackson killed the Second Bank of the United States in the 1830s, calling it a "den of vipers" that enriched the connected at the expense of the common man. He wasn't wrong. For the rest of the nineteenth century, the country operated without a central bank — and the banking establishment never stopped trying to get one back.[1]

Their argument wasn't frivolous. Between 1873 and 1907, a series of financial panics rattled the American banking system — bank runs, liquidity crunches, cascading failures that wiped out depositors. The Panic of 1907 was the worst: a speculative bet on copper stocks went bad, triggered a run on the Knickerbocker Trust Company, and nearly brought down the entire New York financial system. J.P. Morgan himself had to step in, locking bank presidents in his private library until they agreed to pool funds and stop the bleeding.[2]

The bankers' conclusion was straightforward: the system needed a lender of last resort. An institution with the power to create liquidity in a crisis — to flood the system with cash when confidence evaporated — so that a single bad bet couldn't topple the whole structure. On its face, this sounded reasonable.

---

1. The phrase is widely attributed to Jackson in his battles against the Second Bank of the United States (1832–1836). Its exact origin in Jackson's own writings is debated, but the sentiment is consistent with his documented statements and veto message of July 10, 1832.

2. The Panic of 1907 began with the collapse of the Knickerbocker Trust Company in October. J.P. Morgan organized a private bailout from his library at 219 Madison Avenue. See Robert F. Bruner and Sean D. Carr, The Panic of 1907: Lessons Learned from the Market's Perfect Storm (John Wiley & Sons, 2007).

But not everyone agreed. The economist Benjamin Anderson, writing in the years after the Fed's creation, argued that the panics weren't evidence that the system lacked a central authority — they were evidence that fractional reserve banking itself was unstable, and that a lender of last resort wouldn't fix the instability but would subsidize it. Ludwig von Mises made a sharper point: a central bank that can create money to rescue failing banks doesn't eliminate risk. It socializes it. The losses don't disappear. They're transferred — from the bankers who made bad bets to the public whose currency gets diluted to pay for the rescue. And Murray Rothbard, decades later, would document how the panics themselves were often caused or worsened by earlier government interventions in banking — national bank acts, reserve requirements, and bond-collateral rules that made the system fragile in the first place. The proposed cure was for a disease the government had created.[3 4 5]

But the bankers chose to do it anyway — in secret, without public debate. In November 1910, a group of the most powerful financiers in America traveled to Jekyll Island, Georgia, under assumed names. They told the press they were going duck hunting. What they were actually doing was drafting the legislation that would become the Federal Reserve Act of 1913. The group included representatives of the Morgan, Rockefeller, and Rothschild banking empires — men who collectively controlled a staggering share of the world's wealth. The Federal Reserve Bank of Atlanta will give you a tour of the clubhouse where it happened.[6]

The Federal Reserve was sold to the public as a stabilizing force — a way to prevent the panics and bank runs that had plagued the country. It is worth pausing to examine how well that sales pitch held up.

---

3. Benjamin M. Anderson, Economics and the Public Welfare: A Financial and Economic History of the United States, 1914–1946 (D. Van Nostrand, 1949). Anderson served as economist at Chase National Bank and was a sharp contemporary critic of the Federal Reserve's first decades.

5. Murray N. Rothbard, A History of Money and Banking in the United States (Ludwig von Mises Institute, 2002). Rothbard documents how the National Bank Acts of 1863–1864, which required banks to hold government bonds as collateral for note issuance, created the rigidity that made the system prone to panics.

6. The Jekyll Island meeting of November 1910 is documented in G. Edward Griffin, The Creature from Jekyll Island (American Media, 1994), and confirmed by the Federal Reserve Bank of Atlanta, which maintains historical exhibits about the meeting at the Jekyll Island Club. Attendees included Senator Nelson Aldrich, Abraham Piatt Andrew (Assistant Secretary of the Treasury), Paul Warburg (Kuhn, Loeb & Co.), Frank Vanderlip (National City Bank), Henry Davison (J.P. Morgan & Co.), Charles Norton (First National Bank of New York), and Benjamin Strong (Bankers Trust).

In 1920, barely seven years after the Fed opened its doors, America plunged into a severe depression. Unemployment nearly tripled, jumping from 4% to almost 12%. GDP fell 17%. It was, by some measures, sharper than the initial plunge that would later mark 1929. The historian Thomas Woods called it "The Forgotten Depression," and it's forgotten for a very good reason: it embarrasses everyone who came after.[7]

President Warren Harding did essentially nothing. He cut the federal budget nearly in half. He didn't bail anyone out. The Fed was "largely passive," as one economic historian put it. There was no stimulus. No emergency spending. No fireside chats. Harding told the country to take its medicine: "We will attempt intelligent and courageous deflation, and strike at government borrowing which enlarges the evil."[8][9]

By the summer of 1921, the economy was already recovering. By 1923, unemployment was back to 2.4%, industrial production had hit new highs, and the country was roaring. The depression of 1920 cured itself — not [10] *despite* the absence of government intervention, but *because* of it. It was painful and it was fast, which is exactly how a healthy economy processes a correction.

Then the Federal Reserve made its first catastrophic mistake. Flush with its new powers and eager to prove its usefulness, the Fed began aggressively expanding the money supply throughout the 1920s. As the economist Murray Rothbard documented in *America's Great Depression*, this monetary expansion — not some organic burst of American ingenuity — was the primary fuel for the speculative mania of the Roaring Twenties. The stock market didn't boom because America had suddenly become twice as productive. It boomed because cheap credit flooded the economy, and that credit had to go somewhere.

---

7. Thomas E. Woods Jr., "Warren Harding and the Forgotten Depression of 1920," Intercollegiate Review, Fall 2009. Unemployment and GDP data from the Bureau of Labor Statistics and the Bureau of Economic Analysis historical series.

8. Warren G. Harding, inaugural address, March 4, 1921.

9. The characterization of the Fed as "largely passive" during the 1920–1921 depression appears in multiple economic histories. See James Grant, The Forgotten Depression: 1921, The Crash That Cured Itself (Simon & Schuster, 2014).

10. Bureau of Labor Statistics unemployment data and Federal Reserve industrial production index. The recovery from the 1920–1921 depression remains one of the fastest on record.

It went into stocks, real estate, and leverage — the same places it always goes when money is too cheap.[11]

When the bubble popped in October 1929, the institution that had been created to prevent exactly this kind of crisis was powerless to stop it. Worse — it had *caused* it. Bank runs, the very catastrophe the Fed was designed to eliminate, swept across the country. Between 1930 and 1933, over nine thousand banks failed. Savings were wiped out. Families that had worked for decades to build a modest cushion watched it evaporate in a matter of days. The Fed stood by while the money supply contracted by a third. The institution created at Jekyll Island to end panics had manufactured the worst one in American history and then couldn't even mop up the mess.[12] [13]

What came next is one of the great bait-and-switches in political history. In 1932, Franklin Roosevelt campaigned for president on a platform that would make a libertarian blush. The Democratic Party platform called for "an immediate and drastic reduction of governmental expenditures" of no less than 25%, "a federal budget annually balanced," and — this is a direct quote — "a sound currency to be preserved at all hazards." Roosevelt attacked Herbert Hoover for spending too much. He ran as the fiscally responsible alternative.[14]

He won in a landslide, and then did the opposite of everything he'd promised.

Roosevelt's New Deal was the most dramatic expansion of federal power in peacetime American history. He created agencies to set prices, control production, and manage competition across entire industries. The National Recovery Administration — the NRA — imposed codes on businesses dictating what they could charge, what they could pay, and how much they could produce. A tailor in New Jersey was fined and jailed for pressing a suit for thirty-five cents instead of the NRA-mandated forty cents. The

---

11. Murray N. Rothbard, America's Great Depression (D. Van Nostrand, 1963; 5th ed., Ludwig von Mises Institute, 2000). Rothbard demonstrated that the Fed expanded the money supply by approximately 62% between 1921 and 1929.

12. Federal Deposit Insurance Corporation, "Managing the Crisis: The FDIC and RTC Experience," historical data. The exact count varies by source; the FDIC reports 9,096 bank suspensions between 1930 and 1933.

13. Milton Friedman and Anna Jacobson Schwartz, A Monetary History of the United States, 1867–1960 (Princeton University Press, 1963). Friedman and Schwartz documented a roughly 33% contraction in the money supply between 1929 and 1933.

14. Democratic Party Platform of 1932, adopted at the Democratic National Convention, Chicago, June 27, 1932. The full text is archived at the American Presidency Project, UC Santa Barbara.

Agricultural Adjustment Act paid farmers to destroy crops and slaughter livestock [15] *while Americans went hungry* — all to keep prices artificially high.[16]

If this sounds familiar, it should. It's Diocletian's Edict on Maximum Prices, minus the death penalty but plus an army of bureaucrats. And it worked about as well. The Supreme Court eventually struck down the NRA as unconstitutional in 1935, but the impulse — the belief that the government can fix broken money by controlling what people charge for things — survived and metastasized.

But Roosevelt saved his masterpiece for April 5, 1933, barely a month into his presidency. Executive Order 6102 made it a federal crime — punishable by up to ten years in prison and a $10,000 fine — for any American citizen to own gold. Not to steal it. Not to counterfeit it. To [17] *own* it. The government ordered citizens to surrender their gold coins, gold bullion, and gold certificates to the Federal Reserve, in exchange for paper dollars at the official rate of $20.67 per ounce.

Most people complied, because most people trusted the government. The paper dollars they received had always been redeemable for gold in the past, so what was the difference?

The difference became clear the following year. In January 1934, Roosevelt signed the Gold Reserve Act, which changed the official price of gold from $20.67 to $35 per ounce. In one stroke, the government devalued every paper dollar in circulation by roughly 41%. The gold that citizens had surrendered at $20.67 was now worth $35 — but the citizens didn't get the difference. The government did. It was the largest peacetime wealth transfer

15. Jacob Maged, a tailor in Jersey City, New Jersey, was arrested in April 1934 for charging 35 cents to press a suit, five cents below the NRA code price. He was fined $100 and sentenced to 30 days in jail. The case became a national embarrassment for the NRA. See Amity Shlaes, The Forgotten Man: A New History of the Great Depression (HarperCollins, 2007).

16. The Agricultural Adjustment Act of 1933 authorized payments to farmers for reducing acreage and destroying crops. In 1933 alone, the government paid farmers to plow under ten million acres of cotton and slaughter six million piglets. See Jim Powell, FDR's Folly: How Roosevelt and His New Deal Prolonged the Great Depression (Crown Forum, 2003).

17. Executive Order 6102, signed by President Franklin D. Roosevelt on April 5, 1933. Citizens were required to deliver their gold to a Federal Reserve Bank by May 1, 1933, at the rate of $20.67 per troy ounce. Exemptions existed for small amounts (up to $100 in gold coin), jewelry, and industrial or professional uses.

in American history up to that point, and it was legal because the man who did it was the same man who wrote the law.[18]

Read that sequence again, because it's the playbook. The government creates a crisis through monetary expansion. The crisis destroys savings and wrecks the economy. The government uses the crisis to seize emergency powers. It confiscates the one form of money it can't print. Then it devalues the paper it gave you in exchange. The people who trusted the system got robbed, and the people who ran the system got more power.

Oresme warned you. Diocletian tried it with death threats and failed. Roosevelt tried it with executive orders and succeeded — because by 1933, the exit option had been closed. You couldn't walk away from the dollar. There was nowhere to go.

But the gold standard, even in this debased form, still imposed *some* constraint. Dollars were still nominally redeemable for gold in international transactions, which meant the government couldn't print without limit. It could stretch the tether. It couldn't snap it entirely.

Until it did.

Stage Five: The Tether Snaps.

In 1944, representatives from forty-four countries gathered at Bretton Woods, New Hampshire, to redesign the global monetary system after World War II. The deal they struck was elegant on paper: the U.S. dollar would be pegged to gold at $35 per ounce, and all other currencies would be pegged to the dollar. America, holding the world's largest gold reserves after the war, would serve as the anchor.[19]

This made the dollar the world's reserve currency — a position of extraordinary power. Every country needed dollars to trade, which meant America could run deficits that no other country could. We could spend more than we earned because the world had no choice but to accept our paper.

The problem was predictable to anyone who understood the incentives. America spent. Lavishly. The Korean War. The Vietnam War. Lyndon Johnson's Great Society programs. The deficits mounted, and foreign governments started to notice that America

---

18. Gold Reserve Act of 1934, Public Law 73–87, signed January 30, 1934. The revaluation from $20.67 to $35.00 per ounce represented a 40.94% devaluation of the dollar. The Treasury's profit on the revaluation — approximately $2.8 billion — was deposited into the Exchange Stabilization Fund.

19. The Bretton Woods Conference (officially the United Nations Monetary and Financial Conference), held July 1–22, 1944, at the Mount Washington Hotel, Bretton Woods, New Hampshire. The agreement established the International Monetary Fund and the World Bank alongside the dollar-gold peg.

was printing far more dollars than it had gold to back them. France, under Charles de Gaulle, began demanding gold for its dollar reserves. Other countries followed.

On August 15, 1971, Richard Nixon went on television and announced that the United States would no longer redeem dollars for gold. He called it temporary. He called it necessary. He said it was to protect the American economy from "international money speculators."[20]

It was none of those things. It was the final stage of the heist. The last tether between money and reality was cut, and from that moment forward, the dollar — and by extension every currency pegged to it — was backed by nothing but the promise of the government that issued it. The same government that had just broken its most important promise.

The Machine Turns On

What happened after 1971 is not subtle, and it is not debatable. It is visible in every data set that measures the relationship between money, prices, and wages.

I was on vacation with my family a while back, and one of our stops was at a famous cavern on the East Coast. For reasons I still don't understand, there was a carriage and auto museum next door. Inside, I found a 1925 Rolls-Royce Silver Ghost — the crème de la crème of Gatsby-era wealth. Its sticker price in 1925 was $12,209.[21]

In 1925, $20 was redeemable for one ounce of gold. That Rolls-Royce cost 610 ounces.

If you'd stored those 610 ounces in a vault for a hundred years, today they'd be worth roughly $2,000,000. For that, you could fill a garage with Bugattis, Ferraris, and McLarens — all with more power and features than that Silver Ghost ever dreamed of. Gold held its value. Actually, it did better than that. It appreciated in real terms, because productivity improvements made the things you buy with it cheaper over time.

But if you'd held the dollars instead? If you'd listened to the people who told you gold was a barbarous relic, a pet rock, that you can't eat gold? Twelve thousand two hundred and nine dollars today buys you a used Honda Civic with over a hundred thousand miles on it and possible cigarette burns in the floor mat.

At the other end of the museum, I found a Ford Model T — the car that built the American middle class. Its sticker price in 1915 was $490, or roughly 24 ounces of gold.

---

20. Richard Nixon, televised address to the nation, August 15, 1971. Nixon announced the suspension of dollar-gold convertibility as part of a broader package of economic measures that also included a 90-day wage and price freeze — Diocletian would have recognized the impulse. The "temporary" suspension was never reversed.

21. Rolls-Royce Silver Ghost pricing from period sales literature and auction house records. The Silver Ghost was produced from 1906 to 1926 and was considered the finest automobile in the world during its production run.

That gold today is worth over $80,000 — enough for a new BMW or Mercedes. The $490 in cash wouldn't cover a month of groceries.[22]

The gold didn't get smarter. The dollar got dumber. And it got dumber because, after 1971, there was nothing stopping the people who control the money supply from making more of it whenever they wanted.

Since 1981 — the earliest period for which the Federal Reserve reports M2 money supply on its website — M2 has grown at an average annual rate of 6.01%. That means the money in circulation has been increasing by roughly six percent every year for over four decades.

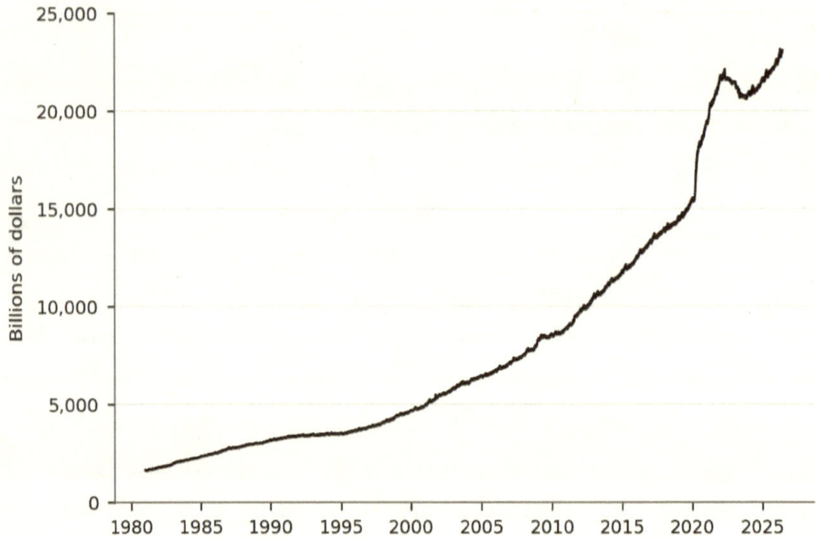

M2 Money Supply (WM2NS). Source: Board of Governors of the Federal Reserve System via FRED.

This is not inflation in the way most people think of it. It's not prices going up because of supply and demand. It's prices going up because the money is worth less, because there's more of it, because someone created it out of nothing. The price of bread didn't change. The price of money did.

The Slow Poison

22. Ford Motor Company historical pricing. The Model T's price fell from $850 at its 1908 introduction to $260 by 1925, a dramatic illustration of what happens to prices under honest money and increasing productivity.

Here is where most people check out. Here is where the eyes glaze over, where the brain files inflation under "boring economic stuff," where you tell yourself it's only a couple percent a year, how bad can it be?

This is exactly what they're counting on.

The Federal Reserve has trained the American public to evaluate its performance against one standard: did they blow up the economy? Did we get hyperinflation — wheelbarrows of cash, Weimar Germany, Zimbabwe? No? Then they must be doing a good job. The whole conversation about central banking in this country is framed around catastrophe avoidance, as though the relevant question is whether the pilot crashed the plane into a mountain, not whether he's been slowly descending for fifty years and is about to run out of altitude.

Hyperinflation is the boogeyman. It's the thing they hold up every time someone questions the system. "It could be worse — look at Venezuela!" And they're right, it could be worse. But "not Venezuela" is not a standard of competence. It is the lowest bar imaginable, and the fact that this is what passes for success tells you everything about how the game is played.

The real damage doesn't require hyperinflation. It doesn't require double digits. It doesn't even require the kind of inflation that makes the evening news. The real damage is done by ordinary, quiet, "under control" inflation — the kind the Fed is *trying* to create — compounding silently over decades and generations until the working class wakes up one morning and can't afford to live.

Let me show you what I mean.

The Federal Reserve targets two percent inflation. That's the goal. That's what they're *aiming for* — the number Jerome Powell says seven times per press conference, the number Don Brash plucked out of thin air, the number they tell you is healthy, necessary, optimal. Let's take them at their word. Let's pretend they actually achieved two percent inflation, consistently, every year.

At two percent inflation, your money loses half its purchasing power every thirty-five years. A hundred thousand dollars saved today is worth fifty thousand in 2060. A young woman who earns her first paycheck at twenty-two will see that money lose half its value before she retires. If she's disciplined enough to save it — in a system that punishes savers — her reward is to watch it quietly dissolve while the people running the system call it "price stability."

That's the *target*. That's the *best case*.

But they can't even do that. According to the Federal Reserve's own data — published on their own website, calculated by their own economists — the Consumer Price Index has increased at an average annual rate of 3.94% since the end of the gold standard in 1972. Not two percent. Nearly four. Almost double what they tell you they're aiming for.

At 3.94%, your money loses half its purchasing power every eighteen years, not thirty-five. A dollar saved the year you were born is worth twenty-five cents by the time you're thirty-six. A hundred thousand dollars set aside for your children is worth less than fifteen thousand by the time they're grown.

And remember: this is the government's own number, calculated by the government's own statisticians, using the government's own methodology — a methodology that has been revised repeatedly over the decades in ways that consistently produce lower readings. If you suspect that the number they publish understates the inflation you actually experience when you buy groceries, fill your gas tank, pay your rent, or take your kid to the doctor — you're not paranoid. You're paying attention.[23]

But let's stay with their number. Let's give them every benefit of the doubt and just use what they publish.

Every number I'm about to show you comes from the Federal Reserve's own database.

Since 1972 — the year after Nixon severed the dollar from gold — the M2 money supply has grown at roughly six percent per year. That means the number of dollars in circulation has been increasing by six percent, every year, for over fifty years. At that rate, money loses half its purchasing power every twelve years. A hundred thousand dollars saved today will have the purchasing power of roughly fifteen thousand dollars in thirty years.

So where did all that new money go?

It didn't go to you. Median household income — the amount the typical American family earns — has grown at 4.23% per year since 1972. That sounds respectable until you realize the money supply was growing at six percent. Your raise didn't keep pace with

23. Bureau of Labor Statistics Consumer Price Index for All Urban Consumers (CPI-U), FRED series CPIAUCSL. Average annual rate calculated from 1972 to 2025. Notable methodological changes include the shift to geometric weighting (1999), hedonic quality adjustments, and the substitution effect — each of which lowered the reported rate relative to earlier methods.

the printer. Every year, the gap between what you earn and how many dollars exist gets a little wider. Over fifty years, that gap becomes a canyon.[24]

Some of it went into housing. The median home sale price has grown at 5.23% per year since 1972 — faster than your income, but slower than the money supply. In 1972, the median home cost about 2.7 times the median household income. Today it costs 4.8 times. A house that took your grandparents less than three years of income to buy now takes you nearly five. Not a bigger house. Not a nicer house. The same house.[25]

But the real story is in the stock market. The NASDAQ has grown at 11.01% per year since 1984. Every dollar in the NASDAQ in 1984 became eighty-two dollars by 2026. Every dollar in your paycheck became less than nine.[26]

Read that again. Eighty-two to nine.

---

24. Median household income for 1972 ($9,697) from U.S. Census Bureau, Current Population Survey, Annual Social and Economic Supplements, Historical Income Tables (Table H-5). Data from 1984 onward from FRED series MEHOINUSA646N. The 4.23% compound annual growth rate spans 1972–2024.

25. Median sales price of houses sold from FRED series MSPUS (https://fred.stlouisfed.org/series/MSPUS). The 5.23% compound annual growth rate spans Q1 1972 ($26,200) to Q4 2025 ($405,300). Price-to-income ratios calculated by dividing MSPUS by median household income for the corresponding year.

26. NASDAQ Composite Index from FRED series NASDAQCOM (https://fred.stlouisfed.org/series/NASDAQCOM). The 11.01% compound annual growth rate spans January 3, 1984 (277.63) to February 27, 2026 (22,668.21). This does not include dividends, which would make the total return even higher.

NASDAQ Composite (NASDAQCOM). Source: Nasdaq, Inc. via FRED.

This is not an accident. It is not a mystery. It is the predictable, mathematically inevitable result of a system that creates money and hands it to the financial sector first. Economists have a name for it. They call it the Cantillon Effect, after Richard Cantillon, an eighteenth-century economist who observed that newly created money doesn't enter the economy evenly — it enters at a specific point, and the people closest to that point benefit at the expense of everyone else.[27]

Here is what the Cantillon Effect looks like in the Federal Reserve's own data, using their own numbers, published on their own website:

The NASDAQ — where Wall Street parks its money — grew at 11.01% per year.

The money supply grew at 6.01% per year.

Home prices grew at 5.23% per year.

Your income grew at 4.23% per year.

27. Richard Cantillon, Essai sur la Nature du Commerce en Général (Essay on the Nature of Trade in General), written c. 1730, published posthumously in 1755. Cantillon observed that when the Spanish brought gold from the New World, prices rose first in Seville, then spread outward — enriching those nearest the new money and impoverishing those furthest from it. The mechanism is identical today; only the source of new money has changed.

Growth of $1 since 1984, by asset class. All data from Federal Reserve Economic Data (FRED).

The closer an asset is to the money printers — to the banks, to Wall Street, to the trading floors — the more of that new money it captured. The further you are from the printers — the more your wealth depends on a paycheck rather than a portfolio — the less you got. The new money didn't trickle down. It pooled at the top.

And here is what that meant for the family that didn't own a home, didn't own stocks, and depended entirely on a paycheck. Since 1972, a homeowner watched their asset grow 15.5 times. A worker watched their income grow 8.6 times. The homeowner — simply by owning the right asset at the right time — gained nearly twice as much as the person who worked for every dollar. And the person who owned stocks? Eighty-two times. The investor class didn't just beat the working class. They lapped them. Multiple times. Using money the Federal Reserve created out of nothing.[28]

A normal hospital childbirth cost $200 in 1960. Today it costs nearly $19,000. Your salary, priced in childbirths, is going to zero. Priced in homes, going to zero. Priced in education, going to zero. Priced in anything real — anything that matters to a family trying to build a life — your salary is on a long, slow slide toward worthlessness.[29]

This is what "two percent" actually means. This is what "price stability" looks like over time. Not a crisis. Not a collapse. A slow bleed — a percent or two each year, just enough that you don't notice, just enough that you blame yourself instead of the system, just enough that by the time you realize what happened, decades have passed and the wealth is gone.

The Standard Is Wrong

This is the thing I need you to understand before we go any further. The debate about inflation in this country is rigged from the start because the standard is wrong.

The question has never been: will the Federal Reserve cause hyperinflation? The answer to that question, at least in the near term, is probably no. The U.S. dollar's reserve

---

28. All growth multiples calculated from Federal Reserve and Census Bureau data cited above. Home prices: 15.5x ($26,200 to $405,300). Household income: 8.6x ($9,697 to $83,730). NASDAQ: 82x (277.63 to 22,668.21). These figures are nominal; they reflect the actual dollar amounts families experienced.

29. Childbirth cost data from the Health Care Cost Institute and historical records compiled by the Bureau of Labor Statistics. The $200 figure for 1960 reflects an uncomplicated vaginal delivery; the current average of approximately $18,865 is from HCCI's 2020 analysis of commercial insurance claims. Costs vary significantly by region and type of delivery.

currency status, the structure of the debt markets, the Fed's ability to raise rates in an emergency — these things make Weimar-style hyperinflation unlikely, at least for now. And the Fed will be happy to remind you of this at every opportunity, because it is the only test they can pass.

The right question — the question nobody in power wants you to ask — is this: does even "moderate" inflation, sustained over decades, destroy the wealth of the working class?

The answer is yes. Obviously, mathematically, irrefutably yes. Not in a dramatic explosion. In a quiet erosion that takes everything — your savings, your purchasing power, your ability to buy a home, your ability to raise a family on one income, your ability to retire, your ability to pass anything on to your children — and grinds it down to nothing over the course of a lifetime.

And here's what makes it worse than hyperinflation, in one specific and devastating way: at least in hyperinflation, everyone knows the money is broken. The crisis is visible. People react. They find alternatives. They demand change. In slow inflation, nobody knows. The theft is invisible. You blame your boss for not paying you enough. You blame yourself for not saving more. You blame the grocery store for charging too much. You blame everything except the one institution that is, by design and by policy, making your money worth less every single day.

Inflation doesn't just destroy wealth. It transfers it — from those who earn money to those who create it, from those who save to those who borrow, from those who work to those who own. It is, in its purest form, a mechanism for moving resources from the productive to the powerful without the inconvenience of asking permission. It is the political means dressed in a lab coat, wielding a spreadsheet, and calling itself science.

And it grows the state. Every dollar of purchasing power that inflation takes from you is a dollar of real wealth that flows toward the institutions closest to the money printers — the government, the banks, the favored corporations. The state doesn't need to raise your taxes to take more from you. It just needs to print, and the inflation does the rest. That is why every government in history has eventually debased its currency. Not because the people in charge were stupid. Because they were *incentivized*. The debasement is the point. The inflation is not a bug. It is the product.

Nicole Oresme told you this in 1360. Diocletian demonstrated it in 301 AD. The Roman emperors proved it over three centuries of declining silver content. And now the Federal Reserve is proving it again, in real time, to three hundred and thirty million

Americans who have been told that two percent is normal, four percent is temporary, and everything is fine.

Everything is not fine.

But here's the thing about slow poisons: they work until they don't. The frog sits in the pot until the moment it can't anymore — and by then it's too late to jump.

Unless someone changes the water.

Chapter Five

Yacht Party

In the summer of 2019, Kylie Jenner turned twenty-two on a chartered superyacht called the *Tranquility* in the Mediterranean Sea. The *Tranquility* rents for $1.2 million a week. It has a crew of eighteen, a helipad, a beach club, a spa, a cinema, and a swimming pool on the deck. There were fireworks. There was a rented helicopter. There were roughly thirty guests, most of them famous, all of them documenting it. Her then-boyfriend Travis Scott gave her a Rolls-Royce. This was described in the press, without irony, as a low-key celebration.[1] Kylie posted the photos to Instagram, where she had 145 million followers—a built-in distribution network more valuable than most broadcast television deals, assembled at zero cost because she happened to be born into a family that had already figured out how to turn fame into capital before she could legally drive.

Kylie Cosmetics was moving lip kits and eyeshadow palettes through her Instagram account. In November of that same year, Coty Inc. paid $600 million for a 51% stake, valuing the whole company at $1.2 billion.

Coty is a hundred-year-old beauty conglomerate. It owns CoverGirl, OPI, Sally Hansen, and Clairol. It is headquartered in Amsterdam. But it is listed on the New York Stock Exchange and financed through American credit markets. A foreign company, borrowing American dollars, from American banks, to buy an American celebrity's lipstick brand. The fiat pipeline does not check passports.

---

1. Widely reported at the time. See, e.g., "Inside Kylie Jenner's 22nd Birthday Celebration on a Superyacht," People, August 2019. The Tranquility (now renamed Equanimity) is a 300-foot vessel originally built for the Malaysian financier Jho Low, later seized by the US Department of Justice as part of the 1MDB fraud investigation—a detail worth noting for what it says about who commissions these things.

Kylie Cosmetics had earned about $177 million in revenue that year. Coty paid roughly 6.8 times revenue for it.[2] For context, the S&P 500 as a whole traded at about 2.2 times revenue in 2019. Coty paid more than triple the market rate for a lipstick brand whose primary distribution channel was a twenty-two-year-old's Instagram account. The only way that math works is if you believe the growth will be enormous—or if money is so cheap that nobody is particularly worried about the math. In 2019, money was cheap.

What made it cheaper still was how Coty financed the deal. By 2019, Coty was already a slow-motion disaster. Three years earlier, flush with cheap post-financial-crisis credit, it had borrowed heavily to acquire 41 beauty brands from Procter & Gamble for $12.5 billion.[3] The integration was a catastrophe. Revenues fell. Costs ballooned. The company took a $4 billion write-down. Its stock price dropped 50% between 2016 and 2019. Coty's board decided what the company really needed was to borrow more money to buy a celebrity's lipstick brand at a valuation that assumed everything would go perfectly.

When Coty borrowed to fund the Kylie acquisition, the bank did not reach into a vault and count out $600 million in existing savings. It created new deposits—new dollars, conjured from nothing, backed by Coty's promise to pay them back with interest. Those new dollars flowed to Kylie Jenner.

Then Forbes reported that Kylie's team had been inflating the company's revenue figures for years—actual e-commerce sales had peaked at $68 million, not the hundreds of millions that had been implied. Coty's shareholders sued. The manufacturer sued. The stock fell another 68% in 2020. Both Kylie and her sister Kim Kardashian eventually sought to buy their brands back from the company that had overpaid for them with borrowed money that had been created out of thin air.

It is a story about what cheap credit does to judgment. In a world of hard money—where loans require actual savings, where interest rates reflect actual scarcity—Coty could not have borrowed its way into a $12.5 billion P&G deal and then borrowed again

---

2. Kylie Cosmetics trailing twelve-month revenue of $177 million reported in Coty's press release of November 18, 2019, and confirmed in subsequent SEC filings. Coty paid $600 million for a 51% stake, implying a $1.2 billion enterprise value—roughly 6.8 times revenue. The S&P 500 price-to-sales ratio stood at approximately 2.2x at year-end 2019, per Siblis Research and Standard & Poor's market data.

3. Coty completed the acquisition of Procter & Gamble's specialty beauty business in October 2016 for approximately $12.5 billion. The portfolio included 41 brands, among them CoverGirl, Max Factor, Clairol, and Wella. The financing was led by Bank of America Merrill Lynch and JP Morgan. Coty subsequently took over $4 billion in write-downs on the acquired brands as integration faltered and drugstore cosmetics fell out of favor. See Coty Inc. Form 10-K, fiscal years 2017–2019.

to buy a celebrity brand at triple the market's valuation rate. The cost of the money would have stopped them. Instead, the fiat system handed them a weapon they were not qualified to use, and they used it enthusiastically, and the new dollars they created rippled outward into the economy while their own equity evaporated.

Kylie Jenner did not design this machine. She just surfed it better than most.

That same year, Craig Hall hosted a fundraiser for presidential candidate Pete Buttigieg in the wine cave beneath his Napa Valley estate. The cave sits thirty feet underground. It is lit by a chandelier made with 1,500 Swarovski crystals and furnished with onyx tables. Tickets ran from $500 to $2,800. The $1,000 ticket got you a photograph with the candidate. The $2,800 option—the legal maximum for an individual campaign contribution—conferred co-host status, meaning you got to tell people you co-hosted a fundraiser in a crystal-chandelier wine cave for a man who wanted to be president. Senator Elizabeth Warren, also running for president at the time, called out the event during a nationally televised debate: "Billionaires in wine caves should not pick the next president of the United States."[4] Buttigieg pointed out that Warren had raised money the same way. Both of them were right, which is the kind of thing that happens when you're arguing about symptoms while agreeing on the disease.

Craig Hall started the way a certain kind of American story always starts—with hustle, borrowed money, and good timing. At eighteen, he used his savings and a loan to buy a boarding house in Ann Arbor, Michigan. That became the seed of Hall Financial Group, which grew into a substantial real estate empire: commercial development, hotels, retirement communities, oil and gas, venture capital. Through the 1970s and early 1980s, credit was available and real estate was booming and Hall borrowed heavily to expand. This is the part of the story that gets told at fundraisers and in business school case studies—the scrappy kid who built something from nothing.

The part that doesn't get told as often is what happened next. In the late 1980s, the Savings & Loan crisis hit. Thousands of thrifts had been deregulated and allowed to pour money into speculative commercial real estate, and when that market collapsed it took most of them with it. Craig Hall's partnerships owed over $1 billion to more than 200

---

4. Democratic presidential primary debate, December 19, 2019, Loyola Marymount University, Los Angeles. Moderated by PBS NewsHour and Politico. The exchange between Warren and Buttigieg over the wine cave fundraiser became one of the most widely discussed moments of the primary campaign.

banks.[5] This is the part of the story where, under the rules that govern the rest of us—the rules that govern a small business owner who can't make payroll, or a homeowner who falls behind on their mortgage, or a family farmer who borrowed at 14% in the 1980s and watched the crop prices collapse—the story ends. The creditors call the loans. The assets get liquidated. You lose what you built and you start again from zero.

What Craig Hall got instead was the Resolution Trust Corporation. Congress created the RTC in 1989 through a law called FIRREA—the Financial Institutions Reform, Recovery, and Enforcement Act—to manage the wreckage of the S&L collapse. The RTC became a kind of federal warehouse for bad loans and foreclosed real estate, empowered to sell or settle distressed assets below face value in order to, as the legislation put it, "expedite resolution." For Hall, this meant he could negotiate to buy back the very loans his partnerships had defaulted on—not at full value, but at a discount. He raised $102.5 million in ninety days and repurchased hundreds of millions of dollars in defaulted debt at roughly ten cents on the dollar. The properties stayed his. The losses transferred to the public balance sheet. The RTC was funded through a combination of Treasury appropriations and bond issuances guaranteed by the federal government. The S&L crisis cost American taxpayers approximately $124 billion in total. Hall paid ten cents on the dollar and got to keep the assets.[6]

He did not break any laws. He used the laws that existed. That is precisely the point. A system that creates money by decree will use that power to rescue the people who owe the most of it—because the alternative, allowing the full weight of those defaults to fall on the system, threatens the system itself. The firefighter who misses a property tax payment gets foreclosed. The developer who owes a billion dollars to two hundred banks gets a federal agency, a ninety-day runway, and the legal right to buy his own debt back at ten cents on the dollar. This is not corruption. It is the machine operating as designed.

The machine treats the working class different.

---

5. Hall Financial Group's debt load and creditor count reported in Craig Hall, Timing Is Everything (1994), and covered in contemporaneous reporting. See also FDIC, History of the Eighties — Lessons for the Future, Vol. 1: An Examination of the Banking Crises of the 1980s and Early 1990s (1997).

6. Financial Institutions Reform, Recovery, and Enforcement Act of 1989 (Pub. L. 101-73). The RTC operated from 1989 to 1995, resolving 747 failed thrifts with total assets of $394 billion. The $124 billion taxpayer cost figure is from the FDIC's final accounting. Hall's debt repurchase at approximately ten cents on the dollar is described in his memoir Timing Is Everything (1994) and confirmed in FDIC resolution records.

In April 2024, Business Insider published a profile of a woman named Cherie Tobias. She was forty-eight years old, living in Hastings, Michigan, and working full-time as a server at an Applebee's.

She earned just over $25,000 a year. She limited herself to one meal a day to keep the household together—her son, her disabled fiancé, her future mother-in-law.[7] To the people she served, she was the one who brought the food. To her family, she was the only thing between them and eviction. She had an associate's degree in Business Administration. She did what she was told to do and arrived here anyway—just above the government's paper poverty line.

This was not how it was supposed to work. The local diner your grandmother waited tables in did not make her wealthy, but it kept her housed and fed and out of debt. Fiat money changed that — cheap credit built the chains that consolidated the industry and replaced the local diner,[8] and the federal tipped minimum wage has been frozen at $2.13 since 1996, while the prices of everything those workers buy compounded with the money supply.[9]

Cherie wasn't failing to save. She was behaving rationally in a system that punishes saving.

In July 2024, a CBS affiliate in Austin, Texas reported that a fourth-grade teacher named Bill Atkinson had been living in his car.

---

7. Business Insider, "Middle-Class Americans Say They Can't Afford Food or Medicine Despite Earning Above the Poverty Line," April 2024. The article profiles Cherie Tobias, an Applebee's server in Hastings, Michigan.

8. Chain restaurant market share figures from Dorothy Sue Cobble, Dishing It Out: Waitresses and Their Unions in the Twentieth Century (1991): "in 1931 fewer than three percent of the nation's restaurants were chain operated; in the 1980s, McDonald's alone accounted for 17 percent of restaurant visits." Applebee's founding (1980) and 1,000th location (1998) per company history. IHOP acquisition of Applebee's for $2.1 billion (2007) per Dine Brands corporate filings. Chili's founding year: 1975; TGI Fridays: 1965.

9. The federal tipped minimum wage was first established by the Fair Labor Standards Act amendments of 1966 at half the regular minimum wage. The Small Business Job Protection Act of 1996 (Pub. L. 104-188) raised the regular federal minimum wage to $5.15 but froze the tipped minimum at $2.13, where it has remained ever since despite subsequent increases to the regular minimum wage in 2007–2009. See U.S. Department of Labor, Wage and Hour Division, "Minimum Wages for Tipped Employees: Historical Tables"; and Economic Policy Institute, "Twenty-Three Years and Still Waiting for Change" (2014).

He showered at the YMCA before school. He graded papers in the passenger seat. He kept it from his students, his colleagues, everyone—until the story aired and a GoFundMe raised over $25,000 in days.[10] He earned $54,000 a year.

Bill's debt—a few thousand dollars on credit cards—made him homeless.

Craig Hall's debt—over a billion dollars—made him a Napa Valley vintner with a crystal chandelier.

In 1960, the average fourth-grade teacher earned about $4,815 a year.[11] The median American home cost $11,900—roughly two and a half years of a teacher's salary. A young teacher could save for a house. Could plan for it. Could get there. Today, Bill Atkinson earned $54,000. The median American home costs over $400,000. That is more than seven years of his salary.

The money that should have reached Bill went elsewhere. Between 1970 and 2018, inflation-adjusted per-pupil spending more than doubled — while real teacher salaries fell. The system was not underfunded. It was redistributed upward, away from the classroom and toward the people who administered it.[12]

Bill Atkinson was not failing a broken system. He was the classroom. The people who outgrew him were the ones who ran the building.

In November 2023, a registered nurse in Pennsylvania named Mackenzie Moan posted a tearful video to TikTok. She and her husband brought home around $120,000 a year. Four days after payday, they had $200 left.

She was taking classes toward an advanced nursing degree while raising two children. Her husband worked full time and picked up security work, personal training, and office cleaning on the side. Four days after payday, they had $200 to $300 left in the account

---

10. Reported by KEYE-TV (CBS Austin), July 2024.

11. National Center for Education Statistics, Digest of Education Statistics, Table 78: average salary of public elementary school teachers, 1959–60. Median home price from US Census Bureau, Historical Census of Housing Tables.

12. Inflation-adjusted per-pupil spending data: American Enterprise Institute, "Animated Chart of the Day: Public School Enrollment, Staff, and Inflation-adjusted Cost per Pupil, 1970 to 2018," citing U.S. Department of Education, National Center for Education Statistics. Spending rose from $5,037 per pupil (1970) to $12,905 (2018) in constant dollars. Real teacher salary decline (1992–2014): Reason Foundation, "Inflation-Adjusted K-12 Education Spending Per Student Has Increased By 280 Percent Since 1960" (2020), citing NCES data. Staff growth figures (1950–2009): Heritage Foundation, "How Escalating Education Spending Is Killing Crucial Reform" (2012), citing NCES; students +96%, administrators and non-teaching staff +702%. Non-teaching staff outnumbering teachers by 2015: AEI, ibid.

with ten more days until the next check. "Growing up, we were told: go to college, get a degree, work to support your family. Here we are. Did that. Now what?" The video passed a million views before national outlets caught up with her.[13]

The healthcare system she worked inside had ballooned in cost while systematically squeezing the people actually delivering care. Since 1970, real per-person healthcare spending has increased sevenfold — and most of it did not reach the nurses.[14]

In 1970, a registered nurse earned approximately $6,500 to $8,000 a year. The median American home cost about $23,000—roughly three years of nursing salary.[15] Today, the average RN earns approximately $86,000. The median American home costs over $400,000. That is more than four and a half years of salary—before taxes, before student loan payments for the nursing degree that now requires a bachelor's or master's, and before the childcare costs that consume a meaningful share of whatever remains. Mackenzie's salary had not fallen. The system around it had inflated everything she needed to buy.

The job itself had gotten harder in ways no pay stub captures. The patients were sicker, there were more of them, the beds had been cut, and above every ward a new layer

13. Mackenzie Moan's story was widely reported in November 2023. See, e.g., LADbible, "Mum Breaks Down in Tears over Living 'Paycheck-to-Paycheck' Despite Good Wage," November 25, 2023. Her TikTok handle is @mackmoan1988. The household income of approximately $120,000 and the $200–$300 remaining four days after payday were reported in the coverage.

14. National Health Expenditure data from Centers for Medicare and Medicaid Services (CMS). Total spending in 1970: $74.1 billion; in 2024: $5.3 trillion ($15,474 per capita). In constant 2024 dollars, per capita spending rose from $2,208 in 1970 to $15,474 in 2024. Health spending as % of GDP: 6.2% in 1970 vs. 18.0% in 2024. Source: Peterson-KFF Health System Tracker, "How Has U.S. Spending on Healthcare Changed Over Time?" updated February 2025; CMS National Health Expenditure Accounts historical data.

15. RN salary in 1970: approximately $6,500–$8,000 based on U.S. Department of Health & Human Services National Sample Survey of Registered Nurses and BLS Industry Wage Surveys for the period. Median home price in 1970: $23,000, from US Census Bureau Historical Census of Housing Tables. Average RN salary 2023–2024: $86,070 per BLS Occupational Employment and Wage Statistics (OEWS), May 2023. Median US home price: approximately $400,000+, per National Association of Realtors and US Census Bureau.

of administrators had taken up residence — people who had never held a stethoscope deciding how the budget worked.[16]

We used to call families like hers the backbone of America.

Business Insider ran the story in August 2024. The headline was almost understated: after losing his farm, a seventy-seven-year-old trucker had spent thirty-five years on the road and logged four million miles without a single accident. The subject was Hank Faber, and the headline undersold it. He was still driving. He was fighting chronic lymphocytic leukemia when the story ran, and he was still hauling freight. His monthly debts and living expenses ran nearly $6,000. And his mortgage—recently refinanced—wouldn't be paid off until he and his wife were ninety-nine.[17]

It didn't start with the truck. Hank grew up farming in Indiana, and in the 1980s the farm crisis arrived — soaring interest rates, collapsing crop prices, years of bad weather on top of borrowed money. The Federal Reserve had spent the 1970s allowing the money supply to expand faster than the economy could support, and the resulting inflation forced a brutal correction that detonated the variable rate loans farmers had taken out in better years.[18] When Hank couldn't keep up, the farm was gone.

Note what he didn't receive: a federal agency created to absorb distressed loans at structured discounts. A legal mechanism that let creditors sell his debt for ten cents on the dollar to investors with the right connections. A ninety-day runway to restructure and raise private capital. He got foreclosure. Then he climbed into a truck.

---

16. Physician count vs. administrator count, 1970–2019: Physicians for a National Health Program (PNHP), citing Athena Health analysis of Bureau of Labor Statistics, NCHS, and US Census data; doctors +200%, administrators +3,800%. The figure of 10 administrators per physician widely cited from same dataset. Hospital administrative costs at 20% of hospital spending: New England Journal of Medicine, Woolhandler and Himmelstein, "The Deteriorating Administrative Efficiency of the U.S. Health Care System" (1991), with subsequent updates confirming the trend. Billing and insurance-related costs of approximately $500 billion annually: Center for American Progress, "Excess Administrative Costs Burden the U.S. Health Care System," November 2021.

17. Business Insider, "After Losing His Farm, a 77-Year-Old Trucker Spent 35 Years on the Road. He's Logged 4 Million Miles with No Accidents," August 2024.

18. USDA historical records document the 1980s farm crisis as the worst period for American agriculture since the Great Depression. The Federal Reserve's effective federal funds rate peaked at 19.1% in June 1981 (FRED series FEDFUNDS); the prime rate tracked closely, reaching approximately 21.5% in 1981. Farmers who had borrowed at variable rates in the late 1970s faced catastrophic payment increases as the Fed tightened to combat the inflation it had generated in the preceding decade. See also USDA Economic Research Service, "Agriculture and the Farm Crisis of the 1980s."

Trucking's economics are unforgiving. In strong years he grossed over $100,000 — after fuel, insurance, maintenance, and taxes, roughly a third stayed in his pocket.[19]

For thirty-five years, he hauled food, clothing, and building materials across American highways. Four million miles. Zero accidents. A documented record of genuine value created.

The work was never the problem. The Federal Reserve set the interest rate that foreclosed his farm. The same institution that manufactured the crisis also designed the architecture of the rescue — the federal programs, the structured discounts, the favorable terms that turned the same catastrophe into an opportunity for those positioned close enough to the money to benefit. Hank wasn't positioned close enough. He had a leased Volvo and the highway. His labor was real. The money was the problem.

Fiat and the Working Class

The jobs these people hold are not lesser jobs. The server, the teacher, the nurse, the trucker — these are the people who feed us, educate our children, heal our sick, and move everything we own from one place to another. Every civilization that ever existed needed them. Ours still does. What changed is not the value of the work. What changed is whether the work pays enough to live on.

Fiat made honest work insufficient, and then the culture decided there was something wrong with the people doing honest work.

That is new. It is not ancient wisdom that a waitress is a step below a hedge fund manager on some natural hierarchy of human worth. It is a recent invention — built slowly, over fifty years of inflation making service work feel like a failure of ambition rather than a choice of vocation. When the money worked, the diner waitress owned a house. When the money broke, she became a cautionary tale. Nothing changed about the job. Everything changed about what the job could buy.

The top one percent's share of national income fell from roughly 18 percent before World War I to about 8 percent through the 1950s and 1960s — then began climbing

19. Trucking economics from Business Insider profile of Hank Faber, August 2024. Gross revenue of approximately $100,000 annually in strong years; after fuel, insurance, maintenance, and self-employment taxes, net income of approximately one-third of gross is consistent with industry benchmarks for owner-operators. American Trucking Associations, "Driver Compensation Study" (2022).

again in the 1970s, reaching nearly 15 percent by 1998. Just from 1981 to today, the M2 money supply grew more than fourteen-fold.[20]

America's net savings rate averaged around 11 percent through the 1950s and 1960s. After 1971, it began a steady decline — 8.7 percent in the 1970s, 5.7 percent in the 1980s, 4.4 percent in the 1990s. By 2007 it had fallen below 2 percent. Then it went negative, and stayed negative for three years. Today it hovers near zero.[21] Americans, as a country, stopped being able to save right around the same time the money stopped being worth saving.

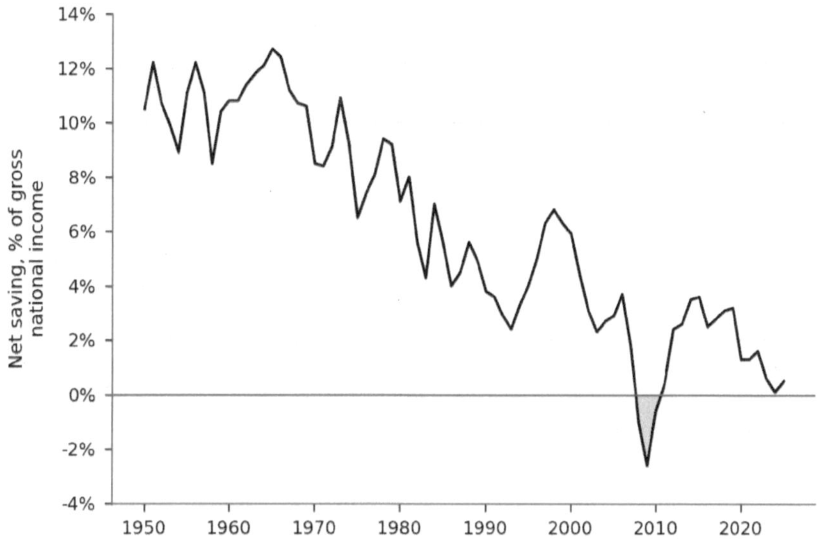

Net Saving as a % of Gross National Income, 1950s–present (FRED / Bureau of Economic Analysis)

The working class needed Bitcoin before anyone else did. They still do. And they are still, largely, the last to know about it.

20. Thomas Piketty and Emmanuel Saez, "Income Inequality in the United States, 1913–1998," Quarterly Journal of Economics 118, no. 1 (2003), Table II, column P99–100. M2 money supply from FRED series WM2NS: $1,620.7 billion (January 1981) to $22,538.7 billion (February 2026), a compound annual growth rate of 6.01%.

21. Net saving as a percentage of gross national income, Bureau of Economic Analysis via FRED. The rate turned negative briefly in 2008–2009, meaning the country as a whole was spending more than it earned—a condition unprecedented in the post-war era.

This is not an accident. The working class is busy working. It takes real effort to survive in a fiat economy, and because of that, working Americans long ago outsourced their financial thinking to experts—advisors, journalists, economists, HR departments, the neighbor who seems to have it figured out. The problem is that the experts promoting the existing system are the same people who benefit from it. The working class handed the keys to the people who built the lock.

The people who most need a tool that protects the value of their labor are the least likely to have it. The people who least need it—institutional investors, treasury departments, hedge funds—are accumulating it aggressively. Michael Saylor is borrowing at near-zero interest rates in a fiat currency to buy Bitcoin with newly created dollars. Larry Fink is selling Bitcoin ETFs to the same pension funds that manage the retirement savings of Hank Faber's peers. The financialization of Bitcoin is well underway. The working class has not been invited to the table—and yet again, they will be asked to fund the invitation through the inflation their labor absorbs.

The people with the highest need and the lowest exposure share a common thread: they were told, repeatedly and by people they trusted, that Bitcoin was a scam. A bubble. A tool for criminals and speculators. The very institutions that destroyed the purchasing power of their savings across fifty years of fiat inflation were the loudest voices warning them away from the one asset those institutions couldn't print more of. The working class listened. They stayed in the dollar. And the dollar kept doing what it has done since 1971.

Cherie Tobias did not have a financial advisor. She had a paycheck that lost ground the moment it cleared. She did not need a sophisticated portfolio. She needed a way to save $25 a week in something that holds its value across the months and years before she can spend it. That is not a complex financial goal.

Bill Atkinson did not end up in his car because he lacked financial sophistication. He ended up in his car because the money system transferred value away from his labor and salary, silently, for decades, while the people who ran the system held press conferences to explain that it was all very healthy and that two percent was nothing to worry about. Meanwhile, the median home in Austin appreciated at five percent per year, and no one in a position of authority told Bill that his path to homeownership was narrowing every year he worked.

Mackenzie Moan's husband was not working three jobs because he lacked ambition or discipline. He was working three jobs because the fiat era made the two-income household the new floor, and the two-income-plus-side-hustle household the one that still couldn't quite make it. He was running faster to stay in the same place.

What they received in return was a monetary system that guaranteed their savings would be worth less every year, while the people nearest to the money printer watched their assets appreciate. They were told this was growth. It was redistribution—carried out at the speed of inflation, too slow to see in any single year, devastating over a generation.

The machine is still running. The only thing that has changed is that an exit now exists.

Everything in this chapter has a name.

The Cantillon Effect we traced does not require malice. It is the natural output of a system that creates money for some people and taxes others with the resulting inflation. The system produces these outcomes because it was built to produce them — and because the people with the power to change it are the same people who benefit most from leaving it unchanged.

For most of human history, if the government controlled the supply of money, there was no alternative. You worked in whatever money your government issued, saved what you could, and watched inflation take what it would.

That is no longer true.

Chapter Six

The Monk and the Cypherpunk

Sometime around 1440, in a workshop in Mainz, Germany, a goldsmith named Johannes Gutenberg figured out the last piece of a puzzle he had been working on for years.

The problem he was solving was not original. Printing had existed in China for centuries. Woodblock printing had been used in Europe for decades. The idea of stamping text onto paper was not new. What Gutenberg discovered — and the word "discovered" is right, because no one person invents a thing that has been gestating for generations — was how to combine existing technologies into something entirely new: a movable metal type system that could be configured, printed, reset, and reconfigured. Fast. Replicable. Cheap.

Before Gutenberg, a book was beyond the reach of any ordinary person. A monk could copy perhaps three or four pages per day, working in a scriptorium from dawn to dusk, and a Bible took years to produce.[1] Literacy was a luxury of the clergy and the nobility, who used their monopoly on written knowledge to shape what ordinary people understood about God, law, and power. The information had always existed. The problem was that it could only travel as fast as a man could walk and only reach people willing to pay for years of a monk's time.

1. Monastic scribes generally worked six hours a day and produced approximately three to four pages of copied text during that time. Joanne Filippone Overty, "The Cost of Doing Scribal Business: Prices of Manuscript Books in England, 1300–1483," Book History 11 (2008): 1–32.

After Gutenberg, a Bible took a few weeks to produce and cost roughly a month's wages for a craftsman. Within fifty years of his press, tens of millions of books were circulating in Europe.[2] Ideas that had been the property of an elite few became the common currency of merchants, tradesmen, and farmers. The Reformation, the Scientific Revolution, the Enlightenment — none of them happen without the printing press. Or rather: the pressures that produced them had always been there, the questions had always been there, the minds capable of answering them had always been there. The press gave those forces a velocity that no institution could contain.

October 31, 2008

The problem Satoshi Nakamoto was solving was not new either. For thirty years before Bitcoin, some of the sharpest minds in cryptography and computer science had been working on it. The cypherpunks — a loose, freewheeling community of mathematicians, libertarians, and privacy advocates who gathered on mailing lists in the 1980s and 1990s — had long understood that the same digital revolution transforming communication could, in principle, transform money. They saw what email did to letters and asked: what does that do to banks?

The attempts came one after another. David Chaum built DigiCash in 1989 — a genuinely brilliant cryptographic payment system that offered real digital privacy. It failed because it required banks to adopt it, and banks had no interest in a system designed to work without them. Adam Back invented Hashcash in 1997, a system requiring a small proof of computational work to send an email — an elegant anti-spam mechanism that would later become one of Bitcoin's core building blocks. Wei Dai proposed b-money that same year, a decentralized digital currency that existed entirely in concept but articulated for the first time the vision of money governed by mathematics rather than institutions. Nick Szabo designed Bit Gold in 1998, a digital asset with genuine scarcity built from cryptographic proof of work — so close to Bitcoin that many still wonder if Szabo was

2. Estimates vary by source and methodology. Britannica's History of Publishing puts the figure at more than nine million volumes by 1500; other historians, including those cited in Wikipedia's entry on the global spread of the printing press, place the total above twenty million. All sources agree on the order of magnitude.

Satoshi. Hal Finney built RPOW — Reusable Proofs of Work — in 2004, bringing the idea closer still. Each attempt solved part of the problem. Each ran into the same wall.[3]

The wall was always the same: the double-spend problem. In the physical world, if you hand someone a dollar bill, you no longer have it. The transfer is self-enforcing. In the digital world, a file can be copied infinitely. If I email you a copy of something, I still have the original. Every prior attempt at digital cash either required a central authority to verify that the money hadn't been spent twice — which meant trusting an institution — or it failed to solve the problem entirely.

Satoshi solved it. The solution was the blockchain: a shared, distributed ledger maintained simultaneously by thousands of independent computers, each holding a complete record of every transaction ever made, secured by a competitive process that makes falsifying the record economically catastrophic. No single institution controls it. No single point of failure can bring it down. The mathematics enforces the rules, and the mathematics cannot be bribed, lobbied, or cajoled into making an exception.

The nine-page whitepaper titled ***"Bitcoin: A Peer-to-Peer Electronic Cash System"*** was not an invention dropped from the sky by a lone genius. It was a discovery — the culmination of decades of searching, the final piece that dozens of brilliant people had been assembling in pieces for a generation.

What Satoshi added, beyond the technical solution, was the wisdom to disappear. He launched the network on January 3, 2009, embedded a news headline in the very first block of the ledger — "Chancellor on the brink of second bailout for banks" — and within two years had vanished from the project entirely, never to be heard from again. He held roughly one million Bitcoin and has never moved a single coin.[4] Every other digital currency that came before or after had a founder who could be pressured, sued, arrested, or bought. Bitcoin has no such person. It is the only monetary asset in history that arrived without a CEO.

---

3. For readers who want to go deeper on the cypherpunk predecessors to Bitcoin, Nathaniel Popper's Digital Gold: Bitcoin and the Inside Story of the Misfits and Millionaires Trying to Reinvent Money (Harper, 2015) covers this history in full. The original technical papers by Back, Dai, Szabo, and Finney are archived at the Satoshi Nakamoto Institute: nakamotoinstitute.org.

4. The estimate of Satoshi's holdings derives from on-chain forensic analysis by cryptographer Sergio Demian Lerner, who in 2013 identified a distinctive mining signature in Bitcoin's earliest blocks — known as the Patoshi Pattern — suggesting a single dominant miner accumulated approximately 1.1 million BTC. A 2018 analysis by BitMEX Research placed the figure lower, at between 600,000 and 700,000 BTC. None of the coins associated with either estimate have ever moved.

The monks who controlled the scriptorium understood, eventually, what Gutenberg had done to their world. The people who manage the money supply have understood, eventually, what Satoshi did to theirs. The information existed. Now it travels at the speed of light, and no institution can stop it.

You do not need to understand how an internal combustion engine works to drive a car. You do not need to understand TCP/IP to send an email. And you do not need to understand the mathematics of Bitcoin to use it, own it, or benefit from it. But you should understand roughly how it works — because the mechanism is the point. The mechanism is what makes the promises stick.

Here is the short version.

There will only ever be 21 million Bitcoin. That number is written into the code. It is not a policy that can be reversed when convenient. It is not a target that the chairman can adjust when the economy needs stimulus. It is a mathematical constant — as fixed as the number of degrees in a circle, as immovable as the speed of light.

The way Bitcoin issues new coins is through a formula written into the protocol itself. Every 210,000 blocks — roughly four years — the reward that miners earn for each new block is cut precisely in half. Satoshi started it at 50 Bitcoin per block in 2009. It dropped to 25 in 2012, to 12.5 in 2016, to 6.25 in 2020, to 3.125 in 2024. It will keep halving, forever, with mathematical precision.

$$\sum_{i=0}^{32} 210{,}000 \times \left\lfloor \frac{50}{2^i} \right\rfloor = 21{,}000{,}000$$

The entire monetary policy of Bitcoin. Summed across all 33 halving epochs, the block subsidy converges to exactly 21 million coins.

Here is the remarkable thing about that formula: even if you keep halving a number forever, it never actually reaches zero — it just gets infinitely smaller. Mathematicians call this *asymptotic* behavior. (That's your one vocabulary word for this chapter. Look it up if you want. It means a curve that approaches a boundary forever but never quite touches it.) Because the reward halves rather than stops, the total supply of Bitcoin converges to exactly 21 million — not a round number arrived at by committee, but a mathematical consequence of the formula itself. The last fraction of the last Bitcoin won't be mined until approximately the year 2140.

You cannot print more. You cannot hold an emergency meeting and vote to issue another round. You cannot declare that extraordinary circumstances require extraordinary measures. The formula runs, automatically, on thousands of computers simultaneously, and has done so without interruption since January 3, 2009.

Those coins are issued through a competitive process called mining. Thousands of computers around the world — in data centers in Texas and Iceland and Paraguay, in warehouses and garages and server farms — compete continuously to earn the right to add the next block of transactions to the shared ledger. To win, each machine must solve an enormous computational puzzle. It runs a cryptographic function called SHA-256 — the same algorithm used to secure classified government communications[5] — billions of times per second, searching for a specific output that the network will accept. The only way to find it is to search. There is no shortcut. There is no smarter approach. The computer that wins is the one that got lucky while working hardest. This is Proof of Work, and the name is exactly right: you cannot fake it, you cannot argue your way in, and you cannot manufacture Bitcoin without burning real energy in the real world.

SHA-256 is worth a brief mention on its own, because it is the spine of Bitcoin's security. It is a one-way cryptographic function — you can run any input through it and get a fixed-length output, but you cannot work backward from the output to find the input. This means that every block of transactions, once confirmed, is locked behind a wall of mathematics that grows stronger with every subsequent block added on top of it. To alter a confirmed transaction, an attacker would need to redo all the computational work for that block and every block that has come after it, faster than the entire honest mining network is adding new valid blocks. By 2025, Bitcoin's mining network had surpassed 800 exahashes per second — that is 800 followed by eighteen zeros — hash calculations every second. The more computing power behind the network, the more

---

5. SHA-256 is a member of the SHA-2 family of cryptographic hash functions, designed by the National Security Agency and published by the National Institute of Standards and Technology (NIST) as a U.S. Federal Information Processing Standard in 2001. It was formally approved under NSA Suite B for protecting Secret-level classified information. The full technical specification is available at nist.gov. For a readable history of SHA-256 and its role in Bitcoin, see Nathaniel Popper, Digital Gold (Harper, 2015), or the SHA-2 entry at Wikipedia, which cites the relevant FIPS publications.

secure it becomes. By that measure, Bitcoin is the most secure computational network ever built.[6]

What keeps the supply schedule on track as more miners join? Satoshi built in a self-correcting mechanism called the difficulty adjustment. Every 2,016 blocks — roughly two weeks — the network automatically recalibrates how hard the computational puzzle is. If more miners are competing, the puzzle gets harder. If miners drop off, it gets easier. The target is always the same: one new block every ten minutes, on average, regardless of how much computing power is pointed at it. The network measures itself and adjusts, automatically, every two weeks — and has done so without fail since 2009.

This is why Bitcoin has the most verifiable security record in the history of financial systems: in seventeen years of operation, processing hundreds of millions of transactions, not a single confirmed transaction has ever been successfully altered or reversed. The ledger is immutable. As a mathematical fact.

That ledger lives everywhere at once. It is not stored in any single location that can be seized, hacked, or shut down. It is maintained simultaneously by tens of thousands of computers called nodes, spread across every continent. Each node holds a complete copy of every transaction ever recorded, going back to Satoshi's first block. No government can confiscate the ledger. No fire can destroy it. No single point of failure can bring it down.

When a massive power blackout knocked out electricity and internet service across Spain and Portugal on April 28, 2025 — the largest grid failure in Spanish history, affecting roughly fifty million people — the Bitcoin network did not notice. Nodes in other countries kept the ledger running without interruption. No block was missed. The network processed transactions throughout as if nothing had happened, because to it, nothing had.[7]

No one controls it. There is no Bitcoin headquarters. There is no Bitcoin CEO. There is no emergency committee that meets when the market moves too fast. The

---

6. Bitcoin's hashrate changes continuously. For current and historical data, see Timechain Stats (timechainstats.com) and the Clark Moody Bitcoin Dashboard (bitcoin.clarkmoody.com), both of which track hashrate in real time alongside other network metrics.

7. On April 28, 2025, a cascading failure in Spain's power grid caused a near-total blackout across the Iberian Peninsula, cutting internet traffic in Spain by as much as 80% within hours. See NPR, "Spain and Portugal Begin Recovering from a Massive Blackout," April 28, 2025; Cloudflare Blog, "How the April 28, 2025, Power Outage in Portugal and Spain Impacted Internet Traffic and Connectivity," April 28, 2025.

whole structure is held together not by trust in any institution, but by mathematics. And mathematics is a harder master than any regulator.

This is possible because of something called a private key. A private key controls whatever Bitcoin is associated with it. That private key can be converted into a twelve or twenty-four word seed phrase — a list of ordinary English words that is the only thing standing between you and your Bitcoin.[8]

To send Bitcoin to someone else, you need two things: your seed phrase and the recipient's Bitcoin address. That's it. No bank. No approval. No middleman. The network handles the rest.

If a miner produces an invalid block — one that breaks the rules of the protocol — the network rejects it instantly. No reward is issued. The electricity was spent, the hardware ran, and the miner gets nothing. The only way to earn a mining reward is to play by the rules exactly as written. The protocol doesn't negotiate. Valid or invalid — that's the entire decision tree. This is what it means to say the system is trustless: not that everyone trusts each other, but that trust is structurally irrelevant. The rules enforce themselves.

How does Bitcoin change its rules? With enormous difficulty, and this is by design.

Any proposed change to the Bitcoin protocol begins as a Bitcoin Improvement Proposal — a BIP. The idea is posted publicly, debated openly by developers, and refined through a transparent review process.[9] If it survives that, it has to be implemented in software that miners and node operators actually choose to run. They don't have to. No one can make them. In Bitcoin's seventeen-year history, several well-funded, well-organized attempts to change core protocol rules have failed, often spectacularly. In 2017, a coalition of major mining companies and crypto businesses tried to increase Bitcoin's block size — a technical change that would have concentrated control in fewer hands. They had

---

8. Seed phrase security, hardware wallet setup, and self-custody best practices are covered in detail in Chapter Fourteen.

9. The BIP process is documented at github.com/bitcoin/bips. A proposed change becomes active only when miners and node operators — the computers that validate transactions and secure the network through hash rate — adopt the updated software. This is what 'consensus' means in Bitcoin: not a popular vote, but agreement among the machines doing the actual work of securing the chain.

enormous economic power and every financial incentive to succeed. They failed. The change died. The network continued as before.[10]

Compare this to how the Federal Reserve changes the rules of your money. Twelve people gather in a room in Washington. They discuss among themselves. They vote. They issue a statement. Your purchasing power, the interest rate on your mortgage, the effective tax on your savings — all of it adjusts, effective immediately, with no public debate, no ratification, no recourse. You find out on the news afterward, if you were paying attention.

Bitcoin's governance is frustrating, slow, and argumentative. It is also why the supply schedule announced in 2008 is the same supply schedule running today. The stubbornness is the feature.

The simplest way to understand Bitcoin is to put it next to the thing it is replacing.

10. The 2017 block size conflict is documented in detail in Jonathan Bier, The Blocksize War (2021). Bier covered the dispute in real time and interviewed participants on both sides. It remains the most thorough account of what happens when powerful economic interests collide with Bitcoin's decentralized governance.

	Fiat Dollar	Bitcoin
Supply	Infinite. Created at will by central banks and commercial lending.	Fixed at 21 million coins. Written in code. Cannot be changed.
Who controls it	The Federal Reserve — a privately governed institution accountable to no voter.	No one. Rules enforced by code and consensus.
Can the rules change?	Yes. Overnight. With no public vote required.	Only by global consensus. Effectively never.
Permission required?	Yes. Banks approve accounts, transactions, and access.	No. A valid transaction cannot be stopped.
Can it be seized?	Yes. Governments freeze and confiscate bank accounts.	Not without the owner's private key.
Can it be inflated?	Yes. The M2 money supply has grown at roughly 6% per year since 1981.	No. The supply schedule is public and cannot be altered.
Who does it favor?	Those closest to the money printer — the Cantillon class.	Everyone equally. The rules are identical for all.
Who sets monetary policy?	12 people, in private, with no ratification.	A public formula, running on thousands of computers, since 2009.

On the Bitcoin network, Jeff Bezos and a school janitor in Memphis are identical. There is no private Bitcoin branch for wealthy clients. There is no relationship manager who waives the fee for the customer with a seven-figure balance. There is no tiered access. A transaction is either valid or it isn't, and the network does not care who initiated it.

This has not been true of any monetary system since governments took control of money. Under a gold standard, no single institution could manufacture the supply at will — the rules were set by geology, not by committee. Once governments severed that connection, a center of gravity appeared. Every system since has had someone positioned at the middle who benefits disproportionately from being there. Bitcoin is the first money since gold — and the first ever with a mathematically enforced supply — that has no center of gravity. That is not a small thing. That is, for the working class especially, the whole argument.

One more thing worth noting: you do not need to buy a whole Bitcoin. This confuses more people than almost anything else about it. Bitcoin is divisible to one hundred-millionths of a coin. The smallest unit — called a satoshi, after the protocol's discoverer — is one hundred-millionth of a coin. Mackenzie Moan, running on two paychecks and a side job to keep her family above water, can put $20 into Bitcoin the same way a hedge fund manager puts in $20 million. The math is identical. The network makes no distinction.

That is the architecture. But the question that matters — the only question that matters if you are living paycheck to paycheck, watching your rent go up and your savings go nowhere — is what any of this does for you.

Chapter Seven

Buying Time

The label that follows Bitcoin around — speculation, gambling, a bet on the greater fool — is precisely backward. Bitcoin is savings technology. It is the first money since the classical gold standard that actually holds its value over time rather than slowly losing it. Understanding why requires accepting something that modern economists spend enormous effort trying to explain away.

Falling prices are good.

When your phone gets cheaper and more capable every two years, you do not consider that a crisis.[1] When grocery stores compete to lower prices, you do not organize a task force to prevent it. Falling prices are the natural result of a productive economy — more goods and services produced by the same amount of human effort, which means each unit of work buys more over time.

We saw in Chapter 1 what this looked like on a gold standard: between 1873 and 1897, through two severe recessions, the real wages of American workers rose thirty percent.

1. The deflationary trend in consumer electronics is well documented. The canonical formulation is Moore's Law (Gordon Moore, "Cramming More Components onto Integrated Circuits," Electronics, April 19, 1965), which predicted that transistor density would roughly double every two years — a prediction that has held for six decades and driven persistent real-price declines in computing power. For an accessible treatment of how technology-sector deflation interacts with aggregate price indices, see W. Brian Arthur, The Nature of Technology (Free Press, 2009). The paradox noted here — that falling prices in consumer goods are celebrated while falling prices in money are feared — is a standard critique in Austrian business cycle theory. See Ludwig von Mises, Human Action (Yale University Press, 1949), Ch. XVII ("Indirect Exchange"), and George Selgin, "Productivity and the Price Level," in Less than Zero: The Case for a Falling Price Level in a Growing Economy (Institute of Economic Affairs, 1997).

Not because wages soared — they didn't — but because the cost of everything around them gently fell.[2] The money worked for the saver.

Bitcoin is hyper-deflationary money. On a Bitcoin standard, prices fall as productivity rises. It is the design. And we already have seventeen years of evidence that it works.

The median American home currently costs roughly four Bitcoin. Five years ago it cost more than forty. A decade before that it cost more than a thousand. This is not because houses are getting cheaper in dollar terms — they are getting more expensive, relentlessly, as we saw with Bill Atkinson's teaching salary. It is because Bitcoin is becoming more valuable relative to everything else, as a fixed-supply money should in a world that produces more value every year. When the supply of money cannot grow but the economy it serves does grow, each unit of money buys more over time. That is not speculation. That is arithmetic.[3]

The modern financial industry calls this a bubble. The financial industry has been calling Bitcoin a bubble every year since 2011. In 2011, when Bitcoin first hit one dollar, commentators explained that the speculative frenzy had driven prices far above rational value, and that collapse was imminent.[4] The same analysis was offered at ten dollars, at a hundred, at a thousand, at ten thousand, and at a hundred thousand. At each price, the collapse was imminent. At each price, the people who held through the volatility came out on the other side owning more real purchasing power than they had before.

---

2. The 30% real wage gain for 1873–1897 is drawn from the same historical wage series examined in Chapter 1. The underlying data comes from Stanley Lebergott's wage estimates in Manpower in Economic Growth: The American Record Since 1800 (McGraw-Hill, 1964), which remains the standard long-run series for U.S. wage history. The NBER Macrohistory Database (nber.org/research/data/macrohistory-database) archives compatible series. The period is sometimes called the Long Deflation; despite persistent price-level declines, real wages rose because productivity gains were not absorbed by monetary expansion. See also Milton Friedman and Anna Schwartz, A Monetary History of the United States, 1867–1960 (Princeton University Press, 1963), Ch. 2.

3. For a continuously updated chart of the median U.S. home price denominated in Bitcoin, see charts.bitbo.io/housing-btc/. The underlying data uses the FRED MSPUS series (median sales price of houses sold for the United States, Federal Reserve Bank of St. Louis) divided by the spot Bitcoin price. Because both figures update continuously, any specific BTC-denominated home price figure in this book is point-in-time. The directional argument — that Bitcoin has appreciated dramatically relative to real assets since inception — holds across the full seventeen-year trading history.

4. The running catalog of Bitcoin death notices is maintained at 99bitcoins.com/bitcoin-obituaries. As of this writing it contains more than 400 separate declarations of Bitcoin's death or terminal decline, spanning every price level from below one dollar to above one hundred thousand dollars. The site attributes each obituary to its original source and publication date. The pattern — confident prediction of collapse at every new price milestone — is the most reliable indicator in Bitcoin's history.

Here is the more useful comparison: set Bitcoin against the alternatives that working Americans have actually been offered as savings vehicles.

The 401(k) that the financial industry sold Cherie Tobias as her path to retirement is quietly eaten by management fees, inflation, and the mathematical reality that a stock market dominated by seven technology companies cannot return 10% annually forever.[5] The Treasury bond that used to be the safe harbor for retirement savings now pays a real return that consistently trails inflation — a politely packaged guaranteed loss.[6] The savings account at the local bank pays 0.5% interest while the money supply grows at 6% per year. The house, as we saw in exhaustive detail in Chapter 2, has become so expensive relative to income that most working Americans can no longer reach it as an asset.

Bitcoin does not compete with gambling. It competes with the savings account, the bond, the pension fund, and every other mechanism the existing system has offered ordinary people to preserve the value of their work across time. Compared to those alternatives — measured over any five-year, ten-year, or twenty-year window you care to name — it has not been speculation. It has been the only instrument that has consistently done what savings is supposed to do: hold your labor so you can use it later.

The number goes up in dollar terms for the same reason the price of a house goes up in dollar terms: because the dollar goes down. The difference is that Bitcoin is going up faster than the dollar is going down — reflecting its growing adoption as people around the world discover that it is a better place to store value than the money their governments issue.

---

5. The claim that passive index investors frequently underperform the index itself due to fees, behavioral timing, and fund selection is documented in J.P. Morgan Asset Management's Guide to the Markets (published quarterly; available at jpmorgan.com/insights/market-outlooks). The Guide's "Investor Behavior" slide historically shows a 20-year annualized return for the average investor well below the S&P 500's return, typically around 2.9% versus ~9–10% for the index, primarily due to market-timing decisions and fund-switching. For the fee drag specifically, Morningstar's annual Mind the Gap report measures the difference between total return and investor return across fund categories.

6. The real yield on U.S. Treasury securities — nominal yield minus inflation — has been negative for extended periods. FRED series DGS10 (10-year Treasury constant maturity rate) and CPIAUCSL (Consumer Price Index for All Urban Consumers) allow this calculation directly at fred.stlouisfed.org. Between 2011 and 2023, the 10-year real yield was negative for multiple extended stretches, meaning holders of "safe" Treasury bonds were paying the government for the privilege of losing purchasing power. For a non-technical treatment, see the Peter G. Peterson Foundation's annual fiscal analysis at pgpf.org.

The number goes up. But more importantly, relative to everything that actually matters — homes, groceries, education, time — the cost of those things in Bitcoin goes steadily, reliably, beautifully down.

That is the technology. That is what the cypherpunks were building toward.

Consider what it means to actually own something.

If you have a dollar in a bank account, you do not own that dollar in any strict legal sense. You own a claim on the bank — a contractual right to receive that dollar on demand. The dollar itself is the bank's asset. The bank operates with the permission of regulators, under rules set by the government, and in extreme circumstances — as we have seen in Cyprus, in Greece, in India, in Canada — those rules can change in ways that prevent you from accessing what you thought was yours. The bank can freeze your account. The government can instruct the bank to freeze your account. Payment processors, who sit between you and every digital transaction, can cut off your access for reasons ranging from genuine fraud prevention to political pressure to a compliance officer deciding your industry looks legally adjacent. It is a description of how the fiat payment system is architecturally constructed. The system requires trust at every layer. And at every layer, that trust can be violated.

Bitcoin is a different kind of ownership.

When you hold Bitcoin in self-custody — your seed phrase written down, stored somewhere only you can access — no institution can touch it. There is no account manager to call. There is no compliance department to satisfy. The Bitcoin lives on the network, untouchable, until you choose to move it. A valid transaction will be processed without asking for your government ID, your credit score, your employment history, or your reason for sending it. (We covered the seed phrase in Chapter 6 — that list of twelve or twenty-four words is the only thing standing between you and your Bitcoin, and the only thing that needs to be protected.)

In February 2022, Canadian truckers drove their rigs to Ottawa to protest vaccine mandates. Whatever you think of the underlying politics, what the government did next was a demonstration that no civics textbook had prepared Canadians for. The government invoked emergency powers and ordered bank accounts frozen — not of people convicted of crimes, but of people who had donated money to a cause the government opposed. Donors who gave fifty dollars to a fundraiser found their accounts inaccessible. The freezes happened without court orders, without due process, without the slow machinery of justice that is supposed to protect citizens from exactly this kind of state action. It happened in Canada — a constitutional democracy with independent courts and rights guarantees that look, on paper, a lot like ours.

The people who had donated Bitcoin were not affected.

The ability to cut someone off from their financial life is the most complete form of control available to a government short of imprisonment. Bitcoin removes that leverage. Not because it is lawless, but because it is trustless. It does not require you to trust anyone, because it is governed by mathematics, not institutions. The network does not take calls from prime ministers. The private key is either in your possession or it isn't, and if it is, no external force can move what it protects.

This freedom matters for more people than the political protester. It matters for the journalist in a country with a corrupt government who needs to store her savings beyond the reach of the people who want to silence her.[7] It matters for the small business owner who has been denied a bank account because a compliance officer decided her industry was too legally adjacent for the bank's comfort. It matters for the immigrant worker sending money to family overseas, currently losing 7% to 10% of every transfer to wire services that exploit their captive market.[8] It matters for the ordinary American who would simply like to save money without watching it evaporate at 0.1% interest while the currency loses 4% per year.

Your keys. Your Bitcoin. No appeals process required, because no one has the authority to deny you in the first place.

---

7. The financial censorship examples are well documented. WikiLeaks: In December 2010, Visa, Mastercard, PayPal, Bank of America, and Western Union all terminated services to WikiLeaks following U.S. government pressure, before any legal finding of wrongdoing. WikiLeaks turned to Bitcoin donations and received funding throughout the blockade. See Glenn Greenwald, No Place to Hide (Metropolitan Books, 2014). Alexei Navalny: The Anti-Corruption Foundation and Navalny's teams repeatedly had accounts frozen and payment processors terminated; supporters used cryptocurrency to continue donating after traditional channels were shut. See reporting from The Guardian and the Navalny Fund's own public statements, 2021–2024. Human Rights Foundation: The HRF's Bitcoin Development Fund (btcdeveloper.fund) specifically supports Bitcoin development in countries with authoritarian financial systems, with documented case studies of activists and journalists using Bitcoin after conventional banking access was revoked.

8. The World Bank's Remittance Prices Worldwide database (remittanceprices.worldbank.org) tracks the average cost of sending money internationally by corridor. As of the most recent available data, the global average cost to send $200 internationally was approximately 6.4%, with many corridors — particularly those serving Sub-Saharan Africa and parts of Latin America — averaging above 8%. The G20 target, set in 2011, was to reduce global average remittance costs to 5%; that target remains unmet as of 2025. Bitcoin Lightning Network transfers between self-custody wallets carry no third-party fee beyond a small on-chain settlement fee, typically a few cents or less.

Here is a question worth asking: if Bitcoin were purely speculative — purely a bet on a number going up — why are businesses using it to pay their employees?

In early 2025, Steak 'n Shake announced that its locations would begin accepting Bitcoin payments at the counter. Not through a third-party app. Not through a crypto debit card. Directly. A customer could walk into a Steak 'n Shake, order a steakburger and a milkshake, and pay in Bitcoin from their phone. The company went further: it offered employees the option to receive a portion of their wages in Bitcoin.

Pause on that for a moment. Steak 'n Shake is not a Silicon Valley startup. It is not a crypto exchange, a technology company, or a platform catering to early adopters. It is a seventy-year-old fast food chain selling hamburgers to working-class Americans for a few dollars a meal. And it decided that Bitcoin was real enough, practical enough, and useful enough to put it at the cash register and on the paycheck.

This matters in ways that go beyond the obvious. When a company offers employees the option to be paid in Bitcoin, something shifts. The paycheck stops being a countdown clock — a number that starts melting from the moment it arrives, losing purchasing power to inflation while it sits in a savings account earning nothing. It becomes a stake in a fixed-supply asset. The employee who takes that option is not speculating. She is making the same decision that anyone who has thought about it long enough eventually makes: given a choice between saving in something that loses value over time and saving in something with a fixed supply and a seventeen-year track record of going up, which do you choose?

Steak 'n Shake is not alone. Microsoft accepts Bitcoin. AT&T accepts Bitcoin. Whole Foods, via the Spedn app, accepts Bitcoin. You can book a flight on Norwegian Air with Bitcoin. You can buy a car from certain Tesla and Subaru dealers with Bitcoin. Home Depot, Nordstrom, and dozens of other major retailers accept Bitcoin indirectly through gift card services like Bitrefill and The Bitcoin Company, where you can convert Bitcoin to store credit and spend it on anything you would normally spend dollars on. The number of businesses and merchants accepting Bitcoin globally now runs into the hundreds of thousands.

The infrastructure for a Bitcoin economy is not being built. It has already been built. The question is not whether Bitcoin can be spent on real things. It can. The question is whether the person who has been told for years that Bitcoin is too risky, too volatile, too speculative — whether that person is going to figure that out before or after the window closes.

People who start saving in Bitcoin report something unexpected: it changes how they think about time.

The economic term for this is time preference.[9] High time preference means you want things now — you'll pay a premium for immediate gratification, you'll borrow against the future, you'll take the smaller reward today over the larger reward tomorrow. Low time preference means you're willing to wait — you'll invest, you'll build, you'll defer consumption in exchange for a better outcome later. Economists have long understood that low time preference is associated with wealth accumulation, stable families, and long-term thinking. High time preference is associated with debt, impulsive decisions, and the inability to escape poverty traps.

Fiat money, by design, punishes low time preference. If your savings lose 4% per year to inflation, waiting is expensive. The rational response to a currency that loses value is to spend it before it loses more. The system trains you, at the level of incentive, to consume now and worry later. An economy built on consumer spending needs consumers who spend.

Bitcoin inverts the incentive. When your savings appreciate over time — when waiting is rewarded rather than punished — the rational response is to wait. To think longer. To ask, before every purchase: is this worth my Bitcoin?[10] That question, asked consistently, changes behavior. It changes what you buy, what you build, what you value. Bitcoiners tend to stop buying things they don't need. They start thinking in decades rather than months. They become, in the language of economics, lower time preference.

The Stanford marshmallow experiment — in which children who could wait for a second marshmallow went on to have better outcomes across almost every life metric —

---

9. For readers who want to go deeper on the personal transformation that Bitcoin tends to produce, Gigi's 21 Lessons: What I've Learned from Falling Down the Bitcoin Rabbit Hole (self-published, 2019; available at 21lessons.com) covers the experience from the inside. For the economic theory behind time preference, Saifedean Ammous addresses it in The Bitcoin Standard (Wiley, 2018, Chapter 5) and goes considerably deeper in Principles of Economics (Saif House, 2023, Chapter 13), which includes dedicated sections on time preference and civilization and time preference and Bitcoin. The original and most rigorous treatment remains Ludwig von Mises, Human Action (1949, Chapter XVIII: "Action in the Passing of Time"). Mises is not easy reading, but any reader who attempts him will be rewarded.

10. For a concrete illustration of this question applied to consumer purchases, see Anand Sinha, "If You Bought Bitcoin Instead of Every New iPhone, You'd Have $250 Million," The Street, August 24, 2025. The calculation covers every iPhone model from the original 2007 launch through the present. For readers who want to run their own numbers on any purchase, Bitbo maintains a free interactive calculator at charts.bitbo.io/if-i-bought/.

has been replicated, challenged, and refined over fifty years of research.[11] The core finding survives: the ability to defer gratification is one of the strongest predictors of long-term success we have ever measured. Bitcoin is a marshmallow machine. It rewards the people who wait.

None of this is guaranteed. Bitcoin is not a life coach. It does not make decisions for you. But the incentive structure it creates — save now, spend later — is the opposite of what fiat money has been training people to do for fifty years. The behavioral changes that Bitcoin advocates report are the predictable result of a changed incentive structure.

The case for Bitcoin is much deeper than price goes up.

There is one more thing the reader of this book deserves to know, and it is perhaps the most clarifying fact in the whole chapter.

While working-class Americans were being advised to diversify into index funds and stay the course with their 401(k)s, the largest financial institutions in the world were quietly accumulating Bitcoin.

Michael Saylor is the most visible example. In 2020, his company — then called MicroStrategy, now renamed Strategy — began converting its corporate treasury from dollars into Bitcoin. Not as a small position. As its primary reserve asset. Saylor borrowed against the company's equity, issued convertible bonds, and used every lever available to him to buy more. By early 2025, Strategy held hundreds of thousands of Bitcoin — a significant percentage of the total supply that will ever exist — making it the largest corporate holder in the world.[12] The company's stock price made it one of the best-performing equities in the entire market over the following five years.

---

11. The original marshmallow studies were conducted by Walter Mischel and colleagues at Stanford University beginning in the late 1960s. The key longitudinal finding — that delayed gratification in childhood predicted better outcomes in SAT scores, educational attainment, and other life metrics — was published in Walter Mischel, Yuichi Shoda, and Monica Rodriguez, "Delay of Gratification in Children," Science, 244(4907), 933–938 (1989). A significant replication and critique appeared in Tyler W. Watts, Greg J. Duncan, and Haonan Quan, "Revisiting the Marshmallow Test: A Conceptual Replication Investigating Links Between Early Delay of Gratification and Later Outcomes," Psychological Science, 29(7), 1159–1177 (2018), which found that socioeconomic background explained much of the effect. The core finding — that the capacity to defer gratification is associated with better long-term outcomes — survived the replication; the causal mechanism and universality remain actively debated.

12. Strategy's current Bitcoin holdings are updated in real time at saylor.app and in the company's SEC filings (8-K disclosures for each purchase tranche, available at sec.gov). As of this writing, Strategy holds more than 800,000 Bitcoin — greater than 3% of the total supply that will ever exist. Both figures will have changed by the time you read this — almost certainly upward.

Saylor's insight was straightforward: holding dollars is a guaranteed slow loss. Holding Bitcoin is a bet on scarcity in a world of abundance. The math, he argued, was not complicated. And the financial world, which had laughed at him when he started, had stopped laughing.

BlackRock — one of the largest asset managers on Earth — launched a Bitcoin spot ETF in January 2024. It was the fastest-growing ETF in the history of the product category. Within twelve months, Bitcoin ETFs had accumulated tens of billions of dollars in assets, a figure that has continued to grow.[13] The same financial institutions that had for years told their clients that Bitcoin was too speculative, too unregulated, and too volatile to hold were now offering it on their platforms and collecting fees for managing it.

El Salvador made Bitcoin legal tender in 2021 — the first nation-state to do so. The IMF warned it would destabilize the country. The financial press predicted disaster. Four years later, El Salvador held several thousand Bitcoin in its national treasury, was in the black on its investment, and was using Bitcoin-linked bonds to finance infrastructure. The disaster never arrived.[14]

In the United States, the conversation shifted from "should the government ban Bitcoin" to "should the government hold Bitcoin as a strategic reserve." Multiple states began passing legislation allowing their pension funds and state treasuries to hold Bitcoin.[15]

---

13. Current Bitcoin ETF assets under management are tracked in real time at bitcointreasuries.net and coinglass.com/bitcoin-etf. The BlackRock iShares Bitcoin Trust (IBIT) reached $10 billion in assets in its first seven weeks — faster than any ETF in history — and was followed by similar products from Fidelity, Ark/21Shares, Bitwise, and others. Both the total AUM figure and the individual fund rankings change continuously with Bitcoin's price and net fund flows.

14. El Salvador's Bitcoin Law took effect September 7, 2021, making it the first country to adopt Bitcoin as legal tender alongside the U.S. dollar. The IMF urged El Salvador to remove Bitcoin's legal tender status as a condition of a $1.4 billion loan program. In early 2025, El Salvador reached an agreement with the IMF that modified the mandatory acceptance provisions — making Bitcoin acceptance voluntary for private businesses — while the government retained its Bitcoin treasury holdings and the Chivo wallet infrastructure. The IMF's concerns about financial stability and fiscal risk are documented in its Article IV consultation reports on El Salvador (imf.org). El Salvador's Bitcoin holdings and unrealized gains are tracked at the National Bitcoin Office (bitcoin.gob.sv).

15. A running tracker of U.S. state-level Bitcoin reserve legislation — including bills introduced, passed committee, signed into law, or failed — is maintained at bitcoinlaws.io. As of early 2026, more than twenty states had introduced legislation permitting or directing state pension funds or treasuries to hold Bitcoin. Oklahoma, Arizona, and Utah were among the furthest along in the legislative process. The policy rationale varies by state but generally cites inflation protection and portfolio diversification.

The political figure who had dismissed Bitcoin as "not money" during his first term was, by 2024, speaking at the Bitcoin conference and pledging to make America the world's Bitcoin superpower.[16]

None of this means that governments or corporations holding Bitcoin is inherently good. It is not. Bitcoin is best when it is held by individuals, by working people, by families — by the people who actually need protection from the system that these institutions built and continue to run. The author of this book believes, without reservation, that the ideal future is one where the working class holds Bitcoin before the governments do. But the fact that governments and the largest institutions in the world are accumulating it tells you something important. It tells you that the people who have spent decades studying the global monetary system — who understand, better than anyone, what the long-term trajectory of fiat currency looks like — have made a choice about where to put their reserves. They chose Bitcoin. The question for Cherie Tobias, and Bill Atkinson, and Mackenzie Moan, and every other working American in this book, is not whether Bitcoin is real. The question is whether they are going to get there before the window closes.

You do not own a share of Bitcoin. You do not own a claim on Bitcoin. You do not own a fund that holds Bitcoin on your behalf, managed by people you have never met, subject to rules you did not agree to, in a jurisdiction that may change its mind about all of it next Tuesday.

Bitcoin held in self-custody is not a claim, not a fund, not a promise. The network recognizes your private key. Nothing stands between you and it. No one can freeze it, dilute it, confiscate it, or tell you that withdrawals are temporarily suspended due to market conditions. It is the first instrument of savings in the modern era that works exactly the way a working person needs savings to work — quietly, reliably, without asking permission from anyone.

The people in this book — Cherie, Bill, Mackenzie, Hank — did not fail. The money failed them. They worked hard, followed the rules, and handed their savings to a system that was designed, from the beginning, to transfer value away from people like them. That

---

16. Donald J. Trump, Twitter/X, July 12, 2019: Bitcoin and other cryptocurrencies are "not money," with value "highly volatile and based on thin air." On July 27, 2024, Trump delivered the keynote address at the Bitcoin 2024 conference in Nashville, Tennessee, where he pledged to fire SEC Chairman Gary Gensler and establish a strategic national bitcoin stockpile. See CNN, "Trump, who once trashed bitcoin as 'based on thin air,'" July 27, 2024.

system is still running. But for the first time in fifty years, there is an escape hatch.[17] It does not require a financial advisor, a brokerage account, or a minimum balance. It requires a decision. There is an escape hatch. The next chapter shows you what that decision looks like across twenty years.

Two families. Same starting point. Different money. One stays in the system. One finds the escape hatch.

17. Christine Lagarde, President of the European Central Bank, said the quiet part out loud in 2021: "If there is an escape, that escape will be used." She meant it as an argument for global regulatory coordination to close that escape hatch before people found it. She was right about the human behavior. Wrong about what to do about it.

Chapter Eight

2046

The Variable

Under sound money, as the economy grows more productive, goods become more abundant, and the money in a working man's pocket buys more goods every year.

That is what technology plus sound money looks like. Prices fall. Wages go further. The workers keep what they earned.

The variable that determines who captures the gains from human ingenuity is not the technology. It was never the technology. It is always the money. The two stories that follow are what happens when the money is wrong — and what happens when one family figures that out in time.

The Fiat Path

The year is 2046. Every number in this chapter represents verifiable trends decades in the making. Federal Reserve data. BLS wages. CBO projections. Run forward twenty years. No crisis assumed. No collapse required. Just the road we are already on.

Inflation is invisible year to year. You only see it when you zoom out. A dollar losing 3% annually is worth 45 cents after twenty years. Twenty years is far enough.

This is the optimistic scenario. Nothing gets worse. The trends just continue.[1]

It is a Saturday morning in March of 2046, and Danny and Sara Vance are sitting at the kitchen table of the apartment they rent in Westerville — a suburb east of Columbus, Ohio, the kind of place described in real estate listings as "family-friendly" and "con-

1. Methodology: All projections apply documented historical trend rates to 2026 base-year data. Home price CAGR from Federal Reserve FRED series MSPUS (median sales price of existing homes, 1963–present). Median income CAGR from FRED series MEHOINUSA646N (real median household income, converted to nominal using the Federal Reserve's CPI data). National debt trajectory from CBO Long-Term Budget Outlook (2024 edition). No structural break, crisis, or policy change is assumed. These are current-trajectory projections only.

venient to shopping," which means it has a Target and a school that is not failing. The television is on in the background. A news anchor is reporting that the national debt has crossed $200 trillion, which sounds enormous until you realize that the last number sounded enormous too, and the one before that. Sara glances at the screen. "Two hundred trillion dollars," she says, "and there are more homeless people on my caseload now than in any year I can remember." Danny does not say anything. She has been a social worker for twenty-two years. She has seen what money running out does to a family, from a desk across the room. She does not connect the number on the television to the number she is about to look at on her phone. Not yet.

She opens her phone. They are looking at a house.

Not a house on the shore of Lake Erie. Not a farmhouse with acreage, not a downtown loft, not anything with a view of anything. A house in Westerville — three bedrooms, two bathrooms, an attached garage, a yard big enough for a gas grill and a small garden. The listing price is $804,000.

That number is not a surprise to anyone who has been paying attention. The median home sales price in Columbus, Ohio in early 2026 was approximately $290,000. According to Federal Reserve and Census Bureau data, home prices nationally have grown at an average of approximately 5.23% per year in nominal terms since 1972.[2] Applied to Columbus — a mid-sized Midwestern city that offers no coastal absurdity as an excuse — for twenty years, that growth produces a median price of approximately $804,000. The house in Westerville, at $804,000, is not a premium property. It is the median.

Danny is forty. He has been a Columbus firefighter for twenty years. He earns approximately $153,000 a year — the result of long shifts, mandatory overtime, and two decades of union negotiation.[3] Sara is forty. She is a licensed independent social worker with

---

2. Columbus, OH median home sale price: $290,000 (Redfin, January 2026, redfin.com). The national median home price (FRED MSPUS) increased at a compound annual growth rate of approximately 5.23% from Q1 1972 ($26,200) through Q4 2025 ($405,300). Columbus trades approximately 32% below the national median, removing coastal-market outliers. Projecting $290,000 at 5.23% annually for 20 years: $290,000 × $(1.0523)^{20}$ ≈ $804,000.

3. U.S. Bureau of Labor Statistics, Occupational Outlook Handbook, Firefighters, May 2024. BLS median annual pay: $59,530. The working figure of approximately $67,000 in 2026 reflects 8–10 years of experience and standard overtime provisions common in municipal departments. Projected at 4.23% annually for 20 years: approximately $153,000 in 2046.

a master's degree from Ohio State. She earns approximately $123,000.[4] Together they earn $277,000, which places them more than 42% above the projected median American household income of $194,000 in 2046.

Same math. Median household income in 2026 was approximately $85,000. It has grown at roughly 4.23% a year for decades.[5] Twenty years at 4.23% gets you to approximately $194,000. Danny and Sara, at $277,000, are doing well by any conventional measure. Their parents tell them this. Their parents are not wrong. They just do not understand what "doing well" means in 2046.

In those twenty years, AI ran through their industries like it ran through everything else. Sara's department was reorganized twice. Both times the result was the same: fewer workers, more cases, same pay. The economy got dramatically more productive. Wages grew at 4.23% a year.[6] Same as always. Same as during the internet boom, when everyone was told the gains would be shared.

Technology plus fiat money looks like Danny and Sara. Their employers captured the productivity. Wages grew at 4.23% annually — while the cost of housing grew at 5.23%. Twenty years of that gap is the story that follows.

The Numbers

Here is what $277,000 looks like in 2046.

---

4. U.S. Bureau of Labor Statistics, Occupational Outlook Handbook, Social Workers, May 2024. BLS median annual pay: $61,330. National Association of Social Workers, Ohio Chapter: mean starting salary for new MSWs, $47,100. The working figure of approximately $54,000 in 2026 reflects several years post-licensure experience. Projected at 4.23% annually for 20 years: approximately $123,000 in 2046.

5. The 4.23% wage growth figure is drawn from U.S. Census Bureau historical income data beginning in 1972 (Table H-5), the same base year used for home price and M2 calculations throughout this book, ensuring an apples-to-apples comparison across all trend lines. The Federal Reserve's own FRED series MEHOINUSA646N shows median household income growing at only 3.34% annually — but the FRED series begins in 1984, cutting off the early post-1971 fiat era. We used the longer Census series for consistency. Had we used the Federal Reserve's own numbers, the gap between wage growth and home price growth would be wider, and the picture in this chapter bleaker still.

6. U.S. Census Bureau, Historical Income Tables: Households (Table H-5), median household income 1972 ($9,697) through 1983; Federal Reserve FRED series MEHOINUSA646N for 1984 onward. The 4.23% compound annual growth rate spans 1972–2024. Bureau of Labor Statistics, Current Employment Statistics Survey, confirms comparable nominal wage growth for full-time workers. Projecting $85,000 at 4.23% annually for 20 years: $\$85{,}000 \times (1.0423)^{20} \approx \$194{,}000$.

After federal taxes, Ohio's flat state income tax, Columbus's city income tax,[7] [8] Danny's mandatory OP&F pension contribution, and payroll taxes, Danny and Sara take home approximately $15,641 a month. Danny contributes 12.25% of his salary — more than $1,562 every month — to the Ohio Police and Fire Pension Fund, a contribution he cannot opt out of. It has come out of his check for twenty years, the price of a retirement promise made in exchange for below-market wages. From take-home, they pay rent, two car payments, health insurance, groceries, utilities, and the rest of a thirteen-line monthly budget. Their expenses total $19,501. Their take-home is $15,641. They run a monthly deficit of $3,860 before any spending they did not plan for.* (For a full breakdown of their monthly budget, see the Appendix at the end of this chapter.)*

Sara still carries student loans. She borrowed $88,220 for the master's degree Ohio's licensing board required for clinical social work practice, completed the degree in 2028, and has been making $657 monthly payments ever since.[9] She is forty years old. She has sixteen years of payments behind her and four in front of her. The balance outstanding is approximately $27,737. She will finish paying in 2050 — age forty-four. By that point she will have paid approximately $157,858 to retire a debt of $88,220 — nearly $70,000 in interest, for a credential she was required to hold.[10]

---

7. Ohio Department of Taxation: beginning with tax year 2026, Ohio imposes a flat rate of 2.75% on all nonbusiness income above $26,050, with income at or below that threshold taxed at 0%. This is the completion of a phased reform enacted in the 2024 Ohio budget bill (H.B. 96), reducing from a top marginal rate of 3.5% (TY2024) through 3.125% (TY2025) to the current flat rate. Source: Ohio IT 1040 instructions; Ohio Dept. of Taxation, tax.ohio.gov.

8. City of Columbus income tax: 2.5% on wages earned within or by residents of Columbus, per Columbus City Code. Ohio municipalities are authorized to levy municipal income taxes under Ohio Revised Code §1718. Columbus has maintained the 2.5% rate since 2009. The combined state-plus-city marginal rate for Columbus wage earners on income above $26,050 is 5.25% (2.75% + 2.5%).

9. Federal student loan interest rate for graduate/professional unsubsidized Direct Loans, 2024–2025 academic year: 8.08%. The 6.5% figure used in this chapter's calculations reflects a midpoint of rates available over the 2020–2026 period. StudentAid.gov, "Interest Rates and Fees."

10. National Center for Education Statistics, Digest of Education Statistics, Table 331.95: average cumulative graduate school debt for master's degree recipients, $77,300 (2019–20). Education Data Initiative estimates average MSW total education debt (including undergraduate) at $88,220. National Association of Social Workers Ohio Chapter: mean total education debt for newly licensed MSWs ranges $79,000–$92,000 against a starting salary of $47,100. Clinical licensure (LISW-S in Ohio) requires an MSW from a CSWE-accredited program; this pathway is mandatory in virtually every state. Sara borrowed $88,220 in 2028; repayment began 2030 on a 20-year extended plan at 6.5%. In 2046 — sixteen years into repayment — outstanding balance is approximately $27,737. Payoff: 2050.

That $3,860 deficit is every month. Not a bad month. Every month. The math does not have a good version.

The house in Westerville requires a 20% down payment. At that price there is no government backing. The bank wants real skin in the game. Twenty percent of $804,000 is $160,800.

Danny and Sara cannot save for it. They spend more than they earn. The $160,800 does not sit at the end of a savings timeline. It sits on the other side of a wall they cannot see over from where they are.

Danny has a spreadsheet. He built it the year they started seriously discussing buying. He has not opened it in six months.

But here is the thing. If Danny and Sara somehow arrived at $160,800 and closed on the house tomorrow, the mortgage on the remaining $643,200 at 5% over thirty years is $3,453 a month.[11] Property taxes in Franklin County add $1,005. Homeowners insurance and a basic maintenance reserve add $700. All-in monthly housing cost: $5,158.

Their rent, projected to 2046, is $6,375 a month. Ownership would cost them $1,217 less per month than renting. The math says buy. The math also requires a closing table, and they cannot reach it. They run a deficit every month. The down payment is not a savings goal. It is a number on the other side of a wall.

The argument "just buy" requires a ramp they do not have. The ramp requires savings. The savings require a surplus. The surplus does not exist.

A Window That Closes on Everyone

Danny and Sara are the lucky ones. The median American household in 2046 earns $194,000. After taxes, they take home approximately $11,400 a month. The house in Westerville does not appear in their budget as a stretch goal. It is not in the conversation at all. The median household in 2046 looks at Danny and Sara — $277,000 combined,

11. Mortgage rate assumption: 5%. We will not pretend to know what thirty-year mortgage rates will be in 2046. This is educated guesswork, and we say so plainly. The 30-year fixed rate averaged approximately 3% during the 2010s and spiked to over 7% in 2023–2024 as the Federal Reserve responded to the inflation its own policies helped create. A rate of 5% represents a rough midpoint between those two regimes. What we can say with more confidence is that the $200 trillion national debt projected on Danny and Sara's television will exert sustained upward pressure on long-term interest rates — the government must compete with private borrowers for the same pool of capital, and the larger the debt, the higher the rate the market demands to hold it. A return to the 3% mortgages of the 2010s would require either a dramatic reduction in federal borrowing or another round of Federal Reserve intervention that suppresses rates artificially. Neither seems likely to persist. We used 5%. The reader who believes rates will be lower should adjust accordingly. The reader who believes rates will be higher will find the picture worse.

two credentialed professionals, twenty years on the fire department — the way Danny and Sara look at the house on Sara's phone. With the recognition that even that is not enough.

Here is what the system took from them.

For twenty years, Danny has contributed 12.25% of his salary to the Ohio Police and Fire Pension Fund. The City of Columbus has contributed an additional 24% on his behalf. Between the two, more than a third of everything Danny has ever earned has gone into a single pool — a pool that, as of its most recent actuarial valuation, is funded at 70.0% of what it owes. On a market-value basis, the funded ratio is 63.5%. The fund carries an unfunded actuarial accrued liability of $7.6 billion. Danny does not contribute to Social Security. OP&F is not a supplement to his retirement. It is his retirement — the only one — and it is short by nearly a third.[12]

He accepted below-market wages for twenty years in exchange for this promise. The promise may not be kept in full.

For sixteen years, Sara has paid $657 a month into a student loan balance that was mandatory collateral for a credential that was mandatory for her job. She did not choose to borrow $88,220. She chose to become a licensed social worker. The state required a master's degree for that license. And tuition has been climbing at roughly 5% a year for fifty years.[13] She still has four years to go. She will finish paying in 2050, at age forty-four, having paid approximately $157,858 to service a debt of $88,220.

And then there is Lucas.

Danny and Sara have one child. Their son Lucas was born in 2028. He is eighteen now, filling out financial aid forms for college the way his mother filled out loan applications eighteen years ago — because Danny and Sara could not save enough to pay for it outright, because the pension contributions and the student loan payment and the rent that grows at 4.2% a year did not leave a margin wide enough for a college fund. Not even with two

---

12. Ohio Police & Fire Pension Fund, "Contribution Rates," op-f.org/employers/contributionrates. As of July 2015, firefighter members contribute 12.25% of gross pensionable salary; employers of firefighters contribute 24%. OP&F 2023 Actuarial Valuation (January 1, 2023): actuarial funded ratio 70.0%; market-value funded ratio 63.5%; unfunded actuarial accrued liability $7.6 billion. A funded ratio below 80% is generally considered distressed by actuarial standards. Ohio firefighters in OP&F-covered positions do not contribute to Social Security; OP&F is their sole defined-benefit retirement vehicle.

13. National Center for Education Statistics, Digest of Education Statistics, Table 330.10: average total cost of attendance at degree-granting postsecondary institutions. In-state public four-year institutions: average total cost increased from approximately $11,000 in 2000–01 to approximately $27,000 in 2022–23, a CAGR of approximately 4.2%. Graduate programs have compounded at similar or higher rates over the same period.

professional salaries. Not even doing everything right. Lucas is not starting from zero. He is starting from negative. And the family that was supposed to break that cycle — two working professionals, twenty years on the job, everything done right — could not.

They wanted two more children. They had the conversation when Lucas was two, and again when he was four, and again when he was seven. The answer was always the same number: childcare for an infant in the Columbus metro in 2028 cost more than $2,800 a month — more than their rent at the time — before a larger apartment, before upgraded insurance, before the pediatric bills. Sara knew the math. She had spent twenty-two years watching what financial pressure does to families. They do not have more children.

This is not a story about poverty. We already know the poor cannot buy homes. This is the story that should concern you if you are the kind of person who has done everything right.

You went to school. You got the degree. You built the career. You make good money. You have been telling yourself that the housing crisis is someone else's problem. That the people being priced out are the ones who did not plan, did not save, did not make the right moves. You are careful. You are responsible. You are succeeding.

The window closes on people like you too. It just closes later. In 2026, first responders in well-off communities across the country were already being priced out of the neighborhoods they served — officers and firefighters who could not afford a starter home within commuting distance of the precinct or station they had worked for years. Twenty years later, the mechanism has not changed. The numbers are just bigger. The window has risen past public safety workers, past credentialed professionals, past households earning 37% above the national median. Danny earns more than those officers did in real terms. It was not enough.

The curve is not bending. The gap between what assets cost and what wages pay has been widening for fifty years, and nothing is stopping it. Every year, the floor rises a little higher. At some point it rises past you.

Danny closes Sara's phone. "Same as last month," he says.

"Same as last month," she agrees.

Continuation, Not Catastrophe

None of this required a catastrophe. It only required continuation. The $200 trillion number on Danny and Sara's television is the result of the same arithmetic that produced the $804,000 house on Sara's phone. The national debt climbed from $6 trillion in 2004 to $36 trillion in 2024 — a six-fold increase in twenty years — and kept accelerating. At a modest average interest rate of 3%, the annual interest payment alone now exceeds $6 trillion — more than the entire federal budget was in 2020. That money services nothing. It builds no roads, teaches no children, funds no military. It is the rent the government pays on the spending it already did, and the mechanism for covering it is always the same: more dollars created, more purchasing power transferred silently from people who earn wages to people who own assets. The debt headline and the house listing are not two different problems. They are the same problem, viewed from two different screens.[14]

Danny and Sara do not know this. Every trend that produced their situation was visible and documented in 2026. None of it was hidden. It was reported quarterly, debated in committee, and then set aside, because the machine had every incentive to keep running. And it ran.

Here is the other road.

A Rabbit Hole on a Tuesday Night

In the spring of 2026 — the same year Danny and Sara Vance were beginning their careers in Columbus — Jake Hartman was thirty-one years old, a licensed electrician, father of two with a third on the way, and about three beers into a Tuesday night when he fell down a rabbit hole on his phone that he would later describe as the best accident of his life.

He was not looking for Bitcoin. He was reading about inflation — specifically about why eggs cost what they cost — and one link led to another and somewhere around midnight he was watching a man drawing on a whiteboard explaining what happens to the value of a dollar when the government prints more of them. He had understood this intuitively for years without having the language for it. He watched the video twice.

Jake made $68,000 a year running electrical on commercial builds. Rachel worked part time as a dental hygienist. Together they cleared around $95,000 — less than half of what Danny and Sara would earn twenty years later, in a world that had gotten significantly more expensive. Jake earned more than Cherie Tobias and less than Bill Atkinson. He was the Chapter 5 people. He just made a different decision about what to do with the money.

---

14. U.S. national debt: Treasury.gov, fiscaldata.treasury.gov. Debt was approximately $6 trillion at end of FY2002 and $36 trillion at end of FY2024. Annual net interest expense on the national debt exceeded $1 trillion for the first time in FY2024 (Congressional Budget Office, The Budget and Economic Outlook: 2024 to 2034). The CBO projects interest expense to continue rising as a share of GDP absent policy changes.

He told Rachel about it the next morning. She was skeptical. She usually was when Jake came home fired up about something at midnight. She asked him to slow down and explain it again. He did. She asked two questions he could not answer. He went and found the answers. That is how they made decisions.

Two weeks later, they bought $400 in Bitcoin on an exchange. Not because they were certain. Because they were curious, and $400 was an amount they could lose without catastrophe, and the alternative was leaving it in a savings account earning next to nothing while their grocery bill climbed every month.

That was the beginning.

The Learning

The learning happened in layers. The first layer was the basics: what Bitcoin is, why the supply is fixed, what that means for its value relative to dollars that can be printed without limit. Jake read. Rachel read. They argued about it at the kitchen table after the kids were asleep — real arguments. By the end of the first month, they had moved past "maybe this is interesting" to "we think this is real." That shift changes everything.

The second layer was process. They set up automatic purchases — $75 every Friday, same amount, regardless of price. Not because they were certain the price would go up that week. Because they understood that trying to time the market was how ordinary people ended up buying high and selling low, and that consistency over time was the strategy that worked. The $75 came out of the budget the way the electric bill did. It stopped feeling like a decision and became a habit.

The third layer was custody. Jake spent a weekend learning what a hardware wallet was and why it mattered — why leaving Bitcoin on an exchange was not the same as owning it, why the phrase "not your keys, not your coins" was not paranoia but basic financial literacy. He bought a hardware wallet. He set it up carefully. He wrote his seed phrase on paper and sealed it in an envelope and put it somewhere only he and Rachel knew. He felt, for the first time in his adult life, like he had something that was genuinely his — not held by a bank, not subject to a terms-of-service update, not dependent on anyone else's solvency.

He moved their stack off the exchange. Then he had a beer to celebrate. Just one.

Twenty Years of Showing Up

Their daughter Emma was three when they started. Their son Cole was one. Their second daughter, born in October 2026, they named Lily.

Before Lily came home from the hospital, Jake had set up a wallet for her. Not a large position — a few hundred dollars' worth of Bitcoin at the time, bought in the weeks before her birth and moved to cold storage. He had done the same for Emma and Cole, consolidating the small amounts he had been setting aside for each since he learned about self-custody. He sat Rachel down and explained what he had done. She looked at the hardware wallets — small, unremarkable devices — and looked at him. "You really believe this," she said. It was not a question.

"I do," he said. "I think this is the most important thing we can do for them."

"Then show me how it works."

He did. After that, they managed it together.

The years between 2026 and 2031 were not dramatic. They were the years of showing up. Jake worked. Rachel worked part time around the kids' school schedules. The $75 a week went in every Friday. The price went up and then down and then up again by more and then down again. Friends asked about it; Jake explained it; some listened and most did not. A coworker told him he was going to lose everything. His father-in-law shook his head at Thanksgiving. Jake did not argue. He had learned that the argument did not work and that the math eventually would.

In 2029, they became whole coiners.

It had been the goal since early on. One full coin. Not a magic number, just a target — and Jake believed that one day whole coins would be hard to come by. They hit it on a Wednesday morning in February. Jake texted Rachel a single number: 1.0. She texted back a single emoji. They did not tell anyone.

They kept buying.

What the Money Did to the Man

The change in Jake happened slowly enough that he did not notice it while it was occurring. Rachel noticed. He drank less. Not dramatically, not all at once — but the Tuesday night beers that had been a reflex became something he thought about first. He started going to bed earlier and getting up earlier. He read more. He made lists. He started thinking in longer time frames — not just what the week looked like but what the year looked like, what the decade looked like, what he was building and whether it was the thing he wanted to be building.

He quit drinking entirely in the spring of 2031. He told Rachel it had started to feel like borrowing against himself — taking the edge off now at the cost of being sharper tomorrow. It was the same argument he made about debt. She got it. She told him she was proud of him. She meant it.

He took up running. He got a physical for the first time in four years. He started a budget spreadsheet that was actually accurate. He and Rachel started actually planning. Not wishing — planning. Numbers. Goals. Things they could check.

"You've changed," Rachel told him one night.

"I think the Bitcoin changed me," he said.

She thought about that. "No," she said. "You changed. The Bitcoin just gave you a reason."

Raising Kids on Sound Money

The children were raised on the concept before they could fully understand it. Jake found a way to explain it to Emma at six: imagine friendship bracelets, he said. If anyone could make them without any work — if they just appeared whenever someone wanted one — you would end up with more bracelets than friendships. They would not mean anything. You would not feel special getting one. But if there was a friendship bracelet that could not be copied, that only existed in a certain number, and someone gave you one — that would mean something. That would be worth keeping. Bitcoin is that bracelet. Dollars are the kind anyone can make.

Emma thought about this. "So if everyone has one it's not special," she said.

"Exactly," Jake said.

"And Bitcoin is special because not everyone can have one."

"There's a limit. That's the whole point."

She nodded slowly. "Okay. I want one."

When Emma was eight, she started getting half her allowance in dollars and half in Bitcoin — automatically purchased and added to her wallet each week. Cole's allowance worked the same way when he was old enough. Lily's was set up before she could ask for it.

The kids understood, as they grew, that money was a tool with properties — that some tools held their value and some did not, and that choosing your tool mattered. Jake took them through the hardware wallet when each was old enough to handle it. He explained seed phrases. He explained why you did not talk about how much Bitcoin you had. He explained the difference between saving and spending, and why saving in something that goes up means your future self has something waiting. These were not abstract lessons. They pointed to actual wallets. They pointed to actual numbers.

Emma started her first real business at fifteen — custom embroidered patches, sold online, payments accepted in Bitcoin and dollars. She preferred Bitcoin. Cole, at thirteen, mowed lawns in the neighborhood and asked to be paid in Bitcoin when the customers would allow it. Lily, the youngest, was quieter and more careful with money than either of her siblings, which Jake took as a good sign without knowing quite why.

The Other Side

It is the same Saturday morning in March of 2046, and Jake and Rachel Hartman are sitting at the kitchen table of the house they own in Terre Haute, Indiana.

Not a large house. A good house. Three bedrooms, a backyard big enough for the dog — a big, ridiculous golden retriever named Biscuit — and a vegetable garden along the fence that Rachel has been expanding every summer for seven years. They bought the house in 2034. Jake offered to pay in Bitcoin. The seller declined. So Jake and Rachel converted a portion of their stack into dollars, wrote a check, and walked out with a key. No mortgage. No bank. No thirty years of interest. Jake is fifty-one now, Rachel forty-nine, and twelve years later it is still the best day of his life.

Emma is twenty-three. She runs her own business now — not embroidered patches but a small product design firm, three employees, profitable in its second year. She does not have student loans. Not one dollar. Jake and Rachel paid for her degree from a Bitcoin wallet they had been building since before she could walk, and when they transferred the funds, the amount was large enough that tuition was a fraction of it.

Danny Vance is sitting in Westerville, forty years old, with a pension fund that is 30% short and no Social Security to fall back on. Sara is still paying student loans — $657 a month, four years left, a finish line visible but not yet crossed. Their son Lucas is filling out the same loan applications his mother filled out eighteen years ago. Emma Hartman started her career from capital. Lucas Vance is starting from the place his mother started — from negative. The difference is not discipline, or intelligence, or even income. It is the money their parents saved in. That is the whole story.

Cole is twenty-one and finishing his last year of engineering school at Purdue. No loans. He has his own Bitcoin wallet, has been managing it himself since he was sixteen, and has made several decisions with it that Jake thought were unwise and did not say so, because Cole had earned the right to be wrong with his own money and the amounts involved meant the mistakes cost less than what they taught him. He has more Bitcoin than his mistakes cost him.

Lily is nineteen, a year into a nursing program, considering a minor in economics. She has questions about monetary theory that Jake can almost keep up with. She is the one who, at twelve, had read the entirety of the book that started Jake's rabbit hole back in 2026, and had come to him afterward with a single question: "If the government can always print more dollars, why doesn't everyone just use Bitcoin?" Jake had thought about how to answer that for a long moment and had finally said: "They will. It just takes time." Lily nodded and went back to her room.

The Fire Pit

The backyard has a fire pit now, added two summers ago. On weekend nights when the kids are home, they sit around it — Jake, Rachel, Emma, Cole, Lily, and Biscuit, who takes up half the bench and contributes nothing — and talk about the future without dread. A small band of humans, figuring out how to survive together. The way it has always been done, when the money is honest.

This is what the other road looks like.

It started with a rabbit hole on a Tuesday night.

It started with a decision to learn.

Danny & Sara Vance

Monthly Budget, 2046

Gross monthly income (combined $277,000)	**$23,000**
Federal income tax (est. effective 16%)	($3,680)
Ohio income tax (flat 2.75% on income > $26,050)	($573)
Columbus city income tax (2.5%)	($575)
Danny: OP&F pension contribution (12.25% of salary)	($1,562)
Danny: Medicare only (no Social Security — OP&F-covered)	($185)
Sara: Social Security & Medicare (7.65%)	($784)
Monthly take-home	**$15,641**
Rent, 3BR Westerville — avg. 4.2%/yr from 2026 base $2,800	($6,375)
Auto insurance, 2 vehicles — avg. 5.5%/yr	($875)
Car payments, 2 vehicles — avg. 2.5%/yr	($1,802)
Gas and fuel — avg. 4.0%/yr	($603)
Health insurance, family plan — avg. 6.1%/yr	($2,451)
Groceries (food at home) — avg. 3.7%/yr	($2,689)
Dining out and entertainment — avg. 4.0%/yr	($1,315)
Utilities (electric, gas, water) — avg. 3.8%/yr	($949)
Phone, internet, streaming — avg. 1.5%/yr	($269)
Clothing — avg. 2.2%/yr	($309)
Out-of-pocket medical, dental, vision — avg. 4.6%/yr	($610)
Vehicle maintenance and registration — avg. 3.5%/yr	($398)
Personal care — avg. 3.5%/yr	($199)
Sara: student loan payment (20-yr extended repayment)	($657)
Total monthly expenses	**$19,501**
Monthly deficit	**($3,860)**

Expense methodology:

Each line item is projected from a documented 2026 base using its own category-specific CPI compound annual growth rate. Rent: BLS CUUR0000SEHA (rent of primary residence), avg. 4.2% since 1972. Auto insurance: BLS motor vehicle insurance CPI, avg. 5.5% since 1947. Car payments: BLS new vehicles CPI (quality-adjusted), avg. 2.5%. Gas/fuel: BLS motor fuel CPI, long-run avg. 4.0%. Health insurance: KFF Employer Health Benefits Survey, family premium CAGR 6.1% (1999–2025). Groceries: BLS food-at-home CPI, avg. 3.7%. Dining/entertainment: BLS food-away-from-home CPI, avg. 4.0%. Utilities: BLS household energy CPI, avg. 3.8%. Phone/internet: telecom costs have been deflationary in real terms; 1.5% applied. Clothing: BLS apparel CPI avg. 2.2% (globalization of manufacturing). Medical OOP: BLS medical care CPI, avg. 4.56% since 1967. Vehicle maintenance: BLS motor vehicle maintenance and repair, avg. 3.5%. Personal care: BLS personal care services, avg. 3.5%.

Student loan detail:

Sara borrowed $88,220 for an MSW (Ohio State University, completing degree in 2028). 20-year extended repayment at 6.5%; monthly payment $657; repayment began 2030. In 2046 — sixteen years into a twenty-year repayment — Sara carries an outstanding balance of approximately $27,737 with four years remaining. Payoff date: 2050 (age 44). Total paid over life of loan: approximately $157,858. Total interest: $69,638. Sara's NASW Ohio starting salary upon licensure: $47,100 — meaning her first monthly loan payment was 16.8% of gross monthly income.

Danny's pension detail:

Danny contributes 12.25% of gross pensionable salary to OP&F (rate set July 2015, op-f.org/employers/contributionrates). The City of Columbus contributes an additional 24%. Danny does not participate in Social Security while in OP&F-covered employment; OP&F is his sole retirement vehicle. OP&F funded ratio: 70.0% actuarial / 63.5% market value (January 1, 2023 valuation). Unfunded actuarial accrued liability: $7.6 billion.

Down payment math:

20% of $804,000 = $160,800. Danny and Sara run a monthly deficit of $3,860 before any discretionary spending. They are not accumulating savings. They are spending more than they earn. The down payment is not a savings goal. It is a number they cannot approach.

All-in housing cost if mortgage obtained:

$643,200 mortgage at 5% / 30 years = $3,453/month. Franklin County property tax (est. 1.5%) = $1,005/month. Homeowners insurance = $350/month. Maintenance reserve = $350/month. Total: $5,158/month. Their projected rent in 2046 is $6,375/month. Ownership would be $1,217/month cheaper than renting — if they could reach the closing table. They cannot reach the closing table.

Chapter Nine

100 Percent

The Power Law

In December of 1566, at the University of Rostock in northern Germany, a twenty-year-old Danish nobleman named Tyge Brahe got into a sword fight with his third cousin over a mathematical formula.

Brahe took a blade across the bridge of his nose. When it healed, the middle of his face was gone. For the rest of his life, the man the world would come to know as Tycho Brahe wore a prosthetic nose — gold and silver for formal occasions, copper for daily wear — affixed each morning with adhesive paste.

Brahe became obsessed with precision. No telescopes existed yet, so he built his own instruments — enormous brass quadrants and sextants, some taller than a man — and from his observatory on the island of Hven he recorded the positions of the planets night after night for nearly four decades. Where previous astronomers measured planetary positions to within ten arc-minutes, Brahe achieved two. He accumulated thousands of observations of Mars, Jupiter, and Saturn.

In 1600, Brahe hired an assistant, a young German mathematician named Johannes Kepler, to build on his data.

Then, in October of 1601, Brahe attended a banquet in Prague. Court etiquette dictated that a guest could not leave the table before the host. Brahe, who had been drinking heavily, needed desperately to relieve himself. He stayed seated. By the time he got home, something had gone wrong. He developed a fever, then a kidney infection, then delirium. Eleven days later he was dead. His last recorded words: ***"Let me not seem to have lived in vain."***

Kepler seized the data.

Now he had the full dataset, and a problem. Everyone assumed the planets moved in perfect circles. Two thousand years of astronomy rested on this assumption. Kepler spent years trying to fit Mars into a circular orbit. He came agonizingly close — at one point, his best model was off by only eight arc-minutes, roughly the width of a quarter held at arm's length.

He abandoned circles. He let the data lead. What he found was an ellipse.

That was his first law. But it was his third law, published in 1619, that matters most for our story. Kepler discovered that the relationship between a planet's distance from the Sun and the time it takes to complete one orbit follows a *power law*: the square of the orbital period is proportional to the cube of the distance. The relationship held for every planet. It held for the moons of Jupiter. Centuries later, it would hold for objects orbiting black holes — systems Kepler could not have imagined, obeying a law he discovered from the observations of a man who glued a metal nose to his face every morning and refused to leave a dinner party.

Kepler did not know *why* the relationship existed. That took another sixty-eight years, until Newton derived it from the law of universal gravitation. What Kepler knew was that the pattern was real, precise, and predictive — and it emerged only when you looked at the data the right way. Plot distance against orbital period on a normal graph and you get a messy curve. Plot them on a graph where both axes are logarithmic — a log-log plot — and the curve becomes a straight line.

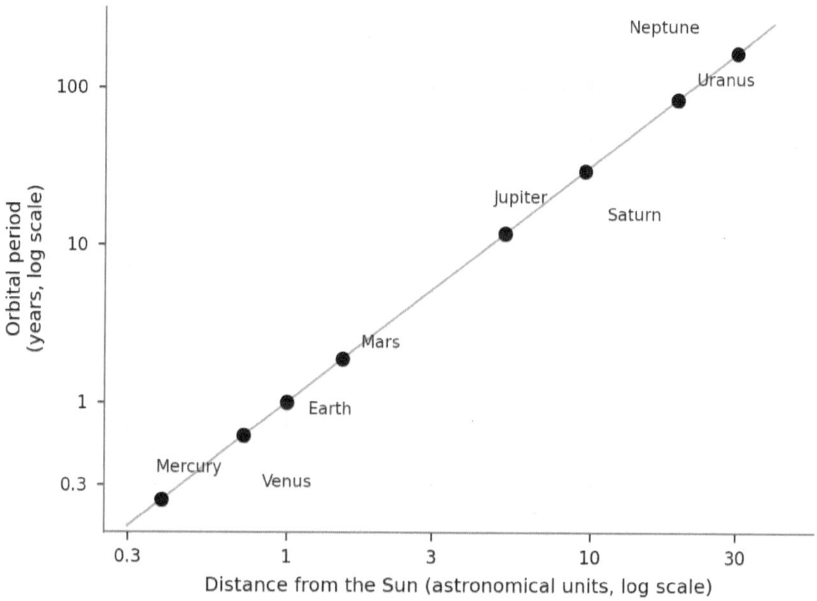

Kepler's Third Law. Plot a planet's distance from the Sun against its orbital period on a log-log scale and the relationship is a straight line. This pattern has held for every orbiting body ever measured — from Mercury to the moons of Jupiter to stars circling black holes.

Reddit Rabbit Hole

In 2018, a physicist named Giovanni Santostasi posted an observation to Reddit's Bitcoin forum that almost no one noticed. Santostasi held a PhD in astrophysics. Power laws describe earthquake frequency relative to magnitude. They describe how city populations scale with city size. They are common patterns in nature.[1]

What Santostasi noticed was that Bitcoin's price, plotted against time since the Genesis Block, displayed the signature of a power law. He posted it. A handful of people read it.

But the data did not stop.

In 2019, an analyst named Harold Burger formalized the observation in a paper that built on Santostasi's work. Burger defined a "corridor of growth" — upper and lower bounds within which Bitcoin's price had traveled since inception. When he published,

1. Giovanni Santostasi, PhD in astrophysics, posted his Bitcoin power law observation to Reddit in September 2018: reddit.com/r/Bitcoin/comments/9cqi0k. Santostasi had been developing the relationship for several years prior to that post. He later formalized the work into the Bitcoin Power Law Theory, available at: giovannisantostasi.medium.com/the-bitcoin-power-law-theory-962dfaf99ee9.

the power law's midpoint — what Burger called "fair value" — pointed to a price of approximately $93,558 five and a half years into the future.

Five and a half years later, the actual price was within one percent.[2]

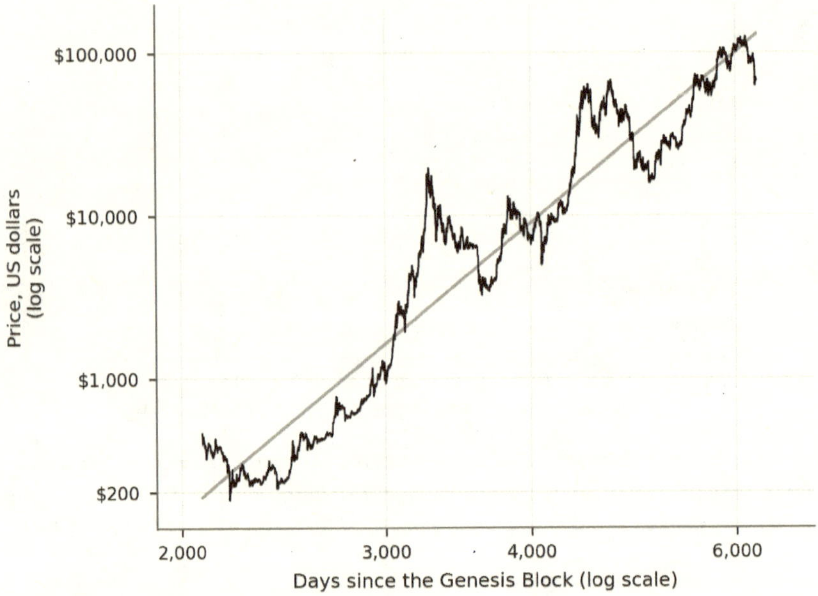

Bitcoin's price history, plotted in log-log space. The same data that looks like chaos on a linear chart resolves into a straight line.

So what is this thing? A power law describes a relationship between two variables that is scale invariant. No matter how large or small one variable gets, the other follows at the same relationship. When you graph Bitcoin's price in log format — representing growth by orders of magnitude rather than by traditional counting — and do the same for time since the Genesis Block, the growth of Bitcoin is linear.

The fit produces an R-squared of approximately 0.95 as of early 2024. That means the relationship accounts for 95% of the variance in Bitcoin's price over its entire history. For

2. Harold Christopher Burger, "Bitcoin's natural long-term power-law corridor of growth," Medium (2019): medium.com/quantodian-publications/bitcoins-natural-long-term-power-law-corridor-of-growth-649d0e9b3c94. Burger's model predicted a "fair value" midpoint price of $93,558 five and a half years from publication. The actual price at that date was within one percent of the prediction.

context, a fit that explains seventy percent of the variance in a financial asset would be considered extremely strong. Nothing in traditional finance comes close.[3]

And this is what makes Bitcoin unique. There are no true power laws identified among financial assets. For brief periods, stock market indices may look like power laws, but no stock, no index, no commodity can say that it has held a power law between price and time *since inception to present*. Only Bitcoin.

Why? Perhaps it has something to do with the lack of a central planner. There is no CEO, no marketing department, no government behind Bitcoin. It spreads purely on incentives. Bitcoin's value is intrinsically linked to the growth of its network — the number of wallets, the transactions between them, the hash rate securing it — and that network has grown in a predictable manner since inception. It is human incentives at work without coercion or manipulation.

The power law is not a model. It is not making predictions. It is an observation that a scale-invariant relationship between Bitcoin's price and time has existed for seventeen years. It is up to us to extrapolate how much that will matter going forward, if it matters at all. If we extend the observation, it suggests a price floor above $1 million sometime around 2036–37. But the extrapolation is ours. The observation is just reality.[4]

The power law could break down. In countries where local currencies have collapsed — Argentina being the most documented example — Bitcoin's price in that currency has broken the power law dramatically to the upside. That is not a win. That is a currency dying. It is not something we hope to see in America. Until it breaks here, it remains

---

3. The R-squared of approximately 0.95 is drawn from Santostasi's fit using Bitcoin's full price history from 2009 inception. Fitting the same relationship to this book's dataset, which begins in September 2014, yields an exponent of 5.948 and an R-squared of 0.921 — consistent with Santostasi's published floor formula, which uses an exponent of 5.9.

4. Price floor calculated using Santostasi's formula: Price Floor = 10 ^ [5.9 × $\log_{10}$(days_since_genesis) – 17.53], where days_since_genesis is the number of days elapsed since January 3, 2009. Applying this formula: the floor crosses $1 million in early 2036 and reaches approximately $1.34 million by January 2037. The formula and methodology are documented in Santostasi's Bitcoin Power Law Theory: giovannisantostasi.medium.com/the-bitcoin-power-law-theory-962dfaf99ee9.

a useful guide for Bitcoin holders, particularly for an asset that people consider highly volatile. In reality, Bitcoin has followed a shockingly predictable price path.[5]

And what does the power law tell you to do? Buy and hold Bitcoin. You were going to do that anyway. The power law does not tell you to trade. It does not tell you to sell. Influencers who follow the power law may tell you to do those things. That is their choice. The power law is a guide, nothing more. But it is a guide that has been right every day for seventeen years.

Bubbles, Credit, and Austrian Theory

Bitcoin does bubble. It has done so spectacularly and repeatedly. The 2011 run from $1 to $31 and back to $2. The 2013 surge to $1,100 and collapse to $200. The 2017 rocket to nearly $20,000 and the grind back to $3,200. The 2021 spike above $69,000 and the slide to $15,500. Each time, the headlines declared Bitcoin dead. Each time, the price ended higher than where the previous bubble started. Each time, the price resolved back to the power law.

So what causes the bubbles?

The conventional answer in the Bitcoin community is the halving cycle. Every four years the mining reward is cut in half — reduced supply, same demand, price goes up. The timing has roughly aligned, and many analysts treat the four-year cycle as an iron law. But there have only been four halvings. That is not enough data points to call anything an iron law. And the most recent cycle has not produced a blow-off top. Bitcoin reached new all-time highs, but gradually, without the vertical parabolic spike. The halving happened on schedule. The blow-off did not.[6]

In Chapter One, we met Ludwig von Mises. The school of thought he represented teaches that the rate of expansion of credit matters. When the central bank accelerates cheap money into the economy, conditions for a bubble exist — not a guarantee, but the conditions. As a bubble develops and grows, inflation emerges as a counteracting

---

5. Argentina's hyperinflationary episode provides the clearest documented example. From mid-2022 through 2023, as Argentina's official inflation rate exceeded 100% annually, Bitcoin's price in Argentine pesos rose from approximately 2.5 million pesos to over 10 million — a 4x increase driven not by Bitcoin's appreciation in dollar terms but by the peso's collapse. The power law, measured in pesos, broke decisively to the upside. Notably, once Argentina's inflation came back under control, Bitcoin's price in pesos settled back into a power law relationship — but at a permanently higher level, reflecting the permanent destruction of peso purchasing power. See: The Bitcoin Report, TBR-31 (August 2023).

6. As of early 2026, the cycle following the April 2024 halving had not produced a blow-off top of the kind seen in 2013, 2017, or 2021. Whether this represents a maturing market or a delayed top remains an open question.

force. Costs go up, interest rates rise, and the projects that only made sense at cheap rates are suddenly underwater. The bust is not a market failure. It is the market correcting a distortion the central bank caused.[7]

In a fiat system, most of what circulates as money was created through lending — mortgages, car loans, credit cards, corporate debt. When credit expands, money flows into the economy and asset prices rise. When credit contracts, that money disappears and prices follow.

This is the primary reason the Federal Reserve is perpetually under pressure to lower interest rates. A fiat economy needs lending to expand. Lower rates make borrowing cheaper, which encourages more lending, which creates more money. When rates rise, lending slows, credit contracts, and the economy stalls. The central bank has no choice but to keep the credit flowing — or watch the whole thing seize up.

Under a sound money system, none of this applies. Expansion is driven by savings — real capital set aside from real production, available to fund real investment. No central bank required. No perpetual pressure to keep rates low. No boom and bust engineered by the cost of borrowed money. Bitcoin is savings-based money. Fiat is credit-based money. That difference is the entire argument.[8]

When you overlay Bitcoin's price history onto the business cycle — using the ISM Purchasing Managers' Index as a proxy for expansion or contraction — the pattern is clear. Every major Bitcoin blow-off has occurred when the PMI was above 50. When credit was flowing into every asset class, it flowed into Bitcoin too.

This is good evidence in support of ABCT. The seventeen-year history of Bitcoin has followed this pattern closely. When the rate of credit expansion is increasing, Bitcoin catches the wave alongside everything else. When credit contracts — when the Fed tightens, when M2 shrinks — Bitcoin does not bubble. It may still appreciate along its adoption curve, but the mania disappears.

---

7. Douglas E. French, Early Speculative Bubbles and Increases in the Supply of Money (Mises Institute, 2009). Critics sometimes point to Tulipmania as proof that bubbles predate fiat money. French shows that even pre-fiat bubbles were preceded by monetary expansion — in the Dutch case, free coinage laws that dramatically increased the money supply. The mechanism differs; the principle does not.

8. Roger Garrison, "The Austrian Theory of the Business Cycle," Mises University lecture. Available at https://youtu.be/5rJceunyCwU — the clearest visual explanation of how artificially low interest rates misallocate capital and make the bust inevitable.

The 2022–2023 period demonstrated this. The Fed raised rates aggressively. M2 contracted for the first time in decades. No bubble. No parabolic top. Just the adoption curve grinding forward without the rocket fuel.

The most recent cycle has been the healthiest in Bitcoin's history precisely because it has not produced a blow-off. Bitcoin reached all-time highs driven by ETF inflows and corporate treasury accumulation — genuine demand, not credit euphoria. The two mini-bubbles — post-ETF and post-Trump election — were pull-forward effects that brought Bitcoin into a new trading range. Not the sustained, credit-fueled mania that creates $69,000 tops followed by $15,500 bottoms.

Some people say Bitcoin needs bubbles for adoption. Number Go Up technology. Without bubbles, it is too hard to bring in new buyers. But why? Why would it not be better to have steady long-term price increases from supply and demand? How does rewarding and then wrecking people help adoption? We do not say that no one will buy Amazon stock unless there are occasional tech bubbles.

The bubbles will likely come again. When US and global M2 accelerate and liquidity opens up, the conditions will be there. But Bitcoin does not need them. So long as people demand Bitcoin, the price will go up because we know what happens to the supply.

Bitcoin's long-term trajectory is adoption-driven. It follows a power law because it is a network growing without a central planner, without marketing, without coercion. That trajectory does not depend on the Federal Reserve.

Bitcoin's bubbles are credit-driven. They are noise layered on top of signal. When Bitcoin drops 40% during a credit contraction, it is not dying. The credit-driven premium is evaporating and the adoption-driven floor is holding. The price is falling toward the power law midline — the same midline it has returned to, without exception, after every bubble in its history.

The reader who understands this will never be shaken out by a correction. The reader who does not will panic-sell at the bottom, watch the recovery from the sidelines, and conclude that Bitcoin is a scam — the same conclusion reached and abandoned by a new group of investors after every single cycle.

The financial experts see the crash and declare the experiment over. They see the volatility and call it proof of worthlessness. They are confusing the credit cycle for the adoption curve. They are looking at an eight-arc-minute error and concluding that the orbit must be circular.

Kepler knew better. And now, so do you.

The DCA Evidence

Dollar cost averaging is not a Bitcoin strategy. It is a savings strategy that works with any asset whose long-term trend is up. You pick an amount, you buy on a schedule, and you do not think about it. When the price is high, your fixed dollar amount buys less. When the price is low, it buys more. Over time, your average cost converges toward a number well below the current price, because the dips — the ones that terrify everyone else into selling — are the weeks your money works hardest. DCA is how your grandfather saved, dropping change into the can every day. The only difference is that his dollar held its value and yours does not, which means you need to save into something better than cash.

DCA matters more with a volatile asset. Bitcoin's price has drawn down 30%, 50%, even 80% from its highs during various cycles. Those drawdowns shake people out. They sell at a loss, swear off Bitcoin forever, and watch from the sidelines as the price recovers and surpasses the previous high — which, so far, it has done every single time. The person who was dollar cost averaging through those drawdowns did not sell. They bought. They bought cheap. And their average cost dropped while everyone else was panicking. The longer you stack, the better your cost basis looks relative to the current price, and the less any given drawdown can touch you. A 40% correction feels very different when your average cost is $14,000 and the price drops from $100,000 to $60,000.

I sourced historical price data on Bitcoin going back to 2014. I then ran dollar cost averaging calculations at $75 per week, every week, for five years, for every starting date I had data available.

There were 2,351 possible five-year windows in the dataset. Every single one of them was profitable — 2,351 out of 2,351. Not most of them. Not ninety-something percent. All of them. The median five-year window returned 266 percent; the average returned 555 percent, pulled upward by a handful of extraordinary runs. The best window, starting in March 2016 and ending in March 2021, turned $19,575 in contributions into $554,467. The worst window — starting in November 2017, one week before the all-time high at the time, right at the peak of the most famous bubble in Bitcoin's history — still returned 48 percent on invested capital. You bought at the absolute worst moment imaginable, endured the 84% crash of 2018, bought through the COVID collapse of 2020, rode the

2021 mania, bought through the FTX catastrophe, and ended with nearly half again what you put in. Not because you were smart. Because you never stopped buying.[9]

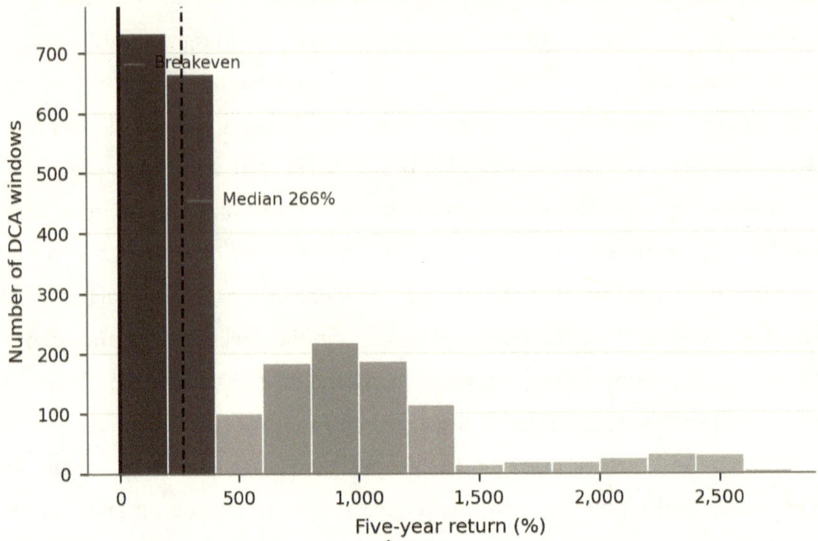

Distribution of all 2,351 five-year DCA windows. $75 per week, September 2014 through February 2026. Every bar sits to the right of breakeven. Worst: 48%. Median: 266%. Average: 555%. Best: 2,733%. Zero losses.

These numbers are not projections. They are not models. They are the actual results of buying $75 worth of Bitcoin every Saturday using real historical prices. No timing. No analysis. No watching CNBC. Just $75, every week, rain or shine.

Here is something worth understanding about volatile assets: they are almost always volatile for the same reason. A rock thrown into a pond makes a much bigger splash than the same rock thrown into the ocean. Bitcoin's market capitalization, while large by any ordinary standard, is still small relative to gold, real estate, or the global stock market. A billion dollars flowing into Bitcoin moves the price in a way that a billion dollars flowing

---

9. Dollar-cost averaging calculations use daily BTC/USD closing prices from Yahoo Finance, September 17, 2014 through February 22, 2026 — 4,176 trading days. Method: $75 purchased every seven days beginning on each window's start date; the window closes exactly five years later; final value equals coins accumulated multiplied by the closing price on the end date. Windows are included only where complete price data exists for the full five-year span. 2,351 windows tested. No transaction fees or taxes are included; actual results would be modestly lower depending on exchange and method. All 2,351 windows ended in profit. Source file: historical_bitcoin_prices.csv.

into the S&P 500 simply cannot. That sensitivity cuts both ways — it is why Bitcoin can drop 30% in a month, and why it can also gain 300% in a year.

But here is the part the frightened observers miss: volatility is not the enemy of the DCA investor. It is his best friend. There is an old Wall Street saying that bulls walk up the stairs and bears run down them — meaning price rises tend to be slow and grinding while crashes are fast and violent. In Bitcoin, I like to say that bulls bound up the stairs and bears jump out the window. The crashes are spectacular, and they make headlines, and they terrify people into selling. But when the price crashes, your fixed weekly contribution buys more coins. Your average cost drops. The dip that sends the headlines into panic mode is the week your dollars work hardest. And when the price recovers — as it has, without exception, after every crash in Bitcoin's history — you recover with a cost basis that was built partly on those cheap coins bought at the bottom. The volatility that punishes the trader rewards the stacker.

There is also a longer arc worth seeing. Assets tend to become less volatile as they grow. When Bitcoin's market cap was measured in the millions, a single large buyer could move the price by double digits in an afternoon. As it grew into the billions, and then the hundreds of billions, and now past a trillion dollars, those swings have gradually — not linearly, but gradually — dampened. The people who stacked early captured the most violent volatility on the way up. Those who stack today still capture meaningful volatility, but with a far deeper, more liquid market beneath them. At some point — no one can say exactly when — Bitcoin's market cap will have grown large enough that its volatility resembles gold's more than a startup's. The pond will have become an ocean. The readers of this book are buying before that happens.

Chapter Ten

The Sultan and the Savant

In 1327, Muhammad bin Tughluq, Sultan of Delhi, decided his capital was in the wrong place. Delhi was too far north, too exposed to Mongol raids. He would move the entire operation 700 miles south to Daulatabad, in the Deccan. Not just the court. Not just the army. The entire population.

Thousands of families were marched through the Indian heat on roads that barely existed. People died on the journey. When the survivors arrived, they found a city with no water supply adequate for a capital. Within two years, Tughluq reversed the order and marched everyone back. The famous traveler Ibn Battuta visited Delhi in 1334 and found entire neighborhoods still deserted. Tughluq had depopulated his own capital, killed untold numbers of his own subjects, and achieved nothing. Central planning at its finest.

But the Sultan was not finished experimenting. His treasury drained from war and extravagance, Tughluq faced a shortage of gold and silver for coinage. His solution: issue copper and brass coins — called *tankas* — and declare them equal in value to gold and silver by royal decree. In theory, a brilliant piece of monetary innovation. In practice, an unmitigated disaster. The coins were simple in design and trivially easy to copy. The historian Barani recorded that counterfeiting became so widespread that homes were effectively operating as private mints. Copper *tankas* flooded the market. Foreign merchants refused to accept them. The coins became worthless.[1]

Tughluq was forced to withdraw the copper currency and exchange it all back for gold and silver at the royal treasury. People who had thrown their worthless copper tankas into corners alongside their pots and pans now brought them in by the cartload and walked out with real money. The treasury was gutted. The Sultan who had debased his currency to solve a fiscal crisis had made it infinitely worse.

Seven centuries later, the lesson has not been learned. But it has been solved.

The most basic law of economics states that supply and demand trend toward an equilibrium price. If supply falls while demand stays the same, the price will rise, because the market will trend toward a new, higher equilibrium. If supply keeps falling while demand holds steady or grows, the price will keep rising toward new equilibrium, again and again.

Part of the problem with supply and demand economics comes from the words themselves. When an economist writes about "supply," he might mean three entirely different things: the *total* supply of an asset in existence, the *rate of new supply* entering the market, or *supply at the margin* — the amount available from sellers who are actually willing to sell right now, at the current price. The same slipperiness applies to demand. These distinctions matter enormously, and it is not always clear which one a given commentator means. Bitcoin critics, in particular, tend to conflate them in ways that produce confident-sounding but ultimately wrong conclusions.

Bitcoin's *total supply* is mathematically capped at 21 million coins. We covered this in Chapter Six. The cap is not a policy choice that can be voted away or overridden by a regulator. It is baked into the protocol. There will never be a 21,000,001st bitcoin. Some analysts argue that because this cap is so widely known, it must already be "priced in" — meaning the market has already accounted for it in the current price, and the cap therefore has no further effect. This argument has some theoretical merit. But it assumes that the market fully understands Bitcoin, which — as anyone reading this book can likely

1. Muhammad bin Tughluq ruled the Delhi Sultanate from 1325 to 1351. The forced capital relocation to Daulatabad and its consequences are documented by the contemporary historian Ziauddin Barani in Tarikh-i-Firuz Shahi. The account is corroborated by Ibn Battuta's Rihla, based on his travels through Delhi in 1334. See also Satish Chandra, Medieval India: From Sultanat to the Mughals (Har-Anand, 1997). Historical sources place the distance of the forced march at approximately 700 miles, with some variance depending on the route taken.

attest from personal experience — is optimistic. Bitcoin remains among the most widely misunderstood assets in the world. The cap being *known* and the cap being *understood* are two very different things.

Bitcoin's *rate of new supply* is where the supply and demand argument becomes most powerful. Every 210,000 successfully mined blocks — roughly every four years — the number of new bitcoins created per block is cut in half. This is the halving. As of April 2024, miners earn 3.125 bitcoin per block, which works out to approximately 450 new coins per day entering circulation. Around March 2028, that drops to 1.5625 per block. The schedule continues, halving by halving, until the last satoshi is mined around 2140. The rate of new supply is always falling. And here is where the basic law of supply and demand does its quiet, inexorable work: as long as demand holds steady or grows, a falling rate of new supply must push the equilibrium price higher. This is not a prediction. It is arithmetic. Tughluq's copper experiment failed precisely because he did the opposite — he flooded the market with new supply, destroying the value of every coin in existence. Bitcoin's protocol makes that failure impossible by design.[2]

When the price of copper rises — real copper, not Tughluq's funny money — copper miners respond. They expand operations, invest in new equipment, open previously uneconomical mines. New supply enters the market and the price comes back down. We see this in just about every commodity and every asset. When housing prices run hot, new construction increases. When stock prices rise, companies issue new shares. When art is selling, suddenly a bunch of artists show up and do more crummy paintings. When baseball cards are hot, new companies pop up and make a bunch of supposedly limited-edition sets. The market always finds a way to produce more supply. Except here. No matter how high the price of Bitcoin goes, the supply schedule will not change. No CEO can issue more shares. No miner can increase production — the difficulty adjustment ensures that more computing power joining the network only makes it harder to earn the same fixed reward. No government can print more. The supply rate is immutable. The halving happens on schedule whether Bitcoin is trading at $1,000 or $1,000,000.

Supply at the margin is the most interesting of the three, at least for understanding short-term price action — and arguably the least understood. At any given moment, the

2. The Bitcoin halving of April 2024 reduced the block subsidy from 6.25 BTC to 3.125 BTC per block, resulting in approximately 450 new coins entering circulation per day. The next halving is scheduled around March 2028, at which point the subsidy drops to approximately 1.5625 BTC per block. The schedule is encoded in the Bitcoin protocol and enforced by the network — it cannot be altered without consensus of the network's participants.

price of Bitcoin is not set by the 21 million total coins or by the 450 new ones mined today. It is set by the most motivated sellers and the most motivated buyers meeting each other at the margin. A long-term holder who swore he would never sell below $200,000 is not supply right now. A miner who needs to cover his electricity bill this week is. A retiree who panics when the price drops 30% is suddenly supply — and his selling meets a buyer who has been waiting for exactly that dip. Marginal supply and demand explain why prices can be volatile in the short run even while the long-run arithmetic is clear. The margin is where emotion lives. The protocol is where math lives. Over time, math wins.

Consider the most recent cycle as evidence of all three at work. Bitcoin's price rose more than 4x from its post-FTX low — and during that same period, the rate of new supply was cut in half by the April 2024 halving. Total supply grew by its scheduled amount. Marginal supply — the coins available from willing sellers — eventually was absorbed by growing institutional demand from ETF inflows and corporate treasury accumulation. The result appeared to be consistent with genuine structural forces rather than a speculative blow-off. The supply schedule rules — not every day, not in every trade, but in every cycle.

The reader who grasps this framework — total supply capped, rate of new supply falling, marginal supply driven by human emotion — has a more complete picture of Bitcoin's price dynamics than most analysts who write about it for a living.

The Macro Dashboard

Nobody knows how many dollars exist.

That is not an exaggeration. The Federal Reserve tracks several measures of the money supply, labeled M0, M1, and M2. It used to track a broader measure called M3, but stopped publishing that number in 2006 — claiming it was too expensive to gather the data and didn't add useful information. One might wonder why the institution responsible for managing the world's reserve currency would stop counting the broadest measure of it. In 2021, the Fed also stopped publishing weekly M2 data and switched to monthly reporting. Again, the institution in charge of the dollar is making it *harder* for the public to see what is happening to the dollar. Compare this to Bitcoin, where anyone with an internet connection can verify the exact supply — down to the last satoshi — at any moment, from anywhere on earth.[3] [4]

Of the money supply measures still reported, M2 is probably the closest thing we have to a useful number. M2 includes everything you would think of as "money available to spend or save": cash in circulation, checking account balances, savings accounts, money market funds, and small certificates of deposit. You can look it up yourself on the Federal Reserve's own website, at the St. Louis Fed's FRED database. As we established in Chapter Four, M2 has grown at roughly 6% per year since the end of the gold standard — doubling the supply of dollars approximately every twelve years.[5] That means the supply of dollars has been doubling approximately every twelve years. In 1980, M2 stood at $1.6 trillion. By 2025, it had swollen past $22 trillion. And remember — that is just what they are willing to report.

But M2 alone does not tell the full story of how many dollars are sloshing through the system at any given time. The Fed has all kinds of tools for parking cash on the sidelines or injecting it back into circulation. The Fed's own balance sheet — the trillions in bonds and mortgage-backed securities it purchased with money created from nothing — is one such tool. The Treasury General Account, which is essentially the government's checking account, is another. Then there is the Reverse Repurchase Facility, which allows the Fed to temporarily drain liquidity from the banking system by parking cash overnight. When you combine these factors, you get what analysts call "net liquidity" — a rough measure of how many dollars are actually available to the economy at any point in time.

Why does this matter for Bitcoin? Because Bitcoin appears to be among the most sensitive instruments to changes in the quantity of dollars in circulation. I want to be careful here — people love to overlay M2 charts on Bitcoin charts and declare a perfect correlation. It is not that clean. You can always find a short time frame where M2 and

---

3. Federal Reserve Bank of St. Louis, FRED Economic Data: M2 Money Stock, series WM2NS. Available at fred.stlouisfed.org. The Federal Reserve discontinued weekly M2 reporting in 2021, switching to monthly data — making real-time tracking of money supply changes more difficult for the public.

4. For a real-time, publicly verifiable window into the Bitcoin blockchain and mempool — including exact supply, transaction activity, block data, and fee markets — see mempool.space. The tool is free, requires no account, and allows anyone to verify the Bitcoin supply and network activity directly from anywhere on earth. No equivalent exists for the dollar.

5. M2 rose from approximately $1,595.2 billion (November 3, 1980) to approximately $22,634.5 billion (December 29, 2025), a compound annual growth rate of approximately 6.01%. Federal Reserve Bank of St. Louis, FRED Economic Data, series WM2NS, fred.stlouisfed.org.

Bitcoin seem to follow each other, fit the scales just right, and declare victory. But the relationship is real in a broader sense: persistent price rips in any asset can only be sustained when new credit is entering the market, and persistent contractions follow when that credit dries up. Bitcoin, being the hardest money in the system, tends to respond to these shifts — but not on a timetable anyone can trade with precision. Understanding this relationship helps explain *why* the price sometimes does nothing for months and then rips higher in a matter of weeks. It is not random. But neither is it as predictable as some influencers would have you believe.

The insight that the *rate of change* in the money supply matters more than the absolute number was the great contribution of my late friend Robert Wenzel. Robert was an Austrian economist, a veteran trader, and one of the sharpest minds I have ever encountered. His weekly investor newsletter was required reading for those of us lucky to know him, and his track record was staggering. Robert called market inflections with remarkable precision — often within hours of their occurrence. His work tracking the explosive M2 increases of 2020–21 helped him predict both the market run-ups and the double-digit inflation that followed.[6]

Robert's method was deceptively simple: track the 13-week annualized rate of change in M2, and compare it to the same period in prior years. Credit expansion tends to be seasonal — people do not start projects in winter — and by watching the *pace* of money creation rather than the headline number, Robert could see inflections before the market priced them in.

Robert passed away before Bitcoin achieved what he would have loved to see — hard money outperforming the very system he spent decades analyzing. When Bitcoin began challenging silver's place as a monetary asset, I thought of him immediately. He would be smiling. He was a true fighter for liberty and sound money, and his insights inform every word of this section. Miss you, old friend.

The takeaway for the reader is simple. You do not need to track M2 or net liquidity or the Fed balance sheet. You need to understand one thing: the supply of dollars is designed to grow, forever, by the very people who control it, and they have made it nearly impossible for the average person to see how fast it is growing. The supply rate of Bitcoin is designed

---

6. Robert Wenzel (1956–2021) published the Economic Policy Journal and the EPJ Daily Alert investor newsletter. His method for tracking the 13-week annualized rate of change in M2 as a leading indicator is described in the Economic Policy Journal archives at economicpolicyjournal.com.

to shrink, forever, the maximum supply will never exceed 21 million coins, and anyone can verify both facts in real time from anywhere on earth. That contrast is the entire argument.

The Investment Mirage

Before we get to what Wall Street thinks of Bitcoin, there is something worth understanding about the stock market itself — something most financial journalists will never tell you, because it makes their entire profession look a lot less impressive. Nearly a hundred years ago, an Austrian economist named Fritz Machlup worked it out in a book called *The Stock Market, Credit and Capital Formation.*[7] The insight is simple enough to explain in five minutes, and once you hear it, you cannot unhear it. The total capitalization of the stock market — the combined dollar value of every publicly traded company in existence — is, in the long run, simply a reflection of the size of the money supply. The money supply grows, and the total market cap grows with it. The money supply contracts, and the market follows. This is not a commentary on whether individual companies are well-run or poorly-run, whether a given stock is cheap or expensive, or whether a particular sector is going to thrive or struggle. Those things matter enormously for individual investors picking individual stocks. Machlup's point operates at a different level. He is describing the tide, not the boats.

There is a saying in investing that a rising tide lifts all boats.[8] What Machlup understood — and what the financial press has never quite gotten around to explaining — is what the tide is made of. It is made of dollars. Every time you see a headline announcing a new all-time high for the stock market, what you are actually seeing is an announcement that more dollars exist than existed before. The companies inside the market did not necessarily become more valuable in any real sense. The pile of dollars available to bid on them got bigger. New money has to go somewhere, and it goes into assets — stocks, real estate, whatever the market believes is worth holding. Prices rise not because underlying

7. Fritz Machlup (1902–1983), The Stock Market, Credit and Capital Formation (William Hodge & Company, 1940; originally published in German as Börsenkredit, Industriekredit und Kapitalbildung, 1931). Machlup was a student of Ludwig von Mises at the University of Vienna and later a professor at Princeton University and New York University. His analysis of the relationship between credit expansion and broad stock market capitalization remains one of the most rigorous treatments of the subject in the Austrian tradition.

8. The phrase 'a rising tide lifts all boats' is commonly associated with Warren Buffett, who has used variations of it over the decades. Its documented origin is a speech delivered by President John F. Kennedy in 1963 in the context of regional economic development — a context quite different from stock market analysis. Machlup's framework, published in 1931, provides the economic mechanism explaining what the tide is made of, predating both attributions by decades.

value increased, but because the unit of measurement shrank. This is why, under a stable money supply, the total stock market capitalization would be roughly flat over time — individual companies would rise and fall on their merits, but the aggregate pile would not perpetually inflate. The only reason it does is that the dollars measuring it are always multiplying.

Which brings us to your fund manager. If the money supply grew at 6% last year and your fund delivered 6%, he did not beat the market. He kept pace with the tide. Your savings bought approximately the same amount of real goods at year's end as they did at the start — and he charged you a fee for that. The benchmark that actually matters — the one the industry has no interest in advertising — is whether your manager outperformed the growth rate of the money supply by enough to cover his fees, his trading costs, the tax drag his activity generated, and still left you with something real. Most do not. The uncomfortable arithmetic, documented exhaustively by academic research spanning decades, is that most actively managed funds underperform a simple passive index over most long time horizons — and a passive index is itself mostly just riding the tide. The fund management industry is, in large part, a very expensive way to tread water.

No one represents that industry more respectably than Vanguard — and no one has been more direct about what Vanguard thinks of Bitcoin.

The CEO of Vanguard — one of the largest asset management firms in the world, a company that controls trillions of dollars in retirement savings — went on television in early 2024 and explained why Vanguard would not be offering Bitcoin ETFs to its customers. His reasoning came down to four words: Bitcoin has no intrinsic value.[9]

The statement was repeated approvingly by financial journalists across the country. It sounded authoritative. It sounded responsible. It was also a category error so fundamental that it reveals more about the speaker than it does about Bitcoin.

---

9. The statement was made by then-CEO Tim Buckley in early 2024, shortly after the SEC approved spot Bitcoin ETFs in January of that year. Buckley retired in July 2024 and was succeeded by Salim Ramji, who joined from BlackRock where he had served as Global Head of iShares and Index Investing and helped bring the iShares Bitcoin Trust (IBIT) to market. In December 2025, under Ramji's leadership, Vanguard reversed course and opened its brokerage platform to Bitcoin and other crypto ETFs — seventeen months after Buckley's declaration. Throughout this entire period, Vanguard's index funds were required by their mandates to hold shares in any publicly traded company — including Strategy (formerly MicroStrategy), the world's largest corporate Bitcoin holder. By mid-2025, Vanguard had become Strategy's largest institutional shareholder, holding over 20 million shares worth approximately $9 billion. The index fund cannot choose its holdings. It just has to own what the market owns.

Intrinsic value is a term from a very specific corner of traditional finance. It originates with Benjamin Graham, the father of value investing, and was popularized by Warren Buffett and Charlie Munger. The concept is straightforward: take a company's historical cash flows, project them into the future with a discount for time, and you have a rough sense of what the business might be worth. That number — the discounted cash flow projection — is what the finance world calls intrinsic value.

Notice what that definition requires. Cash flows. From a business. The entire framework was designed to evaluate *companies* — entities that produce goods or services, collect revenue, and generate earnings over time. It was never designed to evaluate *money*. You cannot run a discounted cash flow model on gold. You cannot run one on a seashell or a block of salt or a warehouse full of grain. These things are not businesses. They are stores of value — and their worth is determined not by what they produce but by what people are willing to hold them as a proxy for.

Bitcoin is not a company. It has no CEO, no earnings call, no quarterly revenue to analyze. What it has is a fixed supply, a predictable issuance schedule, a seventeen-year track record of being one of the best-performing assets in the world,[10] and a protocol that has not missed a single block since the day it launched. Vanguard's framework simply does not apply. Applying it anyway is like criticizing a hammer for being a bad screwdriver.

This matters for the reader not as an academic point but as a practical one. When a financial advisor, a talking head, or a skeptical brother-in-law tells you Bitcoin has no intrinsic value, they are either confused about what intrinsic value means or they are applying a definition they know does not fit. You now understand both the framework and its limits well enough to say so.

But there is something else worth noting about TradFi's hostility to Bitcoin — something that goes beyond honest confusion. The financial services industry is built on fees. Fund managers, financial advisors, retirement plan administrators, ETF providers — all of them earn a percentage of the assets they manage. A 1% annual management fee sounds negligible until you realize it compounds against your savings just as surely as your returns

10. Seventeen years is a meaningful sample but not a definitive one. The pattern holds across four full halving cycles and multiple Fed tightening and easing episodes. Whether it continues to hold as Bitcoin matures and its correlation to broader risk assets evolves is worth monitoring.

do. Over thirty years, a 1% drag on a $100,000 portfolio costs nearly $190,000 in lost compounding.[11] That money does not disappear. It flows to the fund manager.

Bitcoin does not generate management fees. It does not run advertising campaigns. It does not sponsor television programs or pay for endorsements or hire wholesalers to pitch it to financial advisors. It does not court the distribution networks that route ordinary Americans into mutual funds. Bitcoin cannot buy access to the system that decides what your 401(k) holds.

The financial industry that should be most excited about one of the best-performing assets in history has every structural incentive to ignore it. When Bitcoin outperforms the S&P 500, the NASDAQ, and every managed fund over any five-year window — which the data in the previous chapter shows it has, consistently and by enormous margins — it raises an uncomfortable question: if a working-class family can simply buy and hold Bitcoin and outperform the overwhelming majority of professional fund managers, who needs professional fund managers? The industry would rather not have that question asked. It is much easier to point to volatility, to mutter about intrinsic value, and to route your retirement savings into a diversified portfolio of funds that collectively charge you 1% a year for the privilege of underperforming an asset they told you had no worth.[12]

The only people reliably getting rich from the 401(k) system are the people running it.

Which brings us to the 401(k).

The 401(k) was created in 1978, codified through a quirk of tax law almost by accident, and became the dominant American retirement vehicle through a combination of corporate lobbying and IRS guidance over the following decade. Its core promise is simple: contribute pre-tax dollars today, let them grow tax-deferred, and pay taxes when you withdraw in retirement — presumably at a lower rate, since you'll be earning less.[13]

---

11. Computation: $100,000 compounded at 7% gross annual return over 30 years yields approximately $761,226. The same principal compounded at 6% net (after a 1% annual fee) yields approximately $574,349. The difference is approximately $186,877. The 7% gross return is used as a standard long-term approximation for diversified equity market returns. Actual cost of fee drag will vary depending on the fund's gross return and specific expense ratio.

12. See Chapter Nine for the complete dollar-cost averaging analysis of Bitcoin returns across all possible entry points from 2014 onward. The analysis validates that every possible five-year holding window across the data set produced a positive return — 100% of five-year windows profitable regardless of entry point.

13. The Revenue Act of 1978 added section 401(k) to the Internal Revenue Code. Its application as a salary-deferral retirement vehicle was not originally intended by Congress. Benefits consultant Ted Benna devised the first 401(k) plan in 1980, exploiting the new provision to create a tax-advantaged savings account. The IRS issued guidance endorsing the approach in 1981.

That logic was sound in 1978. Tax rates in the late 1970s and early 1980s were punishing — the top marginal rate hit 70% in 1980.[14] Deferring income into the future, when rates were widely expected to fall, was a reasonable bet. Rates did fall. The bet paid off for the generation that made it.

But the period of declining tax rates was an anomaly, not a trend. Across the long arc of American history, tax rates have risen more often than they have fallen. The national debt, which exceeded $38.7 trillion at the time of this writing and continues to climb,[15] now generates interest payments that exceeded one trillion dollars in fiscal year 2024.[16] The federal government faces decades of compounding obligations — Social Security, Medicare, defense, debt service — that are almost mathematically impossible to meet without raising revenue. Deferring your taxes into that future is not obviously a good trade. You are betting that a financially stressed government, desperate for revenue, will tax you *less* than it taxes you today. That is a bet you should examine carefully before making automatically every two weeks from your paycheck.

Then there is the matching myth.

The employer match is the most celebrated feature of the 401(k) — the thing HR departments lead with, the thing financial advisors point to when they say you should contribute at least enough to get the full match. Free money, they call it. Your employer is giving you something for nothing.

They are not. What they are doing is compensating you. The question is the form of that compensation, not whether it exists. In a world without employer matching as a standard corporate benefit, companies competing for workers would be forced to offer higher base salaries to attract the same talent. The money that flows into your 401(k) as an employer match did not appear from a hidden treasure the CEO was hoarding. It came from the same budget that funds your salary. It is your money. It just arrives inside a tax-advantaged account rather than inside your paycheck — which means it is subject to

---

14. The top marginal federal income tax rate stood at 70% in 1980. The Economic Recovery Tax Act of 1981 reduced it to 50%, and the Tax Reform Act of 1986 reduced it further to 28%. Source: IRS Statistics of Income; Tax Foundation, 'Federal Individual Income Tax Rates History,' taxfoundation.org.

15. For a real-time national debt counter, see usdebtclock.org.

16. Net interest payments on the federal debt exceeded $1 trillion in fiscal year 2024, the first time in U.S. history. Source: Congressional Budget Office, 'The Budget and Economic Outlook: 2024 to 2034'; U.S. Treasury, Monthly Treasury Statement.

the account's rules, its investment menu, its withdrawal restrictions, and its underlying fees.

Those fees matter more than most people understand. The typical 401(k) plan offers a menu of mutual funds, and those funds charge annual expense ratios — typically somewhere between 0.5% and 1.5%, sometimes higher.[17] That fee is charged on the entire balance, every year, regardless of performance. A fund that charges 1% and returns 7% costs you about one-seventh of your gains. As covered above, the same compounding logic applies over a thirty-year career — the drag accumulates silently, and the wealth it destroys flows instead to the fund managers who generated it by doing nothing more than maintaining an allocation you could replicate yourself for a fraction of the cost.

Bitcoin removes the logic of the 401(k) the same way hard money always has. Under the gold standard, before the era of inflation made saving punishing, Americans did not need special tax-advantaged accounts to preserve their wealth across decades. Sound money preserved it on its own. You saved, it held its value, and when you needed it in retirement, it was there — no fund managers, no expense ratios, no withdrawal penalties, no bet on future tax rates. The account was your savings and your savings were the account.

Bitcoin is the first sound money available to ordinary people in over fifty years. A working-class family that begins a modest, consistent practice of saving in Bitcoin is not speculating. They are doing what their grandparents did under the gold standard — putting value away in a form that the passage of time cannot quietly steal from them. The volatility is real, and it requires patience. But the alternative — a diversified portfolio of mutual funds inside a tax-deferred account that charges fees, defers your tax liability into an uncertain future, and is managed by an industry with no sufficient financial interest in your outperformance — is not the safe, conservative choice it has been sold as.

It is the Investment Mirage. Bitcoin, held patiently over time, is one of the ways out.

None of the above is financial advice. This book is not telling you what to do with your 401(k). It is telling you how the system works — who benefits, who pays, and where the assumptions break down. What you do with that information is your decision. You are the one who has to live with the number at the end.

What Could Go Wrong

---

17. The Investment Company Institute's annual Investment Company Fact Book documents average expense ratios for mutual funds offered in 401(k) plans. The Department of Labor's annual report on 401(k) plan fees provides additional documentation. Expense ratios vary widely by fund type and plan size; actively managed funds typically carry higher ratios than index funds.

Bitcoin faces two broad risk categories. The first is the risk that you never find real Bitcoin at all — that you get burned by a scam, chalk it up to the whole category, and walk away from the only sound money available to you. This risk is more common and more immediate than anything the protocol itself might do. The second is the risk that the protocol faces genuine threats — technical, political, or otherwise. Both deserve a direct answer.

Bitcoin Is Not Crypto

The single most important thing to understand before you buy your first satoshi is this: Bitcoin and "crypto" are not the same thing. Not even close.

Bitcoin was released in January 2009 by a person or group operating under the name Satoshi Nakamoto. Before launching, Satoshi gave approximately two months' notice to a small cryptography mailing list, mined no coins in advance for personal benefit, never sold, and eventually disappeared entirely from public life. In the seventeen years since the Genesis Block, Satoshi's coins — roughly one million Bitcoin — have not moved a single time. There is no developer fund. There is no foundation collecting fees. There is no CEO to call, no headquarters to raid, no insider who can dump coins on the public.[18]

Every other digital currency in existence has a founder with a financial interest in its success. Ethereum was premined — Vitalik Buterin and his associates held coins before the public could access them. Solana was premined. The entire history of crypto outside of Bitcoin is a history of founders who got theirs before you got yours. The technical differences between these projects and Bitcoin are real but secondary. The moral difference is total.

This matters because the crypto space is home to an active, sophisticated, and well-funded grift industry. Its business model is simple: create a coin, distribute it to insiders, generate hype through social media and celebrity endorsements, and sell into the retail buying frenzy before the inevitable collapse. The victims are not sophisticated investors who should have known better. They are ordinary people — working-class

18. Even if Satoshi Nakamoto were to reappear, he would have no administrative access to the Bitcoin protocol. There is no admin. There is no override. He could propose changes through the same Bitcoin Improvement Proposal (BIP) process available to any developer, and the network would adopt or reject them through the same consensus mechanism that governs all protocol changes. Should he choose to sell after seventeen years of dormancy, the result would not be a collapse — it would be a redistribution of supply to willing buyers at whatever price the market sets. The protocol does not care who holds the coins. It only enforces the rules.

people — who heard something exciting and wanted in. They are your neighbor. They are the reader of this book.

The distinction between Bitcoin and crypto is not a minor technical point. It is the entire difference between sound money with no insiders and a speculative token with insiders who are already waiting to sell to you.

The Hawk Tuah Story

In late 2024, a young woman named Haliey Welch became briefly famous on the internet for a viral video. She seemed likable enough — funny, patriotic, down to earth. She was not a financial sophisticate. She was a regular person who had stumbled into public attention.

Crypto grifters found her before the spotlight faded.

They convinced her to lend her name and image to a meme coin called $HAWK. The mechanics of what followed were not complicated. The coin's creators premined tokens for themselves and distributed more to insiders before the public launch. When $HAWK went live, retail buyers rushed in — many of them people who had never purchased any digital asset before, drawn in by the celebrity association. The market cap briefly hit $500 million. Then the insiders sold. In minutes — not hours, minutes — the value collapsed by more than 95%. Transaction fees alone extracted over a million dollars from buyers in the first moments of trading. The fees went to the creators.[19]

The people left holding the bag were not hedge funds or sophisticated traders with risk capital to lose. They were ordinary people who saw a funny internet personality promoting something and thought they had found an opportunity. Many of them had never touched "crypto" before. After this was their first experience, many never will again — and that means many of them will never find Bitcoin.

That last part is what actually matters. Haliey Welch was not the victim of the story. She was the bait. The victims were working-class people who needed sound money and got a rug pull instead. The grifters did not just steal their money. They poisoned their relationship with the only technology that could actually help them.

Bitcoin does not work this way because Bitcoin *cannot* work this way. There are no insiders with premined coins waiting to sell. There is no Satoshi who can dump on you —

19. The $HAWK meme coin launched in December 2024 associated with internet personality Haliey Welch. Contemporaneous reporting from CoinDesk, The Verge, and others documented: a peak market capitalization of approximately $500 million; a collapse of more than 95% within minutes of launch as insiders sold premined positions; and transaction fees exceeding $1 million extracted from buyers in the opening moments of trading.

his coins have sat untouched for seventeen years and, based on everything we know about the man, they always will. When you buy Bitcoin, you are not buying into a promotional campaign. You are buying a unit of the only monetary network in history that treated every participant equally from the first block.[20]

Know the difference. It will save you from the scam and lead you to the thing worth owning.

Threats to Bitcoin

The following are the objections you will hear from people who have thought about Bitcoin seriously and still have reservations. They deserve serious answers, not dismissal.

Quantum computing. The concern is real in theory and distant in practice. The specific vulnerability is not Bitcoin's mining algorithm — the difficulty adjustment handles that — but rather the elliptic curve cryptography used to sign transactions (called ECDSA). A sufficiently powerful quantum computer could, in principle, derive a private key from a public key, allowing it to steal from exposed Bitcoin addresses. The operative word is "sufficiently powerful." Google's most advanced quantum processor currently operates in the hundreds of qubits. The minimum required to threaten Bitcoin's cryptography is estimated at roughly one million — a gap that represents engineering challenges the world's best computer scientists have not come close to solving. The technology is advancing, but quantum-resistant cryptographic standards already exist — NIST finalized the first set in 2024 — and the Bitcoin network can adopt them through consensus if and when the threat becomes credible. The entire global financial system, every military, and every intelligence agency on earth faces the same quantum threat to the same cryp-

20. Bitcoin has operated continuously since the Genesis Block was mined on January 3, 2009. The network has experienced no complete outage in its seventeen-year history. Individual exchanges and services have failed; the underlying protocol has not.

tographic standards. The incentive to solve it is not Bitcoin's alone to bear. This is a risk to monitor, not a reason to stay out.[21]

Energy. The "Bitcoin kills the planet" argument rests on a confusion that is worth clearing up once and for all. Bitcoin mining consumes energy. This is true. It is also true of every other monetary system humans have ever operated — gold mining, armored trucks, bank branches, data centers, ATM networks, clearing houses, the Federal Reserve's own facilities, and the paper production required to print the dollars in your wallet. The question has never been whether money costs energy. The question is whether the energy is used productively and whether the source matters.

On the source: Bitcoin miners are in the business of finding cheap electricity. Cheap electricity, by definition, is electricity that would otherwise go to waste — power generated far from population centers where transmission costs make it uneconomical to sell, renewable generation that exceeds local demand, natural gas flared at oil wells that would otherwise be released directly into the atmosphere. Mining operations have been documented running on stranded hydroelectric power in remote mountain regions, on excess wind and solar generation that grid operators would otherwise curtail, and on methane capture from landfills and oil fields. Bitcoin miners don't have their own special power plants. They plug into whatever energy source is available at the lowest cost — and the lowest cost sources are increasingly the ones that produce the fewest emissions.[22]

On the broader accusation: Pierre Rochard, then Vice President of Research at Riot Platforms, publicly challenged the New York Times to dispute data showing that Bitcoin

---

21. NIST finalized its first post-quantum cryptographic standards in August 2024: FIPS 203 (ML-KEM, based on CRYSTALS-Kyber), FIPS 204 (ML-DSA, based on CRYSTALS-Dilithium), and FIPS 205 (SLH-DSA, based on SPHINCS+). See: National Institute of Standards and Technology, nist.gov/pqcrypto. The engineering challenges of quantum computing extend beyond qubit counts. Current quantum computers must operate at temperatures approaching absolute zero — roughly 15 millikelvin, approximately 180 times colder than the coldest known region of outer space — requiring elaborate cryogenic infrastructure that makes these machines extraordinarily expensive, physically massive, and impossible to operate outside specialized laboratory conditions. The threat of a quantum attack on Bitcoin assumes not only a dramatic leap in qubit counts and error correction but the ability to operate such a machine at scale under conditions that do not currently exist outside a handful of research facilities worldwide.

22. The Bitcoin Mining Council (bitcoinminingcouncil.com) conducts voluntary surveys of member mining operations documenting sustainable energy use. The Cambridge Centre for Alternative Finance (CCAF) maintains the Cambridge Bitcoin Electricity Consumption Index (CBECI), which tracks mining energy sources globally. Both sources document the use of stranded hydroelectric power, curtailed renewable generation, and methane capture from landfills and oil fields in Bitcoin mining operations.

mining operations can be run as net-zero emissions enterprises. The Times declined to respond. The "Bitcoin boils the oceans" narrative serves a purpose — it gives environmentally-minded people a reason to oppose a technology that threatens centralized financial control — but it does not survive contact with the actual data.[23]

The hallmark of a growing civilization is growing energy production. Humanity has always consumed more energy as it became more capable and more prosperous. The question is never whether we should use energy. The question is whether we use it wisely. Bitcoin uses energy to secure the hardest money ever created and to make it available to every human being on earth equally. That is a productive use of energy. Dismissing it because servers consume electricity is not an environmental argument. It is a political one dressed in green.

Government ban. The most persistent objection, and the one that sounds most threatening to a new holder. No government has ever successfully banned Bitcoin. China — which controls its internet at a level no Western government approaches, which has banned Bitcoin multiple times, and which has the full apparatus of an authoritarian state at its disposal — tried repeatedly and failed. Bitcoin kept mining. The price kept rising. Chinese citizens kept finding ways to hold it.[24] The United States government, having once seized Bitcoin from criminal enterprises, now holds it as a strategic asset.[25] El Salvador and the Central African Republic have recognized Bitcoin as legal tender,

---

23. Pierre Rochard served as Vice President of Research at Riot Platforms, one of the largest publicly traded Bitcoin mining companies in the United States. His public challenge to the New York Times to dispute data on Bitcoin mining's net emissions profile, and the Times' failure to respond, was documented in his public writing. Readers wishing to verify should search his archived posts.

24. China's major Bitcoin crackdowns: September 2017 (ICO and exchange bans); November 2019 (enforcement action against trading and mining); May-June 2021 (near-total ban on mining and trading). Following the 2021 ban, Chinese mining operations relocated primarily to the United States, Kazakhstan, and Russia. The Bitcoin network experienced a temporary hash rate drop before recovering to new highs within months.

25. The United States government accumulated Bitcoin primarily through asset seizures related to criminal enterprises, including the Silk Road and Bitfinex hack. Government Bitcoin holdings have been the subject of ongoing policy discussions regarding their treatment as a strategic asset. Reports as of late 2024 and 2025 indicated significant holdings and active deliberation at the executive level.

and several other nations have granted it varying degrees of regulatory legitimacy.[26] The window for a coordinated global ban — the only kind that could theoretically succeed — has almost certainly closed. Any country that bans Bitcoin now simply cedes the strategic advantage to the countries that don't. Governments can make Bitcoin harder to access for their own citizens. They cannot make it stop.

Protocol failure or replacement. Bitcoin has operated without a single hour of downtime since the Genesis Block was mined on January 3, 2009. It has survived the collapse of major exchanges, multiple hard forks, a coordinated attempt by large mining operations to change its fundamental rules, bans in multiple countries, the disappearance of its creator, and price collapses of 75% or more on four separate occasions.[27] In each case the protocol kept running, the blocks kept coming, and the supply schedule held. No competing protocol has demonstrated anything approaching Bitcoin's combination of decentralization, security, immutability, and network effect. The risk of being "replaced" by a superior technology decreases with every year the network operates without disruption — and it has now been operating without disruption for seventeen years.[28]

The risks are real. They are also manageable, known, and in most cases, declining. The reader who understands them is better equipped than the reader who was never told.

---

26. El Salvador adopted Bitcoin as legal tender under the Bitcoin Law (Legislative Decree No. 57) in September 2021, the first nation to do so. The Central African Republic adopted Bitcoin as legal tender in April 2022. Several additional nations have granted Bitcoin varying degrees of regulatory recognition. The number of jurisdictions with formal regulatory frameworks for Bitcoin has grown substantially since the SEC's approval of spot Bitcoin ETFs in the United States in January 2024.

27. Bitcoin has experienced four major price collapses of 75% or more from peak to trough: (1) 2011: peak approximately $32, trough approximately $2, drawdown approximately 94% (historical record); (2) 2013-15: peak approximately $1,163 in November 2013, trough approximately $152 in January 2015, drawdown approximately 87% (historical record); (3) 2017-18: peak $19,497 on December 16, 2017, trough $3,237 on December 15, 2018, drawdown 83.4% (verified from price data); (4) 2021-22: peak $67,567 on November 8, 2021, trough $15,787 on November 21, 2022, drawdown 76.6% (verified from price data). In each case the protocol continued operating without interruption.

28. Bitcoin has operated continuously since the Genesis Block was mined on January 3, 2009. The network has experienced no complete outage in its seventeen-year history. Individual exchanges and services have failed; the underlying protocol has not.

Chapter Eleven

The Perpetual Machine

Camp Doha, Kuwait. September 2002.

I was walking the base when I noticed the Bradleys. Dozens of them, parked in rows that hadn't been there the day before, as if they'd materialized overnight. There were whispers we were going to war with Iraq. I didn't believe it. America doesn't start offensive wars. Iraq hadn't attacked us. Iraq wasn't friends with bin Laden. *Still — why are all those Bradleys here?*

After the invasion, the troops were asked to secure the country, which mostly meant milling around waiting to get shot at. When they weren't getting shot at, they were getting scammed.

The big scam was the Iraqi Dinar. Before the Gulf War, the Dinar had been pegged to the U.S. dollar at a rate worth more than three dollars to the dinar.[1] By the mid-1990s, UN sanctions and money printing had collapsed it to thousands of Dinars per dollar — and it had never recovered. Clever Iraqis — who understood perfectly well that their currency was finished — began unloading it on young American soldiers and contractors. The pitch was irresistible to a twenty-two-year-old kid sitting in 130-degree heat with money in his pocket and no understanding of what money actually is: *America is rebuilding Iraq. When the country gets back on its feet, the Dinar goes back to where it was. That's a thousand-to-one return. The deal of a lifetime.*

1. The Iraqi dinar was pegged to the U.S. dollar from 1959, initially at one dinar to $2.80, rising to one dinar to $3.22 by the early 1970s — a rate that held through Iraq's oil-boom years until the Gulf War in 1990. Following the war and UN sanctions, Iraq printed money to cover its expenses. By the mid-1990s the black-market rate had collapsed to roughly 3,000 dinars per dollar. The rate remained in the thousands at the time of the 2003 invasion. Wikipedia, "Iraqi dinar."

When the pitch reached me, I didn't bite. Not because I understood monetary economics — I didn't, not then — but because something didn't smell right. I asked the guys buying Dinars a simple question: *What makes a currency valuable? What would cause the Dinar to appreciate a thousand fold?* Nobody could answer. Someone mumbled about oil production, but nobody could explain the mechanism. Nobody could tell me what properties make a good money — scarcity, durability, portability, security — let alone explain why the Dinar scored miserably on all of them.

Those servicemen pissed their money away. The Dinar remains worthless in dollar terms.[2]

But here is the part that haunts me. While those soldiers were getting scammed by bad money in a foreign desert, the money paying their salaries — the U.S. dollar — was being debased at home by the very government that sent them there. The Iraqi scam was crude: a stranger selling you worthless paper in broad daylight. The American version was sophisticated: your own government diluting your purchasing power in the background, year by year, to finance the war you were fighting. Same principle. Different scale.

War

The Iraq War cost approximately $2 trillion. Afghanistan cost $2.3 trillion. Neither was financed by a tax increase. No ballot measure. No line item on a paycheck stub. No vote of any kind. The wars were paid for by money creation — by the slow, invisible confiscation of purchasing power from every American holding dollars. The soldiers who fought those wars came home to an economy where their savings bought less than when they left.

This is new. For most of American history, wars required visible sacrifice. During World War II, Americans rationed meat, sugar, and gasoline, planted victory gardens, and volunteered by the millions. The war was something the whole country bore together, in plain sight, on every kitchen table.

The Korean War was paid for almost entirely by higher taxes. President Truman raised the top marginal tax rate to 92%. The American public could see the cost of the war on every paycheck, and that visibility created political pressure to end it. The Vietnam War was financed by a combination of taxes and inflation. President Johnson — facing a war that was growing faster than he'd told Congress — pushed through a 10% income tax

2. As of the time this book went to press, the Iraqi dinar traded at approximately 1,310 dinars to the U.S. dollar. For a current rate, see xe.com.

surcharge in 1968 after years of resistance.[3] Americans felt it. The war became politically unsustainable in large part because the cost was visible. World War I, World War II, the Civil War, the Spanish-American War — in every case, the government raised taxes and cut non-war spending to pay for the conflict. That was the playbook for 200 years. Wars were expensive in a way that voters could see, and that visibility created political pressure to end them.

The post-9/11 wars broke with every precedent in American history. For the first time, the United States cut taxes while fighting major wars. The cost was not borne by the current generation through higher taxes. It was financed entirely through borrowing and money creation — pushed onto future generations through currency debasement and a national debt that more than tripled during the conflict. The total cost of the post-9/11 "War on Terror," including veteran care, interest on borrowed money, and homeland security, is estimated by Brown University's Watson Institute at $8 trillion.[4] That is more than five times the inflation-adjusted cost of the Korean War. More than five times the cost of World War I. Nearly two and a half times the cost of Vietnam.

And none of them can be called a victory. Afghanistan is back under the Taliban after twenty years — America's longest war. Iraq produced a fractured political system in a decimated country. The wars had no defined endpoint because they had no defined cost. When the money is infinite, so is the war.

This is not an accident. It is what fiat money is designed to produce. A government constrained by a gold standard must do one of two things to fund its operations: tax its citizens or borrow from willing lenders. Both require some form of consent. Taxation is visible, politically painful, and subject to voter backlash. Borrowing under sound money is constrained by the lender's confidence that the loan will be repaid in money of equal

---

3. Truman raised the top marginal income tax rate to 92% via the Revenue Act of 1950 to finance the Korean War. Johnson's Revenue Act of 1964 had previously cut the top rate from 91% to 70%; facing exploding Vietnam costs, he pushed through a 10% income tax surcharge in 1968 — a measure he resisted for years before Congress finally passed it. Tax Policy Center, "Historical Top Tax Rate"; Tax Notes, "Timelines in Tax History: The Korean War" (2022).

4. Costs of War Project, Watson Institute for International and Public Affairs, Brown University, costsofwar.watson.brown.edu. Estimates of post-9/11 war costs vary widely depending on methodology — what is included (direct military spending, veteran care, interest on war debt, homeland security, foreign aid) and the time horizon used. All credible estimates agree the total runs into the multi-trillions. The Watson Institute's 2021 figure of $8 trillion is among the most comprehensive, including projected future veteran care costs through 2050.

value. Neither mechanism allows a government to spend without limit. Neither mechanism allows a twenty-year war.

Fiat money removes the constraint. A government that can create money does not need to ask. It does not need to persuade. It does not need to win a vote. It spends, and the cost is distributed silently across every dollar already in circulation — every paycheck, every savings account, every pension. The people who pay for the spending never see a bill. They just notice, years later, that everything costs more and their money buys less.

And the trend is accelerating. The Congressional Research Service — the official nonpartisan research arm of Congress — has documented every instance of U.S. armed forces deployed abroad since 1798. Between 1798 and 1990, a span of 192 years, the United States conducted 218 military interventions. Then, in just the 31 years between 1991 and 2022, it conducted 251 more.[5] The rate roughly quadrupled. More military interventions after the Cold War ended than during it — the opposite of what you would expect if these deployments were driven by genuine security threats rather than by a government that can project force without limit.

Not all 251 of those are full-scale wars. Many are carrier group deployments, special operations missions, drone campaigns, embassy evacuations, and shows of force. But that is precisely the point. When war is free — when it costs the voter nothing visible — the threshold for military action drops to nearly zero. Every regional dispute becomes an opportunity to deploy. Every crisis becomes a reason to intervene. The standing military becomes a tool that is always in use because there is never a reason to put it down. The money is always there.

Under a gold standard, every one of those 251 deployments would have required a budget line item funded by taxation or borrowing. Every one would have competed against domestic priorities for finite resources. Every one would have faced the question that fiat money eliminates: *can we afford this?* The answer, in many cases, would have been no. And the soldiers who were not deployed would have stayed home, built businesses, raised families, and contributed to their communities instead of serving as instruments of a foreign policy funded by money that does not exist.

COVID

5. Congressional Research Service, "Instances of Use of United States Armed Forces Abroad, 1798–2022," CRS Report R42738 (March 2022), congress.gov/crs-product/R42738. The CRS notes that these figures exclude covert operations and routine overseas stationing — meaning 218 and 251 are conservative counts.

COVID proved the mechanism works identically in peacetime — and revealed just how far a government with unlimited money will go when it smells a crisis.

Between early 2020 and late 2021, M2 — the broadest commonly reported measure of the money supply — grew by approximately 25%.[6] The largest peacetime monetary expansion on record, and likely the largest in American history. Roughly one out of every five dollars in existence had been created from nothing in a matter of months.

Consider the sequence. An unelected bureaucrat proposes that the President and every Governor in the country shut down the economy — close businesses, send workers home, lock children out of schools — based on a projection from a British academic named Neil Ferguson who predicted 2.2 million American deaths if nothing was done. Ferguson's track record on epidemic modeling was, to put it charitably, terrible. The evidence for lockdowns was a single model from a single academic with a well-documented history of overestimating epidemic deaths. No randomized controlled trial evidence supported the idea that locking down a country would slow the spread of a respiratory virus. It was a top-down recommendation from a bureaucracy that faced no consequences for being wrong and stood to gain enormously from being listened to.

And people did listen. Why?

Because fiat money made it possible. Only in a system where money can be printed from nothing and handed out to anyone who needs it will you find business owners willing to shut their doors and workers willing to stay home. The government could afford to pay people not to work because the payment didn't come from anywhere real. It came from a ledger entry at the Federal Reserve. The stimulus checks, the enhanced unemployment benefits, the Paycheck Protection Program loans — all of it funded by money creation, all of it designed to make the lockdowns tolerable enough that the public would comply. The compliance was purchased. The purchase was made with your future purchasing power.

Now imagine that same bureaucrat walking into the same room — but the government is on a hard money standard. Federal revenue comes from taxation. The national purse is

---

6. Federal Reserve Bank of St. Louis, M2 Money Supply (WM2NS), fred.stlouisfed.org. M2 stood at approximately $15.4 trillion in February 2020 and reached approximately $21.7 trillion by July 2022, an increase of roughly 41% over that period. The sharpest single-year expansion — roughly 25% — occurred between early 2020 and early 2021. The Federal Reserve discontinued weekly M2 reporting in 2021; monthly data continues under series M2SL.

finite. Every dollar spent on one thing is a dollar not spent on another. Real opportunity costs, visible to every citizen.

The bureaucrat says: shut down the economy. Immediately, every person in that room understands what that means. It means federal tax revenue collapses — because the businesses that generate tax revenue are closed. It means the government cannot simply print money to cover the gap — because the money is hard and the supply is fixed. It means the bureaucrat is proposing to simultaneously destroy the government's income stream and spend trillions it does not have. He would be laughed out of the room. Not because the people in the room are heartless, but because the math doesn't work and everyone can see it.

On a hard money standard, the decision to lock down would fall where it belongs: with consumers. If a virus is genuinely deadly, people stop going out. They stop shopping. They stop sending their kids to school. They do this voluntarily, because the risk is obvious and the incentive is personal. Businesses that stay open in a genuine pandemic lose customers. Businesses that close lose revenue. The market sorts it out the way markets sort everything out — through millions of individual decisions made by people with skin in the game.

Instead, under fiat, the decision was made by people with no skin in the game at all. The CDC — which had bungled its initial COVID test rollout so badly that it shipped kits contaminated with the virus itself while blocking private labs from developing alternatives — saw its budget grow from roughly $7 billion annually to tens of billions in emergency appropriations.[7] The agency was *rewarded* for the crisis. Its budget did not depend on providing value. It depended on the crisis continuing. On a sound money standard, that agency would have been a fraction of its current size, its recommendations would have carried a fraction of the weight, and its incentive to amplify fear would have been checked by the same budget constraint that checks everything else.

---

7. The CDC's initial COVID test failure is documented in an internal agency review obtained by NPR: officials knew the kits had a 33% failure rate before shipping but chose not to recall them. FDA rules simultaneously blocked private and state labs from developing alternatives. NPR, "CDC Report: Officials Knew Coronavirus Test Was Flawed But Released It Anyway" (November 6, 2020); MIT Technology Review, "Why the CDC Botched Its Coronavirus Testing" (March 5, 2020). On the budget expansion: CDC's pre-pandemic annual budget was approximately $7–8 billion. Through five COVID relief laws (2020–2021), Congress provided CDC with tens of billions in supplemental appropriations. Congressional Research Service, "Centers for Disease Control and Prevention (CDC) Funding Overview," CRS Report R47207.

Local health authorities were no different. They took the CDC's recommendations and turned them into mandates — not because the science supported mandates, but because there was no cost to issuing them. They got paid regardless. And the bigger the crisis, the more paper money they could collect. Bureaucracies did *very well* under the emergency response.

The stimulus checks that arrived in mailboxes were real, and for many families they were desperately needed — needed because the government had just destroyed their livelihoods. But the checks were a fraction of the money created. The bulk flowed into asset markets — inflating stock prices, real estate values, and corporate balance sheets — which is why the billionaire class saw its net worth increase by trillions during a period when working-class Americans were locked in their homes, losing their businesses, and watching grocery prices climb.[8] The lockdowns were enforced by institutions funded with newly created money. The compliance was purchased with it. The entire architecture of COVID policy — the mandates, the funding of compliant media, the suppression of dissent — was made possible by a money printer that required no vote, no debate, and no consent.

And here is the part that should settle the argument permanently: the countries that did the least fared no worse — and in many cases fared better — than the countries that did the most. Sweden refused to lock down and recorded the lowest cumulative excess mortality in Europe over the full pandemic period. Peru imposed one of the strictest lockdowns on earth — military-enforced curfews, severe movement restrictions — and

8. U.S. billionaires' combined wealth grew from roughly $3 trillion at the start of the pandemic (March 18, 2020) to over $5 trillion by October 2021 — an increase of approximately $2.1 trillion, or 70%. Americans for Tax Fairness and the Institute for Policy Studies, "U.S. Billionaires Are Now $2.1 Trillion Richer Than Before the Pandemic" (October 2021), drawing on Forbes real-time billionaire data. The Federal Reserve's own data shows the wealthiest 1% of U.S. households own more than half of all publicly traded stock, meaning asset-price inflation from money creation flows disproportionately to those already at the top.

ended up with the highest per capita COVID death rate globally.[9] The pattern held across dozens of countries: unlimited government intervention, funded by unlimited money creation, did not save lives. In many cases it destroyed them — through delayed medical care, untreated mental health crises, economic devastation, and the downstream effects of isolation on children, the elderly, and the vulnerable.

The *response* to COVID was a feature of fiat. A government with unlimited money has unlimited power to intervene, unlimited incentive to expand that intervention, and zero accountability when the intervention fails. A government on hard money would have been forced, by the constraints of its own budget, to be humble — to weigh the cost of action against the cost of inaction, to defer to the decisions of free citizens rather than impose the preferences of unelected bureaucrats. The virus would have come and gone. The response would have been measured by people with something to lose. And trillions of dollars would not have been created from nothing, inflating every price in the economy and setting the stage for the inflation that followed.

The Administrative Class

The administrative class that manages this system does not grow because the work grows. It grows because the money does. Washington, D.C., and its surrounding counties in Maryland and Northern Virginia are among the wealthiest communities in America. They produce nothing tangible. No cars. No food. No software. No energy. They produce administration, regulation, lobbying, consulting, and compliance — an entire economy built on proximity to the machine that creates money. Four of the ten richest

9. Ferguson's COVID projections were not an anomaly — they fit a pattern. In 2001, his foot-and-mouth model led to the culling of 6 million animals at a cost of roughly £10 billion to the UK economy; 200 people died from the disease. In 2002, he predicted 50,000 to 150,000 BSE ("mad cow") deaths in the UK; fewer than 200 died. In 2005, he predicted up to 200 million bird flu deaths globally; 282 died worldwide between 2003 and 2009. In 2009, a UK government estimate based on his modelling set the "reasonable worst-case" for swine flu at 65,000 UK deaths; 457 died. Ferguson's defenders note that these were framed as worst-case scenarios rather than central predictions. That is true — but a worst-case scenario off by two to three orders of magnitude is not a planning tool. It is noise. Wikipedia, "Neil Ferguson (epidemiologist)"; The Spectator, "Six Questions That Neil Ferguson Should Be Asked" (2020). On the COVID model specifically: Ferguson's Uppsala-adapted projection predicted 96,000 Swedish deaths by July 1, 2020 if Sweden did not lock down. Sweden did not lock down. Actual deaths by that date were closer to 4,000 — a 24-to-1 error. Italy, Spain, and the United Kingdom all imposed severe lockdowns and still recorded among the highest excess mortality rates in Western Europe. Peru's record is the starkest counterexample: one of the world's strictest lockdowns, enforced by military curfew from March 2020, yet the highest per capita COVID death rate globally — over 6,400 deaths per million as of 2023. Wikipedia, "COVID-19 pandemic in Peru"; Johns Hopkins University Coronavirus Resource Center; Statista, "COVID-19 deaths per capita by country" (2022).

counties in America by median household income sit in the Washington, D.C. metropolitan area.[10] That is the Cantillon Effect mapped onto a zip code.

The Federal Register — the daily journal of the federal government's rules, proposed rules, and notices — ran fewer than 10,000 pages per year through the early 1960s. By the mid-1970s, shortly after the gold window closed, it had exploded past 60,000 pages. It has remained in that range ever since, and in recent years has exceeded 100,000 pages annually.[11] More rules require more enforcers. More enforcers require more budget. More budget requires more money creation. The loop feeds itself.

People who live close to the machine understand where their bread is buttered. Washington, D.C., has voted for the Democratic candidate in every presidential election since it was granted the right to vote in 1964. Not most elections. Every single one. In 2016, Hillary Clinton won D.C. with 91% of the vote. In 2020, Biden took 92%. In 2024, Harris took 90%. No Republican has ever won a single electoral vote in the District. The worst Democratic showing in D.C. history was Jimmy Carter's 75% — in the same year he lost 44 out of 50 states.[12]

This is not because D.C. residents are uniquely liberal in their personal values. It is because they are rational. Their mortgages, their children's schools, their careers, their entire economic lives depend on the continued expansion of the federal government. A vote for smaller government is a vote against their own livelihoods. They know it. And they vote accordingly, with a unanimity that would be embarrassing in a one-party state.

The machine is not left or right by nature. But it has a natural constituency: the people it feeds. And those people will always vote to keep the feeding going. Fiat money is what

---

10. U.S. Census Bureau, American Community Survey. Loudoun County, Virginia ranks first nationally in median household income at $178,707; Falls Church city, Virginia ranks fourth; Fairfax County, Virginia ranks fifth; Howard County, Maryland ranks sixth. Santa Clara and San Mateo counties in California rank second and third.

11. Historical Federal Register page counts are tracked by the Regulatory Studies Center at George Washington University and the Competitive Enterprise Institute. For annual page counts from 1936 to the present, see regulatorystudies.columbian.gwu.edu and cei.org/regulatory-studies. The Federal Register itself is searchable at federalregister.gov.

12. Ballotpedia, "Presidential voting trends in the District of Columbia," ballotpedia.org. D.C. has voted Democratic in all 16 presidential elections since gaining electoral votes via the 23rd Amendment in 1961. 2016 result: Clinton 90.9%; 2020: Biden 92.1%; 2024: Harris 90.3% (Wikipedia, "2024 United States presidential election in the District of Columbia"). Carter's 74.9% in 1980 is the lowest Democratic share in D.C. history (Wikipedia, "1980 United States presidential election in the District of Columbia"). Reagan carried 44 states in 1980; Carter won six states plus D.C. National Archives, 1980 Electoral College Results, archives.gov.

makes the feeding possible, and it will continue to grow for as long as the money can be created without constraint.

Chapter Twelve

Culture Wars

Politics as Existential Combat

Americans wonder why politics has become so vicious. Why Thanksgiving dinner is a minefield. Why neighbors who disagree about a presidential candidate treat each other like enemies. Why every election feels like the last stand.

The answer is straightforward. When the government controls over 40% of GDP and can print unlimited money to fund its priorities, politics becomes existential.[1] Every election is a battle for control of the money printer. The stakes are not abstract. They are *your mortgage, your children's school, your healthcare, your job, your retirement.* The person who controls the printer controls the allocation of newly created money, and the allocation of newly created money determines who thrives and who gets crushed.

Under a gold standard, government was smaller, its reach was shorter, and elections mattered less because the government had less power to deploy. You could disagree with your neighbor about tariff policy and still share a beer on the porch, because the outcome of the election would not determine whether your savings were confiscated or your business was regulated out of existence.

Under fiat, every election is a referendum on who gets the next wave of printed money. Teachers' unions or charter schools? Solar panels or oil pipelines? Urban transit or rural highways? Immigration enforcement or sanctuary cities? The answer doesn't come from

1. Combined federal, state, and local government outlays as a percentage of GDP have ranged from approximately 35% to 44% over the past two decades, depending on the year and methodology. Federal spending alone has consistently exceeded 20% of GDP since 2008, and exceeded 30% during the COVID-19 pandemic. See: Office of Management and Budget, Historical Tables, Table 15.3; Federal Reserve Bank of St. Louis, FRED Economic Data, series FYONGDA188S (Federal Net Outlays as Percent of Gross Domestic Product). State and local spending data: National Association of State Budget Officers annual reports.

the market, where voluntary exchange allocates resources. It comes from the state, where political power allocates resources. And because the state can create unlimited money, there is no natural limit on what it can promise — or what it can take.

No wonder everyone is hysterical. Politics has consumed entertainment, sports, education, corporate boardrooms, and family dinners. People who would otherwise mind their own business feel compelled to fight over every school board seat and every zoning variance. When the government is big enough to give you everything, it is big enough to take everything — and fiat money is what made it that big.

I watched this in my own family during COVID. People who had shared Thanksgiving tables for decades were suddenly at each other's throats — not because they had changed, but because the stakes had changed. When the government can shut down your business, mandate what goes into your child's body, and fund the entire operation with printed money, a policy disagreement is no longer a policy disagreement. It is a fight for your life. The people who wanted to exclude family members from the holiday table were not evil. They were terrified — and they were terrified because a government powered by unlimited money had made politics into the arena where every important decision about their lives would be made.

And here is the thing that nobody on either side understands: it does not matter who controls the machine. The machine is the problem. The same people who cheered when the government used its power to enforce their preferred policies during COVID were shocked — *shocked* — when a different administration turned that same power in a direction they didn't like. Voters don't oppose authoritarianism. They oppose losing control. As long as the machine exists, as long as it is funded by money that can be created without consent, whoever does not control it will live in fear of whoever does.

Shrink the government and you lower the stakes. Lower the stakes and people can go back to being neighbors instead of combatants.

Self-Perpetuating

The machine does not want to shrink. It wants to grow. And fiat money is the mechanism that guarantees it will.

Follow the money. The federal government creates dollars from nothing. It spends those dollars — on defense contracts, pharmaceutical subsidies, agricultural programs, regulatory compliance regimes. The corporations and interest groups that receive this money take a portion of it and pour it back into Washington in the form of campaign contributions and lobbying. In 2024, federal lobbying hit a record $4.4 billion — more than double what it was at the turn of the century. The pharmaceutical industry alone has spent over $6 billion lobbying Congress since 1999. Total spending on the 2024 federal elections was approximately $15.9 billion. In 1976, presidential candidates spent a combined $67 million. In 2000, $343 million. By 2024, PACs alone — political action committees funded overwhelmingly by corporations, unions, and industry groups — raised the vast majority of that total in a single cycle.[2]

This is not democracy. This is a feedback loop. The government prints money, distributes it to favored industries, and those industries use a fraction of their windfall to ensure the politicians who sent it keep their jobs. The politicians, in turn, print more money to distribute. Each cycle is bigger than the last because each cycle is funded by money that did not exist in the previous one. It is the Cantillon Effect applied to politics itself: those closest to the money printer do not just get richer. They get to decide who operates the printer next.

And where does the money for all those campaign ads, all those lobbyists, all those PAC contributions ultimately come from? It comes from the same place all fiat dollars come from: the future purchasing power of every American who holds dollars. Every time the government creates money to fund a program that generates a lobbying industry that funds a campaign that elects a politician who creates more money, the loop tightens — and the value of the dollars in your wallet decreases. You are funding your own political disenfranchisement, and you never even get a vote on it.

The Culture of Now

But fiat does not just corrupt our politics. It corrupts *us*.

There is nothing wrong with a grandparent taking that vacation they deferred for thirty years. There is nothing wrong with buying that house in a peaceful place they always dreamed about, or spending a decade doing exactly what they want after a lifetime of doing what they had to. They earned it. I hope I get to do the same.

The problem is not enjoying retirement. The problem is when enjoying retirement becomes the *entire* remaining purpose — when the sum total of a person's ambition for

---

2. Federal lobbying expenditures totaled approximately $4.4 billion in 2024, the highest on record, according to data compiled by OpenSecrets (opensecrets.org/federal-lobbying). The pharmaceutical and health products industry has spent more than $6 billion lobbying Congress since 1999, more than any other sector tracked. Total spending on the 2024 federal elections was approximately $15.9 billion. For historical presidential campaign spending: the combined general election spending of Gerald Ford and Jimmy Carter in 1976 was approximately $67 million; George W. Bush and Al Gore spent approximately $343 million in 2000. All figures: OpenSecrets, opensecrets.org.

their final years is the maximization of personal pleasure, with no weight left on the scale for the people who come after them. That extreme is more common than it used to be, and it is not a coincidence. It is what fiat money produces.

You have probably heard some version of this from someone's grandparents. Maybe your own. "I worked hard all my life. I'm going to enjoy what time I have left. The kids will figure it out." And then they spend down every dollar they have before they die, because why not? What's the alternative — save in a currency that loses half its purchasing power every eleven years? We showed that math in Chapter Four. A $100,000 nest egg set aside for the grandchildren today shrinks to $15,378 in real purchasing power by the time thirty years pass. You cannot build a family legacy in a currency being debased at 6% per year. The grandparents who say "what's the point" are not wrong about the math. They are wrong about what caused it.

And most of them have no idea. That is the part worth sitting with. The retiree who spends every dollar on himself is not making a calculated decision to leave his grandchildren with nothing. He has simply internalized what fifty years of fiat incentive has taught him: saving is irrational, the future is uncertain, and the only real value is what you can enjoy today. He thinks he's being pragmatic. He is actually being managed — by a monetary system that deliberately made thrift feel foolish.

They are also blind to the second half of the equation. It is not just that their savings rot. It is that every succeeding generation faces a harder climb than the one before. The home price-to-income ratio that was 2.5 times salary when these grandparents were young is now 4.84 times salary for their grandchildren. The college degree that a summer job used to cover now requires six figures of debt. The entry-level wages that once supported a family now barely support a single adult in a studio apartment.

The shift in time preference does not stop at personal finance. It reshapes political incentives too. A generation trained by fiat to maximize the present becomes a generation that votes to maximize the present. Any government program that promises a benefit *now* — expanded Medicare coverage, prescription drug subsidies, cost-of-living adjustments to Social Security — becomes an easy vote, even when the math behind the promise is obviously unsustainable. The calculation is not cynical. It is honest: I will likely be gone before the bill comes due. Why would I vote against my own check?

This transforms the role of the elderly in a way that should trouble all of us. In every civilization that preceded ours, the oldest generation was the voice of long-term wisdom — the people who had lived through enough cycles to understand consequences, who counseled patience, who insisted on building durable things because they had seen what happens when you don't. Under fiat, that role has been quietly inverted. The oldest generation becomes another lobbying constituency, fighting for its slice of the pie, increasingly at odds with younger generations who can see the math even when their grandparents cannot. Instead of being honored for their long view, they are resented for their short one.

Fiat did that. It did not make the elderly selfish. It made thrift irrational for them, slowly, over decades, until the cultural posture shifted and nobody noticed because the shift felt like common sense.

One hundred years ago, it would have been unthinkable for a retiree to adopt this posture. Under the gold standard, the money you saved held its value — and often gained purchasing power — over decades. A nest egg was not something to be spent down. It was something to be passed forward. The idea that a person would exhaust their savings and leave nothing to their descendants would have been considered a failure, not a lifestyle. Not because people were more virtuous. Because the money rewarded virtue. It paid to think about the future, so people thought about the future.

With each passing year, young professionals find it harder to acquire what was there for previous generations, and their resentment of those generations grows. With each passing year, the elderly have greater incentive to spend their remaining fortunes on themselves instead of passing it down to a younger generation they view as lazy or entitled, unable to see how the obstacles have grown. The gap will not close on its own. It will widen — until the money changes.

Fiat reversed that incentive, and the reversal did not stop at retirement communities. It infected everything.

Look around. One year Americans are trampling each other on Black Friday to buy televisions they do not need at prices that are not actually discounts. A few years later, one in eight American adults is injecting themselves with GLP-1 weight loss drugs — prescriptions that have tripled since 2020 — because the long-term work of eating well and exercising is too slow, too hard, too *future-oriented* for a culture that has been trained to want everything now.[3] The pattern is the same in both cases. Instant gratification. Present over future. Consumption over investment. The most present-oriented thing a person can do is indulge themselves in every way, and that is exactly what a fiat culture produces.

The personal savings rate tells the story in a single chart. Under the gold standard, Americans saved above 10% of their income. The decline begins — tellingly — just a few years after 1971. Today the savings rate hovers between 3% and 5%.[4] Savings is the act of preferring the future to the present. It is the measurable expression of low time preference. When the savings rate collapses, it is not because an entire nation simultaneously became lazy. It is because the money stopped rewarding patience.

We all know that it is foolish to save in dollars. "Cash is trash" is not a fringe opinion. It is the consensus view of every financial advisor in America. And they are right, within the fiat framework. No savings rate offered at any bank keeps up with the rate of increase in the money supply. So people do the rational thing: they spend, they borrow, they gamble.

The Lottery

Americans spent $113 billion on lottery tickets in fiscal year 2024. That is more than they spent on music, movie tickets, sports tickets, and books combined.[5] It is not a rounding error. It is a staggering transfer of wealth from the people who can least afford it to the government that made them desperate enough to play.

---

3. GLP-1 receptor agonists (including semaglutide, marketed as Ozempic and Wegovy, and tirzepatide, marketed as Mounjaro and Zepbound) saw rapid adoption in the United States beginning in 2021–2022. The KFF Health Tracking Poll (2024) found that approximately 12% of U.S. adults reported having used a GLP-1 medication, and approximately 6% reported current use — a figure consistent with 'roughly one in eight' when accounting for survey methodology and reporting lag. Total GLP-1 prescriptions in the United States tripled between 2020 and 2023, according to IQVIA Institute for Human Data Science.

4. The U.S. personal saving rate (personal savings as a percentage of disposable personal income) is tracked monthly by the Bureau of Economic Analysis (BEA) and is available on the Federal Reserve Bank of St. Louis's FRED database, series PSAVERT. The rate averaged above 10% through the 1960s and 1970s, began a secular decline in the early 1980s following the end of the Bretton Woods gold-exchange standard, and has generally ranged between 3% and 7% in recent years, with spikes during recessions when spending collapses temporarily. The long-term post-1971 trend is clearly visible in the chart.

5. U.S. lottery industry gross revenue in fiscal year 2024 was approximately $113 billion, according to data compiled by the North American Association of State and Provincial Lotteries (NASPL). This figure represents total sales, not net government revenue. For context, the Recording Industry Association of America (RIAA) reported total recorded music revenues of approximately $17.1 billion in 2023. The Motion Picture Association reported U.S. box office revenue of approximately $9.0 billion in 2023. Total U.S. consumer spending on books was approximately $28 billion in 2023 (Association of American Publishers / Book Industry Study Group).

The lottery is a government monopoly. By law, only the state can run lotteries. It is illegal for any private entity to compete. The government sets the odds, runs the advertising, and keeps the profits. And the odds are atrocious. State lotteries return approximately 60 cents for every dollar wagered — far worse than casino slot machines, which return about 90 cents. The odds of winning a Powerball jackpot are roughly 1 in 292 million. You are more likely to be struck by lightning. You are more likely to be struck by lightning *twice*.[6]

The government knows exactly who is buying these tickets. The data is consistent: the lower the income, the higher the share spent on lottery tickets. In the poorest zip codes in America, adults spend an average of $600 annually. In the wealthiest zip codes, they spend $150. One in five Americans believes the lottery is the only way to accumulate significant savings. Not *a* way. The *only* way. This is what happens when fifty years of monetary debasement has made legitimate saving impossible for working people. They are not stupid. They have simply been placed in a situation where a 1-in-292-million longshot feels more realistic than the alternative, which is watching their savings lose half their purchasing power every eleven years while housing prices climb forever out of reach.[7]

And the government has the audacity to market this to them. State lottery commissions spend hundreds of millions on advertising — advertising designed to stoke the fantasy, emphasize the jackpot, and minimize the odds. They target the very communities where financial desperation is highest. They put lottery retailers on every corner of every low-income neighborhood. They trumpet the winners — one winner out of hundreds

---

6. State lotteries typically return approximately 55–62 cents of every dollar wagered in prize money, with the remainder going to state revenue, retailer commissions, and administrative costs. Casino slot machines, by contrast, are typically required by regulation to return 85–98 cents on the dollar, depending on jurisdiction. The odds of winning the Powerball jackpot (matching all six numbers) are approximately 1 in 292,201,338, according to Powerball's published odds. The odds of being struck by lightning in any given year are approximately 1 in 1.2 million (National Weather Service); the odds of being struck twice in a lifetime are considerably lower, but still vastly higher than a Powerball jackpot.

7. A 2008 study of lottery sales and income data by researchers at Carnegie Mellon University found that households in the lowest income quintile spent the highest percentage of their income on lottery tickets. Separately, an investigation by the Howard Center for Investigative Journalism (2020) found that lottery retailers are disproportionately concentrated in lower-income zip codes across every state examined. The $600 annual figure for spending in the lowest-income zip codes and the 1-in-5 statistic on Americans viewing the lottery as their primary path to wealth have been cited widely; the latter originates from polling conducted by Opinion Research Corporation for CNBC and has been reproduced in multiple subsequent studies of lottery behavior.

of millions of losers — and they never, ever mention that the expected return on a lottery ticket is negative forty cents on the dollar.

Then they earmark the revenue for education. This is the final insult. The money flows upward. The poorest households buy the tickets. The revenue funds scholarship programs that disproportionately benefit higher-income students who are more likely to attend college. A 2002 study of the Georgia Lottery found that lower-income households spent more on the lottery than they received in benefits, while higher-income households received a net positive return. The poor fund the education of the comfortable. Through a government-run gambling monopoly. Advertised on billboards in their neighborhoods.[8]

This is fiat in miniature. The government creates the conditions that make saving impossible. Then it offers the desperate a false exit — one it controls, one it profits from, one that makes their situation worse. And it calls the whole operation a public service.

If the dollar held its value — if a working-class family could put $50 a week into a savings account and watch it grow rather than shrink — the lottery would be what it was for most of American history: a minor curiosity. Instead it is a $113 billion industry built on the broken hopes of people whose money was stolen so slowly they never saw it leave.

High time preference is not a character flaw. It is what fiat *produces*. And once you see it, you see it everywhere.

Education

The American university system was, within living memory, a place where a working-class kid could earn a credential that opened the door to a stable career. The cost was manageable. A summer job could cover tuition at a state school. A degree in education, nursing, or skilled trades led to a life that was modest but secure.

Fiat money destroyed that. The mechanism was student loans — specifically, federally guaranteed student loans backed by money that could be created without limit. When the government guaranteed the loans, universities faced no market discipline on price. They could charge whatever they wanted, because the money would always be there. And so

8. A 2002 study published in the Public Finance Review by Mary O. Borg and Paul M. Mason examined the distributional effects of the Georgia Lottery for Education. The study found that lower-income households contributed disproportionately more in lottery revenue than they received in lottery-funded educational benefits, while higher-income households (whose children were more likely to attend college and qualify for lottery-funded scholarships such as the HOPE Scholarship) received a net positive return. The authors concluded that the Georgia Lottery functioned as a regressive tax. Similar findings have been replicated in studies of lottery programs in multiple other states.

tuition rose. It rose faster than inflation. It rose faster than wages. It rose faster than any other major cost category in American life.

The money didn't go to better teaching. It went to administration. Between 1975 and 2008, the number of full-time administrators at American colleges and universities grew by 235%, while the number of full-time faculty grew by only 51%.[9] The universities built compliance offices, diversity bureaucracies, wellness centers, and layers of management that had nothing to do with educating students and everything to do with absorbing the river of money flowing in through the loan system. The students got the debt. The administrators got the salaries.

The total outstanding student loan debt in America now exceeds $1.7 trillion. Larger than all outstanding auto loans. Larger than all credit card debt. Owed overwhelmingly by people between the ages of 22 and 40 — the precise years when a previous generation was buying a first home, starting a family, and building the foundation of a middle-class life. Instead, an entire generation is servicing debt to institutions that used the money to hire more administrators.[10]

The result is a credentialing treadmill that traps working-class families. A college degree that once signaled competence now signals only that you were willing to take on debt. Employers require degrees for jobs that never needed them — not because the work changed, but because the flood of degree-holders made the credential meaningless without a graduate degree on top of it. The working-class parent who tells their child to go to college is following advice that made sense in 1975 and is financially ruinous today.

And here is the cruelest part. When was the last time you heard a parent say, "I hope my kid becomes a teacher"? Never. Yet those same parents will tell you that teachers are vital to society. They know the truth. Being a teacher no longer provides financial security. Under fiat, the professions that hold a civilization together — teaching, nursing, policing, social work — cannot compete with the professions that cluster around money creation.

---

9. Between 1975 and 2008, the number of full-time administrators at American colleges and universities increased by approximately 235%, while full-time faculty grew by approximately 51%, according to data from the Digest of Education Statistics (National Center for Education Statistics) analyzed by the Goldwater Institute. See: Jay P. Greene, Brian Kisida, and Jonathan Mills, "Administrative Bloat at American Universities: The Real Reason for High Costs in Higher Education," Goldwater Institute Policy Report No. 239, August 17, 2010.

10. Total outstanding federal student loan debt exceeded $1.7 trillion as of 2024, making it the second-largest category of household debt in the United States after mortgage debt. Federal Reserve Bank of New York, Center for Microeconomic Data, Quarterly Report on Household Debt and Credit. The majority of this debt is owed by borrowers between the ages of 22 and 40.

The best and brightest are funneled toward finance, consulting, and administration. The people who build things, fix things, and care for people are left behind. That is not a market outcome. It is a monetary one.

Family Both parents forced to work — from 47% of married couples in 1970 to 66% by 2010. Rising single-parent households — from 9% to 33% over the fiat era. Declining birth rates. Delayed marriage. Youth suicide up 62% from 2007 to 2021.[11 12]

More women in the workforce. More choices. More independence. And it is wonderful when women choose to work because they want to. I have three daughters and I would be proud to see them succeed in any career they choose. But that is not what happened for most families. What happened is that fiat money made one income insufficient. Both parents now *must* work — not because the economy expanded to accommodate them, but because the currency was debased until one salary could no longer cover a mortgage, groceries, and childcare. The second income didn't buy a better life. It bought the same life that one income used to provide.

The cost falls on children. Children raised in dual-income households spend more time in institutional care — daycare, after-school programs, organized activities managed by strangers — and less time with their parents.[13] When both parents leave the house at 7 AM and return at 6 PM, there is no one to coach the little league team, sit on the

11. The share of married-couple families with both spouses employed rose from approximately 47% in 1970 to approximately 66% by 2010. Bureau of Labor Statistics, "Working wives: their contribution to family income," BLS Reports. The share of U.S. children living in single-parent households rose from approximately 9% in 1960 to approximately 33% by 2020. Annie E. Casey Foundation, KIDS COUNT Data Center; U.S. Census Bureau, Current Population Survey. Financial stress as a predictor of marital dissolution: multiple studies, including Jeffrey Dew, "Bank on It: Thrifty Couples Are the Happiest," National Marriage Project at the University of Virginia (2012), and Sonya Britt et al., "Financial Arguments as a Predictor of Divorce," Family Relations (2012).

12. Youth suicide rates in the United States increased approximately 62% between 2007 and 2021 among individuals aged 10–24, according to the Centers for Disease Control and Prevention, National Center for Health Statistics, WISQARS Fatal Injury Reports. The increase is concentrated in adolescents aged 10–17, where the rate roughly doubled over the same period. The CDC's data does not establish causation with any single factor.

13. Research consistently links reduced parental presence and increased time in non-parental care to elevated stress markers in children. The NICHD Study of Early Child Care and Youth Development — a longitudinal study funded by the National Institute of Child Health and Human Development tracking more than 1,300 children from 1991 onward — found associations between extensive hours in non-maternal care and elevated cortisol levels and increased behavioral problems in early childhood. See: NICHD Early Child Care Research Network, "Child Care and Child Development: Results from the NICHD Study of Early Child Care and Youth Development" (Guilford Press, 2005). For a synthesis of neurological and psychological research on parental presence and child development, see also Margot Sunderland, The Science of Parenting (DK Publishing, 2006).

school board, check in on the elderly neighbor, or simply be present on the front porch. Community requires *margin* — time and energy left over after the bills are paid — and fiat eliminates margin.

The rise of single-parent families makes this worse. Fiat incentives drive high time preference in relationships the same way they drive it everywhere else. Why plan? Why commit? Why build something durable when the financial ground shifts under your feet every year? Financial stress is the leading predictor of divorce. When every month is a scramble, long-term planning gives way to short-term survival.

The kids are not OK. They are anxious, medicated, glued to screens, and killing themselves at rates that would have been unimaginable two generations ago. Fiat did not cause every one of those problems. But fiat created the conditions — the financial stress, the absent parents, the institutional childhoods, the collapsing sense that the future holds anything worth waiting for — that made those problems inevitable.

The Market, Distorted

When the Federal Reserve holds interest rates below the natural rate — which it has done, with brief exceptions, for the entire fiat era — it sends a false signal to every business in the economy. The signal says: capital is cheap, borrow and expand. The businesses that respond are not making decisions based on genuine savings and genuine demand. They are making decisions based on money created from nothing, and the result is malinvestment — capital allocated to projects that should never have been started and that will fail when the artificial stimulus is withdrawn.

The working-class American sees this as a recurring cycle: boom, bust, bailout, repeat. The boom creates the illusion of prosperity. The bust destroys jobs and savings. The bailout rescues the institutions that caused the bust — because they are "too big to fail" — while the working-class employee who lost their job and their 401(k) is told to retrain and try harder.

Cheap credit also enables corporate consolidation on a scale impossible under sound money. A local hardware store cannot compete with a national chain that borrows billions at near-zero interest to undercut prices and absorb losses for years. A family restaurant cannot compete with a private-equity-backed franchise operation that treats profitability as a long-term luxury funded by debt. The working-class entrepreneur — the plumber who wants to open his own shop, the mechanic who dreams of owning a garage, the baker who wants to stop working for a chain — faces the full weight of this distortion. The cost of commercial real estate is inflated by cheap money. The regulatory burden is funded by the same machine. The competition is not other small businesses. It is debt-fueled corporate operations playing a different game with different money.

Zombie companies — firms that cannot even cover their interest payments from operating income — now represent a significant share of publicly traded companies.[14] They survive not because they create value but because perpetually cheap credit keeps them on life support. Under sound money, they would fail, their resources would be reallocated, and the economy would grow stronger. Under fiat, they persist, consuming capital that could have been employed by the entrepreneurs and small businesses that actually produce things people want.

Community Decay

Every consequence above converges at the community level. Think about what a healthy community actually requires. It requires people who are present — not just physically residing in a zip code, but available, with time and energy and enough financial margin that they can afford to care about something beyond their own survival. It requires parents who show up to school events. It requires neighbors who know each other's names. It requires business owners invested in the town because they live there, not because a spreadsheet in a private equity firm says the location is profitable.

Fiat erodes every one of those requirements. It erodes presence by requiring both parents to work. It erodes neighborliness by making politics so high-stakes that a yard sign becomes a tribal marker. It erodes local business by subsidizing debt-fueled corporate competitors. And it erodes the margin — the financial and emotional breathing room — that allows a person to be a citizen rather than just a worker.

The churches feel this. The volunteer fire departments feel this. The little leagues feel this. The block parties that used to happen on the Fourth of July feel this.

What You Eat

Even the food on your plate has been corrupted by fiat. When a government can fund any research program without constraint, it funds the science that supports its interests and starves the science that doesn't. The result is a half-century of nutritional guidance

---

14. A 'zombie company' is typically defined as a firm whose earnings before interest and taxes (EBIT) are insufficient to cover its interest expenses for an extended period. Research by the Bank for International Settlements (BIS Working Paper No. 894, 2020) estimated that zombie firms accounted for approximately 15% of publicly traded companies in advanced economies, up from roughly 4% in the mid-1980s — a period coinciding with the prolonged low-interest-rate environment following the 2008 financial crisis. IMF research has similarly documented the accumulation of zombie companies as a consequence of extended periods of artificially low borrowing costs.

shaped more by agricultural lobbying and fiat-funded institutional incentives than by honest inquiry into what makes human beings healthy.

How deep does the corruption run? In 2021, Tufts University unveiled its NIH-funded "Food Compass" — a nutrient profiling system three years and millions of taxpayer dollars in the making, touted as the most comprehensive and science-based ranking of foods ever created. Lucky Charms scored a 60 out of 100. Ground beef scored a 26. A fried egg in butter scored a 29.[15] According to the best science that fiat money could buy, a bowl of children's cereal made primarily of sugar and marshmallows is more than twice as healthy as the beef, eggs, and whole milk that built every generation before this one.

This is not an isolated embarrassment. It is the predictable outcome of a system in which government agencies fund the research, the research supports the agencies' preferred conclusions, and the conclusions shape the dietary guidelines that determine what your children eat at school and what your doctor tells you at your next checkup. The full story of how fiat money captured nutrition science — from the demonization of animal fat to the subsidization of corn, soy, and seed oils — is told in devastating detail by Matthew Lysiak in *Fiat Food* and by Saifedean Ammous in *The Fiat Standard.*[16] If you want to understand why 40% of Americans are obese and 88% are metabolically unhealthy

---

15. The Tufts University Food Compass was developed by researchers at the Friedman School of Nutrition Science and Policy at Tufts University and published in Nature Food in October 2021. The system was funded in part by the National Institutes of Health. Published scores included: Lucky Charms, 60 out of 100; plain ground beef (80% lean, 20% fat), 26 out of 100; a fried egg cooked in butter, 29 out of 100. The scores attracted significant criticism from nutrition researchers and clinicians, including Dr. David Katz, Dr. Walter Willett, and others who argued the methodology weighted processing characteristics and plant-origin ingredients in ways that systematically disadvantaged whole animal foods regardless of their nutrient density.

16. Matthew Lysiak, Fiat Food: Why Corrupt Money Is Making Us Fat, Sick, and Poor (BTC Media, 2023). Saifedean Ammous, The Fiat Standard: The Debt Slavery Alternative to Human Civilization (Saif House, 2021). Both books document the relationship between government monetary and agricultural policy, the demonization of animal fat, the subsidization of corn, soy, and seed oils, and the resulting deterioration of the American diet. Ammous is also the author of The Bitcoin Standard: The Decentralized Alternative to Central Banking (Wiley, 2018).

in the wealthiest country in human history, start with those two books.[17] The mechanism is the same one described throughout this chapter: fiat money funds the institutions, the institutions serve the money, and the people who trust the institutions pay the price.

This is the disease. Nearly every societal problem you can think of has been exacerbated — and in many cases caused — by fiat money distorting our time preference. The obesity epidemic. The divorce rate. The anxiety crisis. The addiction crisis. The gambling explosion. The credentialing treadmill. The hollowed-out communities. The children raised by screens instead of parents. The elders who wanted to leave a legacy but were handed a monetary system that made that feel impossible. None of it is random. All of it follows from a single monetary incentive: the future is not worth investing in, so invest in the present.

None of the above is a moral indictment of individuals. The families working two jobs, the young adults delaying marriage, the parents too exhausted to coach a team, the communities that have hollowed out — none of them failed. They responded to incentives. The incentives are set by the money. Change the money and the incentives change. Change the incentives and the culture begins to heal — not overnight, not by government decree, but organically, the way cultures always heal when the conditions for human flourishing are restored.

17. The Centers for Disease Control and Prevention's National Health and Nutrition Examination Survey (NHANES) reported the U.S. adult obesity prevalence at 41.9% (2017–2020 data, published 2022). The 88% figure for metabolic dysfunction originates from a 2019 study by researchers at the University of North Carolina at Chapel Hill: Joana Araújo, Jianwen Cai, and June Stevens, "Prevalence of Optimal Metabolic Health in American Adults,"Metabolic Syndrome and Related Disorders (2019). The study analyzed NHANES data and found that only 12.2% of American adults met criteria for optimal metabolic health across five markers: waist circumference, blood glucose, blood pressure, triglycerides, and HDL cholesterol.

Chapter Thirteen

Sound Government

Government growth is not one thing. It is three things happening simultaneously, each reinforcing the others, each consuming a larger share of your economic life with every passing decade. I want to show you each one.

The coercive apparatus

In the year 2000, the United States spent roughly $300 billion on national defense. By 2024, that number had nearly tripled to $874 billion — and this figure does not include the $326 billion spent on veterans' benefits, which are themselves the downstream cost of prior military decisions. Add the intelligence community — eighteen agencies whose combined budget has grown from an estimated $30 billion in 2000 to an estimated $100 billion or more in 2024 — and you are looking at well over $1.3 trillion per year spent on the security state. The Congressional Budget Office projects defense costs alone will increase another eleven percent between 2029 and 2039.[1]

These are not wartime numbers. The United States is not fighting a World War. It is not responding to Pearl Harbor or D-Day. This is the peacetime cost of maintaining a global

1. U.S. national defense outlays in FY2000 were approximately $294 billion; by FY2024 they reached approximately $874 billion. Department of Defense, Defense Budget Overview (FY2025); Office of Management and Budget, Historical Tables, Table 3.2. Veterans' benefits and services: $326 billion in FY2024, per OMB Historical Tables, Table 3.2. The Intelligence Community currently comprises eighteen member organizations, as listed by the Office of the Director of National Intelligence (ODNI), intelligence.gov. The combined National Intelligence Program budget for FY2024 was $67.1 billion (ODNI disclosed figure); total intelligence spending including the Military Intelligence Program brings the combined estimate to over $100 billion, per Congressional Research Service and public ODNI disclosures. The FY2000 combined intelligence budget is estimated at approximately $30 billion based on retrospective CRS analysis and declassified figures. Congressional Budget Office, The Long-Term Implications of Current Defense Plans, projected defense costs will increase approximately 11% in real terms between 2029 and 2039.

military empire, and it only goes in one direction. Every base built requires maintenance. Every weapons system procured requires upgrades. Every intelligence program launched requires expansion. The bureaucratic logic of a fiat-funded security state is that last year's spending becomes this year's floor, and the ceiling is limited only by the government's ability to create new dollars to pay for it.

Project those rates forward to 2046 at the same pace they have grown since 2000, and the security state's annual price tag approaches $3.6 trillion — nearly equal to the entire federal budget as recently as 2018. That figure includes roughly $2.4 trillion in defense, $885 billion in veterans' costs, and $302 billion in intelligence. No war required. No emergency assumed. Just the same trajectory, continuing.[2]

There is a reasonable debate about how much military spending is necessary. There is no debate about the trend. Under fiat money, the coercive apparatus of the state grows until something stops it, and nothing in the current system is designed to stop it.

The dependency apparatus

In the early 1970s — right around the time Nixon closed the gold window — roughly forty percent of the federal budget went to mandatory spending programs like Social Security and Medicare. Today, that figure is sixty-one percent.[3] More than three out of every five dollars the federal government spends are committed before Congress even votes on a budget. They are on autopilot, growing automatically, year after year, by law.

In 2024, Social Security cost $1.5 trillion. Medicare cost $912 billion. Medicaid and the Children's Health Insurance Program cost another $626 billion. Federal healthcare programs alone are projected to grow from $1.6 trillion today to $2.8 trillion by 2034. Social Security, healthcare, and interest on the debt together account for nearly ninety

2. Projections apply each category's own compound annual growth rate from FY2000 to FY2024 forward twenty-two years to 2046. Defense CAGR: 4.64% ($294B → $874B); intelligence CAGR: 5.14% (~$30B → ~$100B); veterans' benefits projected at the defense CAGR as a conservative proxy. Resulting 2046 estimates: defense ~$2.4 trillion, veterans ~$885 billion, intelligence ~$302 billion, combined ~$3.6 trillion. For reference, total federal outlays in FY2018 were approximately $4.1 trillion (OMB Historical Tables, Table 1.1). No acceleration is assumed; these are straight-line trend projections. Actual figures will vary.

3. Mandatory spending as a share of total federal outlays was approximately 40% in FY1972 and has risen to approximately 61% in FY2024. Office of Management and Budget, Historical Tables, Table 8.4 (Outlays by Budget Enforcement Act Category). Mandatory spending includes Social Security, Medicare, Medicaid, and other entitlement programs whose expenditures are determined by eligibility rules established in law rather than annual appropriations. The shift from roughly 40% to 61% over five decades reflects both the expansion of existing programs and the addition of new ones, compounding automatically regardless of the annual budget process.

percent of all projected spending growth over the next decade. Everything else — defense, education, infrastructure, scientific research — fights over the scraps.[4]

Meanwhile, seventy-two million Americans receive some form of welfare assistance every month. That is roughly one in five people in the country. Forty-one million people are on SNAP. Ninety million are covered by Medicaid. The federal government spent $6.8 trillion in 2024, which works out to roughly $20,000 for every man, woman, and child in the United States — and it still ran a deficit.[5]

Project those numbers forward to 2046 at the same rates they have grown since 2000, and Social Security, Medicare, and Medicaid alone will cost an estimated $11.5 trillion per year. Against a federal budget projected to reach roughly $27.7 trillion by the same year, those three programs consume forty-two cents of every dollar before Congress allocates a cent for anything else. Add the security state's projected $3.6 trillion and more than half the entire federal budget is spoken for — by two of the three apparatus categories — before a dollar is spent on roads, schools, courts, or the interest on the debt that is financing all of it.

This is the dependency apparatus: a system that grows by creating more people who depend on it, then using their dependence to justify its continued expansion. Every program creates a constituency. Every constituency fights to preserve its program. Every preservation ensures the next budget is larger than the last. The fiat money system makes this possible because no politician ever has to answer the question *where is the money coming from?* The answer is always the same: we will print it.

---

4. FY2024 outlays: Social Security, $1.5 trillion; Medicare, $912 billion; Medicaid and the Children's Health Insurance Program (CHIP), $626 billion. Office of Management and Budget, Historical Tables, Table 3.2; Congressional Budget Office, The Budget and Economic Outlook: 2024 to 2034. Federal healthcare programs (Medicare, Medicaid, CHIP, and related) are projected to grow from approximately $1.6 trillion in 2024 to $2.8 trillion by 2034, per CBO baseline projections. Social Security, major health programs, and net interest together are projected to account for approximately 90% of the growth in federal spending over the 2024–2034 period, per CBO. All other discretionary and mandatory programs — including defense, education, infrastructure, and scientific research — compete for the remainder.

5. FY2000 baselines: Social Security ~$409 billion, Medicare ~$197 billion, Medicaid ~$118 billion (OMB Historical Tables, Table 3.2). Compound annual growth rates 2000–2024: Social Security 5.56%, Medicare 6.59%, Medicaid/CHIP 7.20%. Projections to 2046 apply each program's own CAGR forward twenty-two years: Social Security ~$4.9 trillion, Medicare ~$3.7 trillion, Medicaid/CHIP ~$2.9 trillion, combined ~$11.5 trillion. Total federal spending projected at the book's established 6.6% CAGR reaches approximately $27.7 trillion by 2046; the big three entitlements represent approximately 42% of that figure. The security state projection (~$3.6 trillion) is derived in footnote 3 above. No acceleration is assumed; these are straight-line trend projections. Actual figures will vary.

The regulatory apparatus

The third tentacle is the subtlest and in many ways the most insidious, because it does not show up in the federal budget at all.

The Competitive Enterprise Institute estimates that federal regulatory compliance costs the American economy $2.15 trillion per year. The National Association of Manufacturers puts the figure closer to $3 trillion. Either number is extraordinary. If U.S. federal regulation were a country, it would be one of the ten largest economies on Earth.[6]

That $2.15 trillion is a hidden tax. It does not appear on your pay stub. It is not debated during budget season. But it shows up in the price of every product you buy, the hours you spend doing paperwork, and the businesses that were never started because the compliance burden was too high. The average American household pays an estimated $16,000 per year in regulatory costs — more than they spend on food, transportation, or healthcare. Only housing costs more.[7]

In 2024, federal agencies issued a record 3,248 new final regulations and the Federal Register hit a record 106,109 pages — a nineteen percent increase over the prior year. Tax compliance alone costs the economy $536 billion annually and requires Americans to spend 7.1 billion hours — the equivalent of 3.4 million full-time workers doing nothing

---

6. The $2.15 trillion figure is from the Competitive Enterprise Institute's annual regulatory cost report: Clyde Wayne Crews Jr., Ten Thousand Commandments: An Annual Snapshot of the Federal Regulatory State (Competitive Enterprise Institute, 2024). The National Association of Manufacturers estimate of approximately $3 trillion in annual regulatory costs is from NAM, The Cost of Federal Regulation to the U.S. Economy, Manufacturing, and Small Business (2014, updated periodically). At $2.15 trillion, U.S. federal regulation would rank as approximately the 8th largest economy in the world by GDP, ahead of Italy (~$2.1 trillion) and behind France (~$2.8 trillion), per International Monetary Fund, World Economic Outlook Database (2024 estimates). At $3 trillion it would rank 6th, ahead of the United Kingdom. Both figures are estimates derived from bottom-up compliance cost modeling and carry methodological uncertainty; they are cited here as reasonable order-of-magnitude benchmarks, not precise figures.

7. The $16,000 per-household estimate is derived by dividing the CEI's $2.15 trillion total regulatory cost estimate by the approximate number of U.S. households (~130 million), per Crews, Ten Thousand Commandments (2024). For comparison, the Bureau of Labor Statistics Consumer Expenditure Survey (2023) reports average annual household spending of approximately: food, $9,985; transportation, $12,295; healthcare, $6,159; housing, $24,298. On this basis, the $16,000 regulatory cost estimate exceeds average household spending on food and healthcare and is comparable to transportation, with only housing representing a larger single expenditure category. The per-household regulatory cost figure is an allocation of an aggregate estimate and should be understood as an order-of-magnitude illustration rather than a precise individual burden.

but paperwork for a full year. That is roughly the population of Los Angeles engaged in purely unproductive activity mandated by the government.[8]

This is the regulatory apparatus: a system that controls private activity without the political cost of direct spending. It allows the government to dictate how you run your business, what products you can sell, what forms you must file, and what permissions you must obtain — all without appropriating a single dollar. And like the other two tentacles, it only grows. The last time the Office of Management and Budget attempted its own accounting of regulatory costs — in 2001 — it estimated roughly $954 billion. That figure has more than doubled in less than twenty-five years.[9]

At trend rates, the regulatory burden alone reaches an estimated $4.7 trillion per year by 2046.[10]

Force. Dependency. Control. Three systems, each growing independently, each reinforcing the others, each funded or enabled by the ability to create money from nothing. Together they describe a government that is not shrinking, not stabilizing, and not reforming. It is expanding into every corner of economic life, and the expansion is accelerating.

The national debt

The United States crossed the $5 trillion mark in national debt in the mid-1990s and was still under $6 trillion nearly a decade later. In just twenty years since, the debt has gone

8. Federal agencies issued 3,248 final rules in calendar year 2024, and the Federal Register contained 106,109 pages — a 19% increase over 2023 — per the George Washington University Regulatory Studies Center and federalregister.gov. Tax compliance cost estimate of $536 billion and 7.1 billion hours: Internal Revenue Service, IRS Data Book and Paperwork Reduction Act burden estimates, as compiled by the National Taxpayers Union Foundation, Cost of IRS Tax Compliance (2024). The 3.4 million full-time-equivalent figure is derived by dividing 7.1 billion hours by 2,080 annual working hours. The city of Los Angeles had a population of approximately 3.9 million as of the 2020 U.S. Census.

9. Office of Management and Budget, Report to Congress on the Costs and Benefits of Federal Regulations (2001), estimated total annual federal regulatory costs at approximately $954 billion (in 2001 dollars). Adjusted to 2024 dollars the figure would be higher; compared against the CEI's nominal 2024 estimate of $2.15 trillion, the increase represents more than a doubling in nominal terms over approximately twenty-three years, a compound annual growth rate of approximately 3.6%.

10. Regulatory cost CAGR 2001–2024: approximately 3.6% ($954 billion → $2.15 trillion, per OMB 2001 and CEI 2024). Projected to 2046 at trend rate: ~$4.7 trillion. No acceleration assumed; straight-line trend projection. Actual figures will vary.

up more than sixfold and now exceeds $38.7 trillion.[11] Another sixfold increase — which follows the same trajectory, no acceleration required — takes us past $200 trillion.

At $200 trillion in debt and a 3% average interest rate — roughly what the government pays today, a figure that is itself optimistic given that much of the current debt was issued during a period of declining rates that has since reversed — interest payments alone would exceed $6 trillion per year. That is approximately equal to the entire federal budget today.[12]

Government spending has risen at 6.6% per year since 1984 and currently sits at roughly $6.4 trillion annually. Projected forward twenty years at the same rate, the federal budget reaches approximately $23 trillion per year in 2046. The annual interest payment on the national debt will be roughly equal to the entire current federal budget — and the federal budget itself will exceed the total M2 money supply currently in existence.[13] *Where will the money come from?* The same place it always comes from. It will be created. And every dollar created will dilute the dollars you already hold.

The squeeze does not relent. It tightens. The same forces that made housing unaffordable, that forced both parents into the workforce, that priced the middle class out of homeownership and pushed families into debt — those forces compound. The home price-to-income ratio does not reverse. It continues.

CBDCs: the digital endpoint

If fiat money is the operating system of unchecked government growth, then a central bank digital currency is the operating system's final upgrade.

---

11. The $38.7 trillion figure reflects the U.S. national debt as of early 2026. For a real-time counter, see https://www.usdebtclock.org/

12. The weighted average interest rate on U.S. federal debt outstanding was approximately 3.2% as of late 2024 and rising, as lower-rate debt issued during the 2010s and early 2020s matures and is refinanced at current market rates. U.S. Department of the Treasury, Monthly Statement of the Public Debt (MSPD), Table III. At $200 trillion in debt and a 3% average rate, annual interest payments would total $6 trillion ($200T × 0.03 = $6T). Federal outlays in FY2024 were approximately $6.8 trillion (OMB Historical Tables, Table 1.1), making a $6 trillion interest bill approximately equal to 88% of the entire current federal budget. The 3% rate assumption is therefore modestly optimistic relative to the current trajectory.

13. Federal spending CAGR of 6.6% since 1984: derived from OMB Historical Tables, Table 1.1. Baseline of ~$6.4 trillion projected forward twenty years at 6.6% yields approximately $23 trillion by 2046 ($\$6.4T \times 1.066^{20} \approx \$23T$). U.S. M2 money supply as of early 2026 was approximately $21.5 trillion, per Federal Reserve Bank of St. Louis, FRED series WM2NS. A federal budget of $23 trillion would therefore exceed the entire current M2 money supply.

Over 130 countries are in some stage of researching, developing, or piloting a CBDC. The concept: replace physical cash and private bank deposits with a digital currency issued and controlled directly by the central bank. Every transaction visible. Every balance known. Every dollar programmable.[14]

That last word is the one that should get your attention. Programmable money means the issuer can set conditions on how it is used. It can expire — spend it by Friday or it vanishes. It can be restricted by category — approved for groceries but not for ammunition. It can be frozen — your account locked pending investigation, no warrant required. It can be geofenced — your money works in your city but not in the next state. Every complaint you have ever had about the banking system — the fees, the holds, the frozen accounts, the arbitrary rules — amplified by orders of magnitude and administered by the same government that brought you the DMV, the IRS phone line, and HealthCare.gov.

That said, let's be honest about the current state of play. The federal government is not historically excellent at building digital infrastructure. HealthCare.gov — $2.1 billion spent on a website that crashed on launch day and took months to function — is the kind of technological competence we are discussing. Private-sector attempts to build digital currencies with surveillance characteristics have not inspired confidence either. WorldCoin asked users to scan their eyeballs in exchange for digital tokens and was met with the public reception it deserved. The American public has shown consistent, bipartisan hostility to CBDC proposals whenever the concept is explained clearly. People do not want the government watching every purchase they make and holding a switch on

14. As of early 2026, more than 130 countries representing over 98% of global GDP were in some stage of CBDC research, development, or pilot, per the Atlantic Council CBDC Tracker (atlanticcouncil.org/cbdctracker). Of these, more than 60 were in advanced development, pilot, or full launch phases. China's digital yuan (e-CNY) is the most advanced major-economy CBDC, with hundreds of millions of wallets issued. The European Central Bank formally launched the digital euro investigation phase in 2021 and moved to the preparation phase in 2023.

whether their money works. The political appetite for a domestic CBDC in the United States is, at present, approximately zero.[15]

But the architecture is being built elsewhere. China's digital yuan is live. The European Central Bank's digital euro is in advanced development. The global trend is clear even if the American timeline is uncertain. And the incentive is permanent: a government addicted to monetary control will always be drawn toward the tool that maximizes it.

The appropriate response is not panic. It is the same as the response to any serious but distant threat: understand it, monitor it, and own the asset that makes it irrelevant. Bitcoin cannot be programmed. It cannot expire. It cannot be frozen by a bureaucrat. It cannot be restricted by category of purchase. In a world where CBDCs are even possible, Bitcoin is the exit.

What Bitcoin Could Mean for Government

Bitcoin has been running without interruption since January 3, 2009. No government created it. No government controls it. No government can stop it. The protocol does not know or care which party holds the White House.

Governments face a choice — not about whether Bitcoin will exist, but about how their citizens will relate to it.

The strategic reserve

The United States government now holds Bitcoin as a strategic asset. The executive order establishing the Bitcoin Strategic Reserve separated Bitcoin from altcoins — the Digital Asset Stockpile is a junk drawer of confiscated tokens that the government has no plan to add to, which limits the risk of a nation-state-level rug pull. It directed the government to explore revenue-neutral ways of acquiring additional Bitcoin, which is important because the public is not ready for aggressive federal purchasing and, frankly,

15. The Government Accountability Office estimated total federal spending on HealthCare.gov at approximately $1.7–2.1 billion through 2014, with costs continuing thereafter; the $2.1 billion figure reflects the upper range of contemporaneous congressional and GAO estimates. See: U.S. Government Accountability Office, Healthcar e.gov: Ineffective Planning and Oversight Practices Underscore the Need for Improved Contract Management (GAO-14-694, July 2014). WorldCoin — rebranded as 'World' in 2023, operated by Tools for Humanity — collected iris scans from users in exchange for a cryptocurrency allocation (WLD tokens). The project faced regulatory action in multiple countries including Germany, France, Spain, Kenya, and Hong Kong. CBDC opposition polling: a 2023 Cato Institute/YouGov survey found that 34% of Americans supported a U.S. CBDC while 49% opposed it, with opposition consistent across party affiliation once the surveillance implications were explained. Cato Institute, 'The American Public Is Not Ready for a Central Bank Digital Currency' (2023).

it gives individual citizens, businesses, and local governments more time to accumulate Bitcoin before the federal government enters the market in force.[16]

The country that holds the most Bitcoin as the protocol matures holds a structural advantage. This is game theory, not ideology. Every other nation is now forced to consider whether it can afford not to hold Bitcoin, which creates exactly the kind of competitive dynamic that accelerates adoption.

But the real importance of a strategic reserve is political. Once the government holds a meaningful stockpile of Bitcoin, that stockpile becomes a razor in every future election. If Bitcoin appreciates as the power law predicts — and every chapter of this book has argued that it will — then the reserve grows in value over the coming decades in a way that voters can see and measure. Candidates who pledge to protect and grow the reserve will have a structural advantage over candidates who want to sell it or raid it. Candidates who want to spend the reserve to fund one more program, one more war, one more stimulus package, will face an electorate that has watched the value of that reserve climb while their purchasing power eroded year after year.

This is new. This has never existed in American politics. Under fiat, the government's balance sheet is abstract — trillions in debt, trillions in obligations, all denominated in a unit that the government itself controls. Nobody can point to a pile of assets and say protect that. But a Bitcoin reserve changes the equation. It gives voters something concrete to defend: an asset that appreciates precisely because the government cannot print more of it. The political incentive to protect the reserve aligns perfectly with the economic incentive to stop debasing the currency. For a government addicted to spending, that alignment alone makes a strategic reserve a worthwhile endeavor.

A Bitcoin standard

16. Executive Order, 'Establishment of the Strategic Bitcoin Reserve and United States Digital Asset Stockpile,' signed March 6, 2025; published in the Federal Register March 11, 2025 (90 FR 11791, document 2025-03992). The order established the Strategic Bitcoin Reserve, capitalized with all Bitcoin held by the Department of the Treasury forfeited through criminal or civil asset forfeiture proceedings. Government Bitcoin deposited into the reserve shall not be sold. The U.S. Digital Asset Stockpile was established separately to hold other confiscated digital assets, with no directive to add to it beyond future forfeitures. The Secretaries of Treasury and Commerce were directed to develop budget-neutral strategies for acquiring additional Bitcoin without incremental cost to taxpayers. The U.S. government held an estimated 207,000 Bitcoin at the time of signing. Full text: whitehouse.gov/presidenti al-actions/2025/03/establishment-of-the-strategic-bitcoin-reserve-and-united-states-digital-asset-stockpile/

The longer-horizon scenario — one in which the dollar, or the global monetary system, is partially or fully backed by Bitcoin. Not imminent. Perhaps not in the reader's lifetime. But worth understanding as the logical endpoint.

Under a Bitcoin standard, the government cannot create money. It can only spend what it collects in taxes or borrows from willing lenders — lenders who know they will be repaid in money that cannot be debased. Wars become expensive in a way that voters can see. Bureaucracies must justify their budgets against genuine opportunity costs. The administrative state shrinks — not because anyone dismantles it, but because the money to sustain it no longer appears from nowhere.

But it is not just about constraint. It is about transparency. Bitcoin is a public ledger. Every transaction is recorded, permanently, on a blockchain that anyone with an internet connection can read. Imagine a government whose spending is auditable — not by Congress six months after the fact, not by a Government Accountability Office report, but by any citizen, in real time, from their phone. Imagine being able to trace a dollar from the moment it leaves the Treasury to the moment it arrives at its destination. Imagine the end of black budgets, slush funds, and the creative accounting that allows agencies to spend billions with no meaningful oversight.

This is what hard money does to institutions. It does not just limit how much a government can spend. It illuminates how it spends. It makes waste visible. It makes corruption traceable. It makes the $2.15 trillion regulatory apparatus, the estimated $100 billion intelligence budget, and the $6.8 trillion federal budget subject to the kind of scrutiny that the current system is specifically designed to avoid.

Hard money makes government responsive. It ties spending to consent. It restores the feedback loop between the people who pay and the people who spend. And for the first time in human history, it gives ordinary citizens the tools to verify that the loop is working.

A friendly regulatory environment

The most immediately actionable scenario and the one that most directly benefits working-class Americans right now.

The wish list is short. Eliminate or dramatically raise the de minimis exemption for Bitcoin transactions — so that buying groceries with Bitcoin does not generate a taxable event on a $47 purchase.[17] Provide legal clarity for self-custody — make it explicit that holding your own private keys is a right, not a regulatory gray area. Create friendly mining environments that allow American energy producers to capture stranded and curtailed energy. In West Texas, in North Dakota, in Appalachian coal country, there are energy resources that cannot be economically transported to market but that can power a Bitcoin miner sitting next to the wellhead or the plant. Every one of those miners is a job. Every one of those operations is tax revenue for a rural county. Every kilowatt of stranded energy converted to Bitcoin is wealth created in communities that fiat monetary policy has left behind for decades. Establish inheritance rules that treat Bitcoin like property rather than a regulatory landmine, so that a father who stacks sats for his children can pass them on without a legal nightmare.

This costs the government nothing except the control they were never going to have anyway. Bitcoin does not ask permission. The protocol runs regardless of what any legislature decides. The choice is not between having Bitcoin and not having it. The choice is between making it easy for American citizens to benefit and making it hard — and the countries that make it easy will attract the capital, the talent, and the next generation of financial infrastructure.

What Sound Money Rebuilds

Everything fiat corroded — patience, thrift, community investment, generational thinking, the willingness to sacrifice present comfort for future security — sound money restores. Not by decree. Not by ideology. By incentive.

When your money gains value over time instead of losing it, saving becomes rational again. When saving is rational, time preference drops. When time preference drops, people plan further ahead. They invest in durable things — homes, businesses, relationships, children, communities. They think in decades instead of pay periods. They build instead of consume.

Talk to the families that have been stacking for years. They are not just wealthier. They are calmer. They have margin. They have the luxury of thinking about what they want to

---

17. Under current U.S. tax law (Internal Revenue Code Section 1001, and IRS Notice 2014-21), every disposition of Bitcoin — including purchases of goods and services — is a taxable event requiring calculation of gain or loss based on the asset's cost basis. There is no de minimis exemption for small transactions. This creates significant compliance friction for everyday Bitcoin use: a $47 grocery purchase requires the buyer to calculate and record any capital gain or loss on the Bitcoin spent. The Virtual Currency Tax Fairness Act, introduced in multiple sessions of Congress, would establish a de minimis exemption (proposed at $200 or $600 per transaction in various versions) for personal-use cryptocurrency transactions. As of early 2026 no such exemption had been enacted into law.

do instead of scrambling to cover what they have to do. The fathers and mothers in those families have time. Time for their kids. Time for their neighbors. Time for the kind of slow, unglamorous community involvement that makes a neighborhood feel like home.

Local circular economies begin to make sense when the money circulating through them holds its value. The barber who accepts Bitcoin from the diner owner who accepts Bitcoin from the mechanic creates a loop that keeps value in the community instead of leaking it to a corporate headquarters or a government program. Churches and mutual aid networks that could operate on sound money would not need grants from agencies with agendas. They would serve their communities because their communities could afford to fund them directly.

The family heals. Not through any program or policy — through arithmetic. When one parent's income holds its value, the other parent has a choice. When savings grow instead of shrinking, financial stress — the leading predictor of divorce, the leading driver of two-job households, the invisible force behind a thousand forms of family breakdown — loses its grip.[18] When the future looks better than the present, birth rates could recover, marriage makes sense again, and children grow up in homes where someone has time to be present.

The generational wealth transfer that fiat destroyed becomes possible again. A father who stacks sats for twenty years can hand his children something that has not been halved, quartered, and halved again by the time they receive it. The half-life of money under fiat — roughly eleven years at 6% M2 growth — means that $100,000 saved today is worth $15,378 in today's purchasing power by the time it reaches the next generation.[19] Under Bitcoin, that same discipline compounds in the other direction. The inheritance is not a melting ice cube. It is a foundation.

None of this happens overnight. Bitcoin does not fix culture by magic. But it fixes the incentive structure that broke the culture — and when the incentives are right, people tend to do the right things. Not because they are told to. Because it makes sense.

---

18. On financial stress as a predictor of divorce and driver of dual-income households, see sourcing in Chapter Twelve, footnote 11: Bureau of Labor Statistics; U.S. Census Bureau; Jeffrey Dew, 'Bank on It: Thrifty Couples Are the Happiest,' National Marriage Project at the University of Virginia (2012); Sonya Britt et al., 'Financial Arguments as a Predictor of Divorce,' Family Relations (2012).

19. The $15,378 figure is derived from the 6% M2 CAGR established in Chapter Four. At 6% annual monetary debasement, money loses half its purchasing power every 11.9 years (half-life = ln(2) / ln(1.06)). Over thirty years, $100,000 retains approximately $100,000 / 2^(30/11.9) ≈ $15,378 in real purchasing power. Federal Reserve Bank of St. Louis, FRED series WM2NS. See Chapter Four for full methodology.

The machine described in this chapter is powerful. It has been running for over fifty years. It has reshaped government, education, family, community, and the very way Americans relate to time and to each other. But it has a weakness that no machine in human history has ever had to confront: there is now a money it cannot print, cannot confiscate, and cannot debase.

Every day that money exists, the machine gets a little weaker. And the people get a little stronger.

The next chapter shows you exactly how to start.

Chapter Fourteen

Get Off Zero

The Swiss Bank in Your Pocket

In 2016, Barack Obama said something about Bitcoin that was meant as a warning. He asked, with genuine incredulity, why anyone would want to walk around with a Swiss bank account in their pocket.[1]

Bitcoin influencers laughed at him. They posted the clip with fire emojis and thank-you notes, treating it like free advertising. *A Swiss bank account in your pocket? Yes please!* But I think they missed what Obama was actually saying, and I think what he was saying matters — especially for the reader who has made it to this final chapter.

Obama was not making a technical argument. He was making a *responsibility* argument. He was saying: are you sure you want this? Are you sure you want to be in charge of your own money, with no institution standing behind you, no fraud department to call, no FDIC insurance to catch you if something goes wrong? He was speaking to a public that has spent its entire life inside a system where somebody else handles the hard parts. The bank holds your money. The government insures the bank. The credit card company reverses fraudulent charges. Someone is always there. You are never truly alone with your wealth.

And he was right. It *is* a big responsibility. That is the entire point.

1. Barack Obama, remarks at South by Southwest Interactive Conference, Austin, Texas, March 11, 2016. White House transcript: obamawhitehouse.archives.gov/the-press-office/2016/03/14/remarks-president-south-south west-interactive. The remark was made during a panel discussion on encryption and government access to digital devices, in the context of the Apple–FBI dispute over the San Bernardino shooter's iPhone. Obama used the phrase as a warning about the consequences of unbreakable encryption for tax enforcement and law enforcement access, not as a reference to Bitcoin specifically — though it has been widely adopted by the Bitcoin community as an apt description of Bitcoin's self-custody model.

If you have read this far, you know what happens when you hand that responsibility to someone else. You have seen what fiat money does to wages, to housing, to families, to an entire culture's ability to plan for the future. You have watched the government grow along three axes simultaneously — force, dependency, and control — each funded by its ability to create money from nothing. You have seen the math on where this road leads. You know what the responsible parties have done with the trust you placed in them.

So when Obama asks *why would anyone want a Swiss bank account in their pocket,* the answer is no longer abstract. The answer is: because the people who run the current bank are debasing everything in it. Because the institution you were told to trust has been stealing from you in slow motion for more than fifty years. Because the alternative to self-sovereignty is the system you have been living in, and that system is failing you.

Bitcoin. The Swiss bank account in your pocket. Not a joke. Not a slogan. A responsibility. The same responsibility that the wealthiest families in the world have always understood — that if you want to preserve wealth across generations, you do not leave it in the hands of governments that can debase it, banks that can freeze it, or institutions that can change the rules whenever it suits them. You take custody. You take control. You take it seriously.

The Swiss did not build their banking reputation on recklessness. They built it on precision, security, privacy, and long time horizons. That is exactly the mindset this chapter asks you to adopt. Not *download an app and you're set.* This is your family's wealth. Treat it accordingly.

The Most Important Things

If you remember nothing else from this chapter — if you skip every other section and come back to this one — remember this: your Bitcoin must never have a single point of failure.

Not one seed phrase, device, company, or method. Do not put all your eggs in one basket. In Bitcoin, that is not a proverb. It is the difference between generational wealth and an empty address.

1. Know the two risks.

Every custody decision you will ever make is a trade between two risks. The risk of loss: your Bitcoin becomes inaccessible to you. A house fire. A forgotten hiding spot. A death without a plan. A defective device. The risk of theft: your Bitcoin becomes accessible to someone else. A scammer. A burglar. A hacked exchange. A weak key. Every choice that lowers one risk tends to raise the other.

Make extra copies of your seed phrase and it becomes harder to lose — and easier to steal. Memorize it and no burglar on Earth can find it — but it dies with you, and memory fades sooner than people think. Hand your coins to an exchange and the loss risk is no longer yours to carry — and neither are the coins. No arrangement drives both risks to zero. What remains is the discipline of weighing them, and the humility of never betting everything on one answer.

Custodians have lost vastly more coins than self-custody ever has — measured across Bitcoin's entire history, it is not close.[2] Against theft, your own keys remain the strongest position available to anyone. Loss is the honest trade-off, and loss risk depends on you. Your discipline. Your record-keeping. Your household. The method that best protects a meticulous person can endanger a disorganized one. There is no shame in that calculation — only in refusing to make it.

2. Do your own research — and verify what you can.

No one can hand you the perfect setup — not this book, not a podcast, not the friend who brought you here. There is only the arrangement that fits your life: your household, your discipline, your tolerance for being your own bank versus trusting someone else's. For many people the honest answer is a mix — some Bitcoin here, some there, so no single mistake can take it all.

Then verify what you chose. Don't trust, verify is the oldest instinct in Bitcoin, and it is not a slogan for programmers. It means: check that your backup actually restores. Check that the address on the screen matches the address on the device. Check that the company behind your wallet publishes its code, answers its critics, and fixes what it breaks. Trust is a cost. Spend it deliberately.

In the summer of 2026, that instinct was worth a fortune. A firmware bug in one of the most respected hardware wallets — Bitcoin-only, code published for anyone to inspect — quietly weakened the randomness behind its seed phrases for five years. Attackers eventually reconstructed thousands of keys and swept more than a thousand Bitcoin.[3]

---

2. Mt. Gox, 2014: approximately 850,000 BTC lost — more than every hardware-wallet failure combined, by orders of magnitude.

3. Coinkite Inc., 'Coldcard Security Advisory,' July 30, 2026, blog.coinkite.com. A firmware error introduced in March 2021 routed seed generation through a predictable software generator instead of the device's hardware random number generator, reducing effective entropy to roughly 40 bits on affected devices against the expected 128. Galaxy Research attributed more than 1,800 BTC swept from over 5,000 addresses as of August 3, 2026, with sweeps ongoing. Seeds created with at least fifty user-supplied dice rolls were not at risk. Firmware updates cannot repair previously generated seeds.

But the device had always offered an option most users skipped: adding your own dice rolls to seed generation — physical randomness no software bug can fake. The users who rolled the dice were untouched. They had refused to take the machine's word for the one thing they could check themselves.

You will not verify everything. Nobody does. You cannot personally audit firmware, and you cannot see inside an exchange's cold storage. That is fine — as long as you know what you are taking on faith. Every unverified link in your setup is a risk you are carrying, whether you feel it or not. Name them. Count them. Then spread across them or shrink them. What you cannot verify, you must watch — which is the sixth principle's job.

3. Mitigate the risks — and know the steps.

If your research lands on a mix, good — that is the principle working. Here is the menu, with honest trade-offs.

Start with the seed phrase. A seed phrase is twelve or twenty-four ordinary English words that represent the private key to your Bitcoin. Whoever holds the words holds the coins. If the words are lost, the Bitcoin is gone — not frozen, not delayed, not recoverable by customer service. Gone permanently. The coins sit on the blockchain forever, visible to everyone and movable by no one.

A hardware wallet, with the seed phrase on paper or metal in a safe. This is where everyone starts, and for modest holdings it remains sound. Paper burns and dissolves in a flood; steel plates survive both. Choose a Bitcoin-only device whose code is published for inspection, keep the firmware current, and follow the manufacturer's security announcements. This arrangement defends well against theft. Its weakness is concentration: one key, one device, one vendor.

Seedless wallets. A newer generation of wallets eliminates the seed phrase entirely, splitting the key so that no complete set of words ever exists to be photographed, copied, or stolen.[4] Recovery runs through hardware you hold and the provider's process. The trade-off is dependence — on the company's design, and on the company still existing when you need it. That is a different risk, not a smaller one. For the person more afraid of their own record-keeping than of any company, it can be the right trade.

Multi-signature wallets. A multi-sig arrangement requires two or more keys — say, any two of three — to move funds. You hold one. Your spouse or a trusted party holds

4. As of this writing, the most widely available seedless Bitcoin hardware wallet is Bitkey, made by Block, Inc., which splits key material between the user's phone, a hardware device, and a recovery server. Reference is descriptive, not an endorsement; evaluate any product against its current documentation.

another. The third sits in a separate location. No single lost key strands you, and no single stolen key robs you. This is the strongest structure available to an ordinary saver, and July 2026 wrote its fine print in public: the keys must come from different devices made by different manufacturers. Three keys from one vendor's flawed firmware is one point of failure wearing three costumes. The costs — more setup, more to track, harder inheritance — are why multi-sig earns its keep as holdings grow, not on day one.

The exchange — custodial storage — carries risk of its own. Handing coins to an exchange does not eliminate key risk; it transfers it. You cannot lose keys you never held — but the exchange can, and exchanges have.[5] They have also learned brutal lessons from a decade of failures, and the serious ones now run custody with a discipline most individuals never match. You are trading your failure modes for theirs. Small amounts while you learn: sensible. Your life savings: only if you weighed both risks and chose it — never because you drifted.

Whatever you choose, mitigation is only half of this principle. The other half is competence.

Self-custody means moving your Bitcoin off the exchange and into a wallet for which you — and only you — hold the private key. This is the moment you go from having an IOU to having actual Bitcoin. Download a Bitcoin-only mobile wallet. When you set it up, it will generate a seed phrase — write it down and secure it before you do anything else. Then you are ready to practice.

But before you move your whole stack — practice. Send ten dollars' worth. Watch it leave the exchange. Watch it arrive in your wallet. Get comfortable with the process. Send another ten dollars. Do it again. Learn what a receiving address looks like. Learn how confirmations work. Learn the rhythm of it. If you make a mistake — and you might, because everyone is clumsy the first time — you made it with ten dollars instead of ten thousand. That is the entire point of practicing. You would not learn to drive on the highway. Do not learn self-custody with your life savings. Start small, get confident, then move the rest.

---

5. QuadrigaCX, once Canada's largest cryptocurrency exchange, collapsed in 2019 when founder Gerald Cotten died as the only person with access to customer funds. The Ontario Securities Commission later found most of the money was already gone — Cotten had been trading away customer deposits for years, leaving a shortfall of approximately C$169 million. Ontario Securities Commission staff review, June 2020.

The habit I recommend while you learn is simple: buy on the exchange, then transfer to your own wallet on a regular schedule. From there, follow your risk tolerance decisions to determine where your Bitcoin will actually live.

And know the steps in both directions: how to move your Bitcoin, how to recover it, how to sell it. If you do not know them, you are not in control. You are hoping.

4. Know what you own.

There are four ways people say they "own Bitcoin," and only one of them puts the keys in your hand. Know which one you are holding, because they fail in different ways.

When you buy Bitcoin on an exchange, you do not own Bitcoin. You own an IOU. The exchange holds the private key — which is the actual right to move and spend the Bitcoin — and gives you a balance on a screen. This is similar to the relationship you have with your bank. The money in your checking account is not in a vault with your name on it. It is a number in a database, and the bank owes you that number. You trust them to honor the debt.

The question is whether that trust is warranted. In 2022, FTX answered that question for the entire cryptocurrency industry.

FTX was the second-largest cryptocurrency exchange in the world. It was led by Sam Bankman-Fried, who was celebrated by the media, praised by regulators, invited to testify before Congress, and endorsed by celebrities and politicians on both sides of the aisle. It had millions of customers and held billions of dollars in customer funds. It also turned out to be a fraud. Bankman-Fried had been using customer deposits to fund his own trading firm, political donations, and personal spending. When the truth came out, customers tried to withdraw their funds. The money was gone. Billions of dollars — the savings, the portfolios, the futures of ordinary people — simply vanished. Not because Bitcoin failed. Because *custody* failed. The people who lost everything on FTX had Bitcoin on the exchange. They had a number on a screen. They did not have their keys.[6]

Not your keys, not your Bitcoin.

---

6. FTX Trading Ltd. filed for Chapter 11 bankruptcy on November 11, 2022. Sam Bankman-Fried was convicted on seven counts of fraud and conspiracy by a federal jury on November 2, 2023. He was sentenced to 25 years in federal prison on March 28, 2024. Customer losses from the fraud were estimated at approximately $8 billion. The FTX bankruptcy estate subsequently recovered assets — aided in part by appreciation in Solana holdings and the sale of FTX's stake in Anthropic — sufficient to repay creditors at approximately 118–119% of allowed claim values as of their November 2022 dollar-equivalent holdings. Customers who held Bitcoin on FTX did not receive Bitcoin; they received the dollar equivalent of their Bitcoin at November 2022 valuations, missing all subsequent appreciation.

There are two more ways to hold a number that follows Bitcoin. You can buy shares of a company that holds Bitcoin in its treasury — you met the largest one in Chapter Seven. You own the company: its coins, but also its debt, its decisions, its executives. Or you can buy shares of a fund that tracks the price. The fund holds the coins; you hold a claim on the fund, minus an annual fee, inside a brokerage account, on Wall Street's hours. Both are exposure to the price. Neither is Bitcoin. For some savers — inside a retirement account, say — they may be the only door available, and exposure honestly beats zero. But do not mistake the wrapper for the coins. An IOU, a share, and a fund all depend on someone honoring a promise. Bitcoin in your custody depends on no one.

5. Watch for wolves.

Two kinds of wolves circle this market. The first wants the Bitcoin you have. The second wants to sell you his coin instead. Learn both faces, because both count on you not looking closely.

Start with the rule that will save you from the single most common way people lose their Bitcoin:

If someone asks for your seed phrase, they are robbing you. Period. No exceptions. Not your exchange. Not your wallet company. Not someone claiming to be customer support. Not someone who emailed you about a security update. Not a website asking you to "verify" your wallet. Not anyone, ever, for any reason. No legitimate entity will ever ask for your seed phrase. The moment someone does, you are being targeted by a thief.

The wolves wear uniforms now. They call as your exchange's fraud department, text as your wallet's support team, and buy ads so their fake login pages outrank the real ones. All of them manufacture urgency — act now, your account is at risk — because urgency turns careful people into careless ones. Slow down. Legitimate companies do not call you.

The second wolf is friendlier. He does not want your Bitcoin. He wants to sell you his.

The pitch is always the same: the next Bitcoin — earlier, cheaper, faster. Remember what you already know. Bitcoin has no founder waiting to sell, no insider allocation, no developer fund. Every other digital asset in existence was built by someone who got theirs before you got yours.

Complexity is where this wolf hunts, and it is why this book keeps saying Bitcoin only. In early 2025, North Korea stole $1.5 billion in Ethereum from Bybit, one of the largest cryptocurrency exchanges in the world. The attack did not crack a password. It targeted the complexity of the Ethereum protocol itself: the man signing the transaction — the man safeguarding the funds — could not tell where the money was going, because on a protocol that complex, you often cannot verify what you are authorizing. He did not know what he was signing. That is not a personal failure. It is a design failure.[7]

A Bitcoin transaction is simple: a specific amount, from one address to another, verifiable before you sign. That simplicity is not a limitation. It is what makes Bitcoin securable by ordinary people using ordinary tools.

Bitcoin only. Open source. Don't trust, verify. These are not bumper stickers. They are survival tools.

6. Monitor the ecosystem.

Your setup is not a crockpot. You cannot set it and forget it. Whatever mix you chose, news that affects it will break somewhere — and you want to be standing where it lands. That place is almost never the evening news.

News about your wallet, your exchange, or Bitcoin itself hits social media hours or days before it reaches any other medium. Follow the companies behind your setup. Follow the researchers who scrutinize them. The Bitcoin community is vocal, opinionated, and ruthless about calling out anything that falls short — use that to your advantage. You do not need to be online all day. A few minutes, a few trusted sources, a habit of checking before you assume: that is the whole discipline.

Here is why it pays. In the summer of 2026 — the firmware bug from the second principle — the flaw was disclosed within hours of the first theft. Fixed firmware shipped the next day. Competing vendors published their own analyses of a rival's product. Volunteer researchers began combing every major wallet for the same class of bug. And one week before the attack, nine of Bitcoin's largest firms — rivals among them — had

---

7. Federal Bureau of Investigation, Public Service Announcement, 'North Korea Responsible for $1.5 Billion Bybit Hack,' February 26, 2025; fbi.gov/investigate/cyber/alerts/2025/north-korea-responsible-for-1-5-billion-bybit-hack. The attack occurred February 21, 2025, and was attributed by the FBI to North Korean state-sponsored hackers operating under the designation TraderTraitor. The attack exploited a compromised developer's machine at a third-party software provider to inject malicious code that altered the displayed destination of a multi-signature Ethereum transaction — making the transaction appear legitimate to the human signers while redirecting funds to attacker-controlled addresses. The Bybit hack is the largest cryptocurrency theft in recorded history.

already committed millions to fund exactly this kind of security work.[8] The holders who were watching moved first. And no one was bailed out, which is the point: in the fiat system, failure is hidden, socialized, and repeated. In Bitcoin, failure is public, paid for, and fixed. Nobody can print away the lesson.

Get Off Zero

The most important number in Bitcoin is not the price of a single coin or twenty-one million total supply. The most important number is the distance between zero and one — between owning no Bitcoin and owning any Bitcoin at all.

If you own zero Bitcoin, you are fully exposed to everything described in this book. Your savings lose purchasing power every year. Your wages fall behind the cost of housing, education, healthcare, and food. You are on the wrong side of the Cantillon Effect, watching your labor eroded by a monetary system designed to benefit the people closest to the money printers. You have no exit.

If you own *any* Bitcoin — ten dollars' worth, fifty dollars' worth, whatever you can afford this week — you have an exit. You have crossed the line. You are no longer at zero. Everything after that is a matter of degree. Getting off zero is the only step that is truly binary, and it is the only step that matters today.

Bitcoin is divisible to one hundred millionth of a coin. The smallest unit — a single satoshi — is worth a fraction of a penny. You do not need to buy a whole Bitcoin any more than you need to buy a whole share of Berkshire Hathaway to invest in the stock market. Unit bias — the psychological trap of thinking that because a single Bitcoin is out of reach you cannot afford it — is exactly that: a trap. It keeps you at zero. It keeps you on the wrong side of the line.

You saw the data. Every five-year window of dollar-cost averaging in Bitcoin's history — every single one — was profitable. The person who put in $50 a week made money. The person who put in $25 a week made money. The person who put in $10 a week made

---

8. Bitcoin Security Consortium, announced July 23, 2026: nine firms, fifteen million dollars over three years to fund open-source Bitcoin security research. The volunteer response to the July attack was organized in part by security researcher Rob Hamilton, whose Bitcoin Red Team coordinated bug hunts across major wallets in the weeks that followed. AI-assisted code analysis now accelerates vulnerability discovery for attackers and defenders alike. The next year or two will be turbulent as old code meets new scrutiny; after that, expect systems hardened like never before, and new code shipped hardened from the start.

money. The returns ranged from 48% to 2,733%. The amount does not need to be large. It needs to be consistent, and it needs to start.[9]

Here is what getting off zero looks like:

Choose a Bitcoin-only exchange and set up automatic recurring purchases on a schedule you can live with — weekly, biweekly, monthly. The money comes out of your bank account automatically and you do not have to think about it. It becomes a habit, like the electric bill. You stop wondering whether this is the right week to buy. Every week is the right week, because you are not trying to time the market. You are trying to leave it behind.

There are other on-ramps as well. Peer-to-peer Bitcoin apps let you buy directly from other users. Bitcoin ATMs exist in most American cities.[10] Some services send Bitcoin directly to a self-custody wallet you already control, skipping the exchange entirely. The on-ramps exist. They are simple. The hardest part is the decision, and if you have read this far, you have already made it.

Set your amount. Make it something you will not miss — something that, if it went to zero, would not change your life. Twenty-five dollars a week. Fifty dollars a week. Whatever fits. Then do not touch it. Do not check the price every day. Do not panic when the price drops thirty percent, because it will drop thirty percent, probably more than once, and the data from Chapter Nine tells you exactly what happens to people who keep buying through the dips: they end up ahead. Every single time, in every five-year window, in the entire history of the asset.

Get off zero. Everything else flows from that.

How Bitcoin Moves

One of the most common objections to Bitcoin as everyday money is speed. *You can't wait ten minutes for a block confirmation to buy a cheeseburger.* This is true. You also can't wait three days for your bank to settle a wire transfer, but you use a credit card anyway. The solution in both systems is the same: layers.

The Bitcoin base layer — the blockchain itself — is designed for final settlement. When a transaction is confirmed on-chain, it is permanent. Irreversible. Secured by more computing power than any network on Earth. But it takes roughly ten minutes per block,

---

9. Dollar-cost averaging methodology and full results are documented in Chapter Nine. Summary: 2,351 five-year windows tested, September 2014 – February 2026. Every window profitable. Worst return approximately 48%; median 266%; average 555%; best 2,733%.

10. Bitcoin ATM locations are searchable at coinatmradar.com. As of early 2026, more than 30,000 Bitcoin ATMs were operating across the United States, representing the largest Bitcoin ATM network in the world.

and it can cost anywhere from a few cents to several dollars depending on how many transactions are competing for space. The base layer is the vault. It is where large amounts move with maximum security.

For everyday transactions — the cup of coffee, the grocery run, the Steak 'n Shake steakburger — there is the Lightning Network. Lightning is a second-layer protocol built on top of Bitcoin that enables instant, near-free transactions. You can send a few dollars' worth of Bitcoin across the world in less than a second for a fraction of a penny in fees. If the base layer is the Federal Reserve settling accounts between banks, Lightning is the debit card you use at the checkout counter.

The analogy to the existing financial system is direct. When you swipe your Visa card, the merchant does not receive dollars in real time. Settlement between the merchant's bank, Visa, and your bank happens days or weeks later. You experience an instant transaction, but final settlement is deferred. Lightning works the same way — transactions are instant, and final settlement to the base layer happens when participants choose to close their payment channels. The difference is that Bitcoin's final settlement takes minutes instead of days, and no one takes a two to three percent processing fee.

Transaction fees on the base layer deserve a brief explanation because they confuse newcomers. Bitcoin fees are not based on the dollar amount you send — you can send a million dollars for the same fee as sending ten dollars. Fees are based on the data size of the transaction and the current demand for block space. When many people are competing to get their transactions confirmed, fees rise. When demand is low, fees drop to near zero. For a long-term holder who is simply moving Bitcoin from an exchange to a personal wallet, timing the transfer during a low-fee period is easy and saves money. For someone spending Bitcoin through Lightning, base-layer fees are largely irrelevant. Bitcoin transaction fees are one of the most authentic examples of a free market in action.

Taxes

In the United States, Bitcoin is classified as property by the IRS. This means that every time you sell Bitcoin, spend Bitcoin, or exchange Bitcoin for another asset, you create a taxable event. If you bought Bitcoin at $30,000 and spent it when it was worth $100,000, you owe capital gains tax on the $70,000 difference — even if you just used it to buy a cheeseburger. The gain is the gain, regardless of what you bought with it.[11]

This is not a reason to avoid Bitcoin. It is a reason to be smart about it.

The most important distinction is between short-term and long-term capital gains. If you hold Bitcoin for more than one year before selling or spending, you pay long-term capital gains rates — which, for most working-class Americans, are significantly lower than ordinary income tax rates and may be as low as zero percent depending on your income. If you hold for less than a year, you pay your ordinary income tax rate. The strategy practically writes itself: buy and hold for at least a year before you spend anything.[12]

If you are dollar-cost averaging — buying small amounts every week — each purchase has its own cost basis and its own holding clock. This creates a record-keeping burden that can get complicated if you are making frequent purchases and occasional sales. Several software services connect to your exchange accounts and automate the tracking. They are worth the modest subscription fee. The alternative — ignoring it and hoping the IRS does not notice — is how good people turn a Bitcoin success story into a tax nightmare.

One more thing, and I want to be direct about this: do not try to hide your Bitcoin gains from the IRS. Do not skip reporting. Do not convince yourself that because Bitcoin is decentralized, the government cannot find you. They can and they will. Exchanges report to the IRS. The blockchain is a public ledger. The tools for tracing transactions

---

11. Internal Revenue Service, Notice 2014-21 (2014-16 I.R.B. 938). The IRS classifies Bitcoin and other convertible virtual currencies as property for federal tax purposes. General tax principles applicable to property transactions apply to all transactions using virtual currency. Every disposition — including sales, exchanges, and purchases of goods or services — is a taxable event requiring the taxpayer to calculate and report gain or loss based on cost basis. There is no de minimis exemption for small transactions.

12. Long-term capital gains tax rates for tax year 2024, per IRS Revenue Procedure 2023-34 and IRS Publication 550: 0% for single filers with taxable income up to $47,025; 0% for married filing jointly with taxable income up to $94,050. The 15% rate applies up to $518,900 (single) or $583,750 (married filing jointly); the 20% rate applies above these thresholds. A Bitcoin holder who has held for more than twelve months and whose taxable income falls below the 0% threshold pays no federal capital gains tax on the sale. State capital gains taxes vary and may apply regardless of the federal rate.

get better every year. And the penalties for tax evasion are not a fine and a stern letter — they are federal charges that can end with you in a cell.[13]

I am not saying this because I love taxes. You have read this entire book. You know exactly how I feel about a government that debases your currency and then taxes you on the nominal gains that debasement creates. The game is rigged, and the tax code is part of the rigging. But I also know what the government *is.* I have spent this entire book showing you what it is. It is a machine with the power to destroy your life if you give it a reason to, and it does not fight fair. You do not beat that machine by cheating on your 1040. You beat it by building wealth it cannot debase. That is what Bitcoin is for. Pay your taxes. Stack your sats. Play the long game.

Find an accountant who understands Bitcoin. They exist in every state now, and the consultation is worth the cost.

Spending and Living on Bitcoin

There is a paradox at the heart of being a Bitcoiner: why would you spend an asset you believe is going up in value?

The answer is that you should not think of spending Bitcoin the way you think of spending dollars. You are not reaching into a depreciating pile and hoping there is enough left at the end of the month. You are reaching into an appreciating one. That changes the psychology entirely. Every purchase made in Bitcoin carries a question that never occurs when you swipe a credit card: *is this worth my Bitcoin?*

That question — *is this worth my Bitcoin?* — is a more powerful financial filter than any budget app ever invented. It is a discipline mechanism that operates at the point of purchase. The frivolous expense that would have gone on the Visa without a second thought now gets scrutinized. The impulse buy pauses. The time preference lowers. You are not being asked to live like a monk. You are being asked to consider whether what you are buying is worth the future purchasing power you are giving up. Sometimes the answer is yes. Buy the steak dinner. Take the vacation. Live your life. But ask the question first.

---

13. Cryptocurrency exchanges are required to report customer transactions to the IRS pursuant to the Infrastructure Investment and Jobs Act of 2021, which expanded the definition of 'broker' to include digital asset trading platforms. Broker reporting on Form 1099-DA began with transactions in calendar year 2025. The blockchain is a public, immutable record of every Bitcoin transaction; specialized blockchain analytics firms provide government agencies with tools to trace Bitcoin flows between addresses. The IRS Criminal Investigation division has successfully prosecuted numerous cases of cryptocurrency tax evasion using these tools.

The merchant ecosystem for Bitcoin is growing rapidly. Steak 'n Shake accepts Bitcoin directly at the counter. Major retailers, telecoms, and technology companies accept Bitcoin through payment processors and gift card services. Bitcoin merchant adoption grew more than fifty percent in 2025 alone.[14] The infrastructure exists. It is expanding every month.

Most serious Bitcoiners handle spending the same way: they maintain a small amount of Bitcoin in a Lightning-enabled mobile wallet for daily purchases, while their core savings stack — the long-term wealth, the generational wealth — stays in cold storage and does not get touched. This is not complicated. It is the same principle as having a checking account for daily expenses and a retirement account you do not raid for pizza money. One is for living. The other is for building.

And for the reader who wants to take this further — who wants to live on a Bitcoin standard, not just invest in one — you can get paid in Bitcoin. Services exist that allow you to route a portion of your paycheck directly into Bitcoin without your employer needing to do anything different. Your employer pays you in dollars the way they always have. The service converts the portion you specify into Bitcoin and deposits it into your wallet. You choose the percentage — ten percent, fifty percent, all of it. The conversion happens automatically every pay cycle. You are dollar-cost averaging with your paycheck, which is the most natural DCA rhythm there is, because it is tied to the thing that actually generates your wealth: your labor. As adoption grows, more employers will follow. But you do not have to wait for your employer to figure it out. The infrastructure exists today for any worker in America to receive part or all of their compensation in Bitcoin.

And once you have been in the Bitcoin world for a while — once you understand what it means to save in something that appreciates rather than depreciates — you may find yourself wanting to earn it directly. Not just convert your paycheck, but sell your products and your labor in exchange for Bitcoin. If you are a small business owner, a freelancer, a contractor, a farmer at a Saturday market, or a retailer with a storefront, this is remarkably simple. Generate a Bitcoin receiving address or a Lightning invoice, convert

---

14. Bitcoin merchant adoption grew approximately 53% in 2025, driven in significant part by Block Inc.'s Square point-of-sale platform enabling merchants to accept Bitcoin payments with no processing fees through 2027. Benzinga, January 5, 2026, citing BTC Map data and Block Inc. figures. River Financial, 'What's Driving Bitcoin Adoption in 2026' (2026), reports Lightning Network volume grew 300% in 2025 as the average Lightning transaction size increased from $24 to $223, indicating expansion from micropayments into mainstream commercial transactions.

it to a QR code, and post it. On your website. On a card by the register. On a sign at your booth. A customer scans the code with their phone, confirms the amount, and the Bitcoin arrives in your wallet in seconds. No credit card processor taking two to three percent. No chargeback risk. No waiting days for settlement. You provided the value. You received sound money in return. That is the oldest and most honest transaction in the world, and Bitcoin makes it available to any business of any size with nothing more than a phone and a printed QR code.

The Family Bitcoin Plan

In Chapter Eight, Jake Hartman started giving his daughter Emma half her weekly allowance in dollars and half in Bitcoin. By the time she was fifteen, she had started her first business. By twenty-three, she was running it. The allowance was not a lottery ticket. It was an education — in saving, in responsibility, in the difference between money that loses value over time and money that gains it.

The Saturday allowance ritual is one of the most powerful tools a parent has for teaching children about money. A few minutes each week. A few satoshis into a wallet. The child watches the number grow. They learn that patience has a payoff — that the sats they earned mowing the lawn last month are worth more today than they were then. They learn to guard a private key, and sometimes they fail, and the failure costs them a few dollars instead of a few thousand, and the lesson sticks. They learn that their money cannot be confiscated or censored or debased. They learn economic sovereignty before they learn to drive.

In a fiat world, allowance teaches kids how to spend. In a Bitcoin world, allowance teaches them how to build.

But the family plan is bigger than allowance. It is about the conversation every family building wealth in Bitcoin must eventually have — the one nobody wants to have and nobody can afford to skip.

Bitcoin inheritance and estate planning.

Your seed phrase is your estate. If you die without having made arrangements for someone to access it, your Bitcoin dies with you. This is not a metaphor. It is a mathematical certainty. The coins will sit on the blockchain, visible to anyone, movable by no one, forever. For a working-class family building generational wealth — the whole reason many readers picked up this book — this is not an abstract concern. It is the entire point, and it can be undone by a single oversight.

Here is what the plan looks like:

The simplest approach is a sealed envelope — your seed phrase written clearly, stored in a secure location that a trusted family member or attorney can access upon your death. A safe deposit box with a named beneficiary. A fireproof safe whose combination your spouse knows. The method matters less than the existence of the plan.

For larger holdings, multi-signature setups provide both security and redundancy. A two-of-three multi-sig wallet means any two of three keys can authorize a transaction. You hold one. Your spouse holds one. Your attorney or a third trusted party holds one. If one key is lost, stolen, or compromised, the wallet is still accessible. If you die, the remaining two keyholders can recover the funds without any single person having unilateral control.

You do not have to figure this out alone. Several companies now specialize in Bitcoin inheritance planning, and they have built products specifically designed to help families pass Bitcoin to the next generation without requiring heirs to be technically sophisticated. Some hold one key in a multi-sig arrangement while you hold the others, working with your executor when the time comes. Others guide your designated beneficiary through the process step by step through a mobile app, even if they have never touched a hardware wallet. This is a growing industry, and by the time you read this there may be additional options. But the services exist, they are accessible, and any family serious about generational wealth should look into them.

One critical note: never put your seed phrase in your will. Wills become public documents during probate. Anyone who reads the will could access your Bitcoin before your heirs do. The seed phrase must be stored separately, securely, and communicated through a private channel — a sealed envelope with an attorney, a multi-sig arrangement, or a dedicated inheritance service. Not in the will. Ever.

Have the conversation. Make the plan. Write it down. Do not leave it for tomorrow.

The government will not help you with this. There is no FDIC for a lost seed phrase. There is no probate court that can compel the Bitcoin network to release funds. This is the trade-off of self-sovereignty — the same trade-off that protects your wealth from every institution in the world also means that *you* are the last line of defense. Act like it.

Epilogue

Generation Zero

On August 15, 1971, Richard Nixon severed the last link between the U.S. dollar and gold. As of this writing — early 2026 — that is fifty-four and a half years ago. An entire human career. A full working lifetime.

Which means that anyone who graduated college in the early 1970s and entered the workforce that decade spent their *entire professional life* under a fiat monetary system. Every paycheck they earned, every dollar they saved, every mortgage they signed, every retirement contribution they made — all of it denominated in a currency that was no longer anchored to anything real. They were the first generation in American history for whom this was true. Every generation before them had at least some tether to gold, however thin. This generation had none.

They were Generation Zero of the American fiat experiment. And they had no idea.

They worked hard. They got screwed. They worked harder. They got screwed more. They followed the rules — save, buy a house, invest in the market, trust the institutions. And for the most part, the institutions told them it was working. The numbers on the statements went up. The house appreciated. The 401(k) grew. Everything *looked* fine, because everything was measured in the same depreciating unit that was causing the problem. It is hard to notice you are being robbed when the ruler they hand you to measure your wealth is shrinking at the same rate as your purchasing power.

They do not want pity from you or me. And many of them made it out just fine — grinding away, working hours that most of us would find unbelievable, refusing to complain because that is what their generation did. My father was one of them. He made it. But in the end, his wealth — and the wealth of everyone in his generation who played by the rules — was eroded constantly. It mostly evaporated, silently, through inflation.

Only those sharp enough to drop every spare dollar into gold or the S&P 500 index came out roughly even in purchasing power terms, and even they lost ground once taxes were factored in. The IRS does not distinguish between real gains and nominal gains. If inflation pushes your investment from $10,000 to $20,000 but your purchasing power has not changed, the government still taxes you on the $10,000 "gain." You did not get wealthier. You got taxed for staying in place.[1]

Even homeownership — the great American wealth-building strategy, the one thing everyone told Generation Zero to do — did not go as planned. Home prices increased at roughly 5.2% annually since 1972.[2] That sounds good until you remember that M2 money supply was being debased at roughly 6% per year on average.[3] Property taxes exploded. Maintenance costs compounded. Insurance premiums climbed. What Generation Zero was left with was a feeling of being stuck. Lots of equity on paper. No realistic chance of buying something nicer. Most would end up downsizing at retirement. Some because they no longer needed the space. Many because they could no longer afford the space and then rationalized that they did not need it. The rationalizing is the cruelest part. The system trained an entire generation to mistake shrinking options for personal contentment.

Very, very few of them were fortunate enough to invest so spectacularly that they actually gained wealth through their unspent income. Those people exist, but they are the exception so rare that it proves the rule. For the overwhelming majority of Generation Zero, the best-case outcome of a lifetime of disciplined saving was *not falling behind too badly.*

---

1. IRS Publication 550 (Investment Income and Expenses); Internal Revenue Code §1001. The U.S. tax code contains no inflation adjustment mechanism for capital gains. A taxpayer who holds an investment whose nominal value doubles while purchasing power holds flat owes tax on the full nominal gain — despite having experienced no real increase in wealth. This means that in a high-inflation environment, disciplined savers who hold assets can be taxed into negative real returns even on positions that merely kept pace with inflation.

2. Median U.S. home sale price, quarterly data: Federal Reserve Bank of St. Louis (FRED), series MSPUS (U.S. Census Bureau / HUD). Compound annual growth rate calculated from Q1 1972 through Q3 2025: approximately 5.23%. Source dataset: MSPUS.csv.

3. M2 money supply: Federal Reserve Bank of St. Louis (FRED), series WM2NS (weekly, seasonally adjusted). The compound annual growth rate of M2 since 1984 — the earliest date available in the FRED weekly series — has averaged approximately 5.75% through early 2026, reflecting significant deceleration during the Federal Reserve's 2022–2024 quantitative tightening cycle. In the decades prior to QT (1984–2022), the CAGR was approximately 6.23%. The text uses 'roughly 6% per year on average' as a durable characterization of the full-period trend. Source dataset: WM2NS.csv.

And those were the ones who did well.

The members of Generation Zero on fixed incomes today fare even worse. Social Security cost-of-living adjustments are pegged to the Consumer Price Index[4] — the government's own measure of inflation, which has averaged 3.94% annually since 1972 by the government's own data.[5] But CPI systematically understates the real cost of living. It does not capture the true rate at which housing, healthcare, and groceries have climbed. It is a thermometer designed to read low. The adjustments that are supposed to protect retirees from inflation are based on a number that was engineered to minimize the appearance of the very problem it claims to measure.

The result is that retirees on fixed incomes are the bottom feeders at the Cantillon Effect trough. They get the newly created money last — after the banks, after the asset holders, after the corporations, after the government itself has already spent it into existence and driven up the prices of everything these retirees need to buy. Their standard of living does not hold steady through retirement. It perpetually declines. Every year, the same check buys a little less. Every year, the gap between what they were promised and what they can afford widens. The golden years — that phrase the financial planners loved to use — turn out to be the years when the theft accelerates, because the people being robbed no longer have the option of earning more to keep up.

Few of them will be able to afford the care they deserve at the end. And the deepest irony is this: the safety nets that supposedly guarantee them dignity in their final years are part of the reason they will not get any. Social Security, Medicare, Medicaid — these programs are symptoms of a government run amok, creating dollars out of thin air in an attempt to provide financial well-being to everyone. The programs grow. The dollars they are funded with buy less. The gap between promise and reality widens with every passing year. And the people at the bottom of the Cantillon chain — the elderly, the disabled, the fixed-income retirees who played by every rule — are the ones who pay the difference.

---

4. Median U.S. home sale price, quarterly data: Federal Reserve Bank of St. Louis (FRED), series MSPUS (U.S. Census Bureau / HUD). Compound annual growth rate calculated from Q1 1972 through Q4 2025: approximately 5.23%.

5. M2 money supply: Federal Reserve Bank of St. Louis (FRED), series WM2NS (weekly, seasonally adjusted). The compound annual growth rate of M2 since 1984 — the earliest date available in the FRED weekly series — has averaged approximately 5.75% through early 2026, reflecting significant deceleration during the Federal Reserve's 2022–2024 quantitative tightening cycle. In the decades prior to quantitative tightening (1984–2022), the CAGR was approximately 6.23%. The text uses "roughly 6% per year on average" as a durable characterization of the full-period trend.

Not in taxes. In purchasing power. In dignity. In the slow, quiet erosion of a retirement they spent a lifetime earning.

Generation Zero deserved better. They did not get it.

The Man Who Did Everything Right

This book began with one of them — a man who came home from Vietnam in 1971, the same year Nixon closed the gold window. He had lost a leg. He had not lost his work ethic, his discipline, or his faith that the system would reward him for doing the right thing. He got a job. He paid his mortgage. He maxed his 401(k). He lived within his means. He did everything the responsible parties told him to do.

He arrived at retirement with less than he was promised. Not because he failed. Because the money failed him. Every year, quietly, invisibly, the dollars he saved bought a little less. The house he could have afforded at thirty was out of reach by forty. The retirement he planned for at fifty looked different by sixty-five. The purchasing power that should have been waiting for him at the end of a lifetime of honest work had been siphoned away — not by a thief he could see, but by a system he was told to trust.

His son wrote this book.

Not because he has all the answers. Not because Bitcoin solves every problem. But because for the first time since the end of the gold standard, there exists a form of money that cannot be debased by the people who are supposed to protect it. A form of money with a fixed supply that no government, no central bank, no Federal Reserve chairman can inflate away. A form of money that a working-class father can save in today and know — with mathematical certainty — that no one can print more of it tomorrow.

That father deserved this tool. He did not have it. You do.

The Road

You do not need to be a technologist. You do not need to understand cryptography or hash rates or elliptic curve mathematics. You need to understand what you already understand: that your labor has value, that saving is the foundation of a good life, and that the money you save in matters as much as the amount you save.

You need to get off zero. Any amount. This week.

You need to take custody. Your keys, your Bitcoin. Do not trust someone else with the keys to your wealth.

You need to protect your seed phrase as if your family's future depends on it — because it does.

And you need to start. Not when the price is lower. Not when you understand more. Not when your brother-in-law stops making fun of you. Now. One paycheck at a time. One satoshi at a time.

The game was rigged. The money was broken. The institutions you trusted failed you.

But the hardest money ever invented is available to anyone, anywhere, at any time, with no permission required. It has been running for over seventeen years without a single minute of downtime. Every five-year window of regular investment has been profitable. The math works. The network works. The people closest to it — the ones who have studied it the longest and held it through the worst drawdowns — are more convicted than ever.

Generation Zero did not have this option. You do. Do not waste it.

About the Author

Grant Amagi has spent nearly two decades working in cybersecurity. He publishes The Bitcoin Roll on Substack, where he writes against the grain of optimistic Bitcoin commentary in favor of rational analysis and accuracy. Generation Zero is his first book and his proof of work.

Data Sources

Federal Reserve Economic Data (FRED)

All FRED data retrieved from fred.stlouisfed.org. Series used:

WM2NS — M2 Money Supply (weekly, seasonally adjusted). https://fred.stlouisfed.org/series/WM2NS

MEHOINUSA646N — Real Median Household Income in the United States (annual). https://fred.stlouisfed.org/series/MEHOINUSA646N

MSPUS — Median Sales Price of Houses Sold for the United States (quarterly). https://fred.stlouisfed.org/series/MSPUS

NASDAQCOM — NASDAQ Composite Index (daily). https://fred.stlouisfed.org/series/NASDAQCOM

FPCPITOTLZGUSA — Inflation, Consumer Prices for the United States (annual, World Bank via FRED). https://fred.stlouisfed.org/series/FPCPITOTLZGUSA

BOGZ1FL075035503Q — Commercial Real Estate Loans, All Commercial Banks (quarterly). https://fred.stlouisfed.org/series/BOGZ1FL075035503Q

Bitcoin Price Data

Daily Bitcoin closing prices sourced from Yahoo Finance (BTC-USD). Data covers September 17, 2014 through February 22, 2026 — 4,176 trading days. DCA analysis computed across 2,351 rolling five-year windows using $75 weekly purchases. Every window produced a positive return. Return range: 48% to 2,733%; median 266%; average 555%. Source file: historical_bitcoin_prices.csv.

Income Data

Historical median household income data from the U.S. Census Bureau, Current Population Survey, Annual Social and Economic Supplements. https://www.census.gov/topics/income-poverty/income.html

Books Referenced

The Bitcoin Standard by Saifedean Ammous (Wiley, 2018)

The Fiat Standard by Saifedean Ammous (Saif House, 2021)

The Blocksize War by Jonathan Bier (self-published, 2021)

Early Speculative Bubbles and Increases in the Supply of Money by Douglas E. French (Mises Institute, 2009)

Principles of Economics by Saifedean Ammous (Saif House, 2023)

The Ethics of Money Production by Jörg Guido Hülsmann (Mises Institute, 2008)

Man, Economy, and State by Murray N. Rothbard (Mises Institute, 2004)

Human Action: A Treatise on Economics by Ludwig von Mises (Yale University Press, 1949)

The Theory of Money and Credit by Ludwig von Mises (1912; Liberty Fund, 1981)

End the Fed by Ron Paul (Grand Central Publishing, 2009)

Live Resources

U.S. National Debt Clock: https://www.usdebtclock.org

Bitcoin Mempool & Block Explorer: https://mempool.space

Federal Reserve Economic Data: https://fred.stlouisfed.org

Bitcoin live price dashboard: https://bitcoin.clarkmoody.com/dashboard/

Bitcoin Power Law Model (Giovanni Santostasi): https://giovannisantostasi.medium.com

Podcasts Referenced

The Fall of Civilizations Podcast, hosted by Paul Cooper. https://fallofcivilizationspodcast.com

The Bitcoin Standard Podcast, hosted by Saifedean Ammous. https://saifedean.com/podcast

The Tom Woods Show, hosted by Tom Woods. https://tomwoods.com/podcast

www.ingramcontent.com/pod-product-compliance
Lightning Source LLC
LaVergne TN
LVHW100314210926
848480LV00003B/1115
9798995844709